Vygotsky

Lev Vygotsky's approach to children's learning and development centers on adult mediation: adults engage children in age-appropriate activities and promote in this context the development of new motives and tools for thinking, problem solving, and self-regulation. Although this approach has earned widespread recognition in the global scientific community, English-speaking educators remain relatively unfamiliar with its contemporary elaborations for practical application. Yuriy V. Karpov offers the first comprehensive English-language introduction to contemporary elaborations of Vygotsky's ideas and their practical applications from birth through adolescence. He demonstrates the advantages of the Vygotskian approach over both traditional and constructivist education. This volume will prove an invaluable resource for educators and students in teacher education programs, as well as for everyone interested in educational and developmental psychology.

Yuriy V. Karpov is Professor of Psychology and Education and Associate Dean at the Graduate School of Education of Touro College. He is the author of *The Neo-Vygotskian Approach to Child Development* (2005), as well as numerous journal articles and book chapters in English, Russian, French, and Spanish. He serves on the editorial board of the *Journal of Cognitive Education and Psychology* and is a member of the American Educational Research Association and the International Association for Cognitive Education and Psychology.

Vygotsky for Educators

Yuriy V. Karpov

Touro College

CAMBRIDGE
UNIVERSITY PRESS

CAMBRIDGE
UNIVERSITY PRESS

32 Avenue of the Americas, New York, NY 10013-2473, USA

Cambridge University Press is part of the University of Cambridge.

It furthers the University's mission by disseminating knowledge in the pursuit of
education, learning, and research at the highest international levels of excellence.

www.cambridge.org
Information on this title: www.cambridge.org/9781107637498

First published 2014

Printed in the United States of America

A catalog record for this publication is available from the British Library.

Library of Congress Cataloging in Publication data
Karpov, Yuriy V., 1957–
Vygotsky for educators / Yuriy V. Karpov, Touro College.
    pages   cm
Includes bibliographical references and index.
ISBN 978-1-107-06542-0 (hardback) – ISBN 978-1-107-63749-8 (paperback)
1. Child development.   2. Educational psychology.   3. Developmental psychology.
4. Learning, Psychology of.   5. Vygotskii, L. S. (Lev Semenovich), 1896–1934.   I. Title.
HQ767.9.K366   2014
153.1'5–dc23   2014001823

ISBN 978-1-107-06542-0 Hardback
ISBN 978-1-107-63749-8 Paperback

This book is dedicated to my wife, Lora Gornaya

Contents

List of Figures

Acknowledgments

My interest in and knowledge of the Vygotskian theory of children's learning and development was formed during my seventeen-year affiliation with the School of Psychology of Moscow State University, which was the center of Vygotsky-based research in the former Soviet Union. I am deeply indebted to my former teachers, especially to Daniel Elkonin, Piotr Galperin, Alexey Leontiev, Alexander Luria, and Nina Talyzina, whose writings, lectures, and generous sharing of their ideas with students and younger colleagues have shaped my entire professional life.

My efforts to produce this book have benefited from all kinds of support from colleagues and administration at Touro College. I am especially grateful to Inna Rabinovitch, Inna Smirnova, and Daniel Stein for their help with the production of photos and charts that illustrate the book.

My deepest gratitude must be reserved for my friend and colleague Ronald Lehrer, who provided extremely useful scholarly consultations, commentary, and suggestions on my analysis and presentation of the material.

I am also grateful to the anonymous reviewers of an early draft of the manuscript for their helpful feedback.

Finally, I want to thank David Repetto, the book editor, and other staff at Cambridge University Press who dedicated their expertise, time, and effort to the preparation of this book for publication.

Introduction: "There Is Nothing More Practical Than a Good Theory"

"There is nothing more practical than a good theory," a statement made by the famous psychologist Kurt Lewin in the 1950s, is especially relevant to the field of children's education. Every educator adopts, implicitly or explicitly, a certain theory of child learning and development, which greatly determines what methods he or she uses when educating children. In the best seller of the 1970s, *Future Shock*, Alvin Toffler observes how a replacement of one fashionable theory by another resulted in a change of child rearing practices:

> At the turn of the [20th] century in the United States, for example, the dominant theory reflected the prevailing scientific belief in the primacy of heredity in determining behavior. Mothers who had never heard of Darwin or Spencer raised their babies in ways consistent with the world views of these thinkers. Vulgarized and simplified, passed from person to person, these world views were reflected in the conviction of millions of ordinary people that "bad children are a result of bad stock," that "crime is hereditary," etc.
>
> In the early decades of the [20th] century, these attitudes fell back before the advance of environmentalism. The belief that environment shapes personality, and that the early years are the most important, created a new image of the child. The work of Watson and Pavlov began to creep into the public ken. Mothers reflected the new behaviorism, refusing to feed infants on demand, refusing to pick them up when they cried, weaning them early to avoid prolonged dependency.[1]

1

Similar shifts from one set of practices to another as a result of replacement of one fashionable theory of child learning and development by another take place in the field of instruction. For example, in the 1960s–1970s, growing disappointment with Watson's and Skinner's behaviorism and the embracing of Piaget's constructivist theory resulted in many abandoning conditioning and advocating discovery learning instead as the major method of instruction.

If, as discussed, the theory of child learning and development that one has adopted significantly determines his or her educational practices, would it not be reasonable to assume that the better this theory, the more successful the educational practices will be? The most influential theories of child learning and development have been mentioned earlier; let us review them in more detail.

The Nativist (Maturational) Approach

Nativism appeared at the end of the 19th century. Heavily influenced by Charles Darwin's evolutionary theory, early nativists saw heredity as the major (if not only) determinant of children's development. For example, one of them, Francis Galton, advocated the idea of the inheritance of intelligence. Another early nativist, Karl Bühler, even insisted that criminal behavior is a result of "bad" heredity.

The views of contemporary nativists are not very different from the views of their predecessors. For example, Christopher Ferguson and Kevin Beaver recently published an article with a title that speaks for itself: "Natural born killers: The genetic origins of extreme violence." Martin Daly and Margo Wilson explain incidents of violence and abuse in stepfamilies as a result of our "selfish genes" that are driven to reproduce themselves: Stepparents view their stepchildren as diminishing their opportunities to pass along their own genes through their biological children, which leads them to abuse their stepchildren. Another contemporary psychologist, Frank Sulloway, advocates the idea that inheritance determines political attitudes, so that some people are born liberals and some conservatives.

To be sure, these examples of contemporary nativist views are somewhat exotic. A much more mainstream idea in contemporary nativism is the one that was formulated by Francis Galton: the idea of inheritance of intelligence. To support this idea, nativists refer to empirical studies that have revealed a high correlation between Intelligence Quotient (IQ) scores of genetically related people.

The view of human development as a process predetermined by heredity leads nativists to grossly undermine any opportunity to influence the developmental processes through parenting and teaching. Sandra Scarr, a renowned nativist, writes:

> Ordinary differences between families have little effect on children's development ... Children's outcomes do not depend on whether parents take children to the ball game or to a museum so much as they depend on genetic transmission, on plentiful opportunities, and on having a good enough environment that *supports children's development to become themselves* [italics mine] ... Feeding a below-average intellect more and more information will not make her brilliant.[2]

Thus, according to Sandra Scarr, each child is born predisposed to "become somebody" and to enjoy a certain level of intelligence; therefore, the role of educators is limited to simply providing a child with "plentiful opportunities" to develop in accordance with hereditarily predetermined fate.

Of course, as Scarr herself mentions, this position may be very "comforting" to some parents by giving them "more freedom from guilt when they deviate ... from culturally prescribed norms about parenting"[3] and, I want to add, by relieving them from guilt if the outcomes of their parenting do not meet their expectations. Some teachers may find this position comforting as well, because it implicitly relieves them from responsibility for poor learning outcomes of their students. Other educators, however, will be happy to learn that this fatalistic position of nativists is far from the truth. Yes, some abilities are indeed inherited, but, as discussed later in the book, higher-level human abilities, including cognitive and metacognitive abilities, are not. Rather, they develop in children, and educators can and should promote the development of these abilities.

The Behaviorist (Environmental) Approach

Behaviorism appeared at the beginning of the 20th century, and its development was strongly influenced by studies of animal learning by Ivan Pavlov and Edward Thorndike. As these studies demonstrated, new responses can be developed in animals through conditioning, that is, the creation of new associations between stimuli and responses as a result of practice (trial and error) and reinforcement (reward). Having applied the results of these animal studies to humans, behaviorists came to advocate conditioning as the major mechanism of learning and development in children. A newborn child, in their view, is a tabula rasa, a blank slate, and the child's learning and developmental outcomes are the result of conditioning. In other words, a child is a piece of clay in the hand of an adult, and it is up to the adult to choose how to shape this piece of clay. A classic quote from John Watson, a prominent behaviorist, is very revealing in this respect: "Give me a dozen healthy infants, well-formed, and my own specified world to bring them up in and I'll guarantee to take any one at random and train him to become any type of specialist I might select."[4]

Behaviorism lost its popularity among psychologists long ago: It turned out that it fails to explain learning in animals, not to mention children. For example, the German psychologist Wolfgang Köhler demonstrated that apes are able to learn without trial and error but rather through insight, the "aha" experience. Or, as the American researcher Edward Tolman found, even rats can learn without any reward.

Although behaviorism is not a fashionable theory any longer, its ideas are still broadly used in education. In the field of instruction,

> behaviorist learning theory emphasized arranging the student environment so that stimuli occurred in a way that would instill the desired stimulus-response chains. Teachers would present lessons in small, manageable pieces (stimuli), ask students to give answers (responses), and then dispense reinforcement ... until their students became conditioned to give the right answers.[5]

As I discuss in detail later, it is the implementation of behaviorist ideas in American education that is most responsible for the poor learning outcomes and the problems with the cognitive and metacognitive development of American students.

Behaviorist methodology used to resolve children's behavioral or learning problems at school or at home is often referred to as behavioral therapy or behavioral modification. For example, to eliminate a child's aggressiveness toward classmates, the teacher gives him a token for every day that he behaves. Similarly, parents may give tokens to their children for doing their homework. Having accumulated a certain number of tokens, the child can exchange them for a specific attractive reward.

No doubt, behavioral modification often results in the desired changes in children's behavior. It is important, however, to be aware of several important shortcomings of this methodology. First, you can hardly expect that the child will be rewarded for not being aggressive or for doing his "homework" indefinitely. What is going to happen when the rewards are withdrawn? Sometimes, the child will not return to the former bad behavioral pattern: He or she has already come to appreciate the social advantages of not being aggressive or has developed intrinsic learning motivation, and the external rewards are not needed any more. Often, however, a return to the undesirable behavior does take place upon the reward's withdrawal. Second, and most important, behavioral modification may work if the child is able to behave himself but simply does not want to. But it is useless to reward the child, for example, for attending to the teacher's explanation if the child is not able to make herself attentive – in other words, if he or she is lacking tools for self-regulation. In this book, I am advocating other ways to resolve children's behavioral or learning problems that relate to developing intrinsic motivation in children and teaching them cognitive and metacognitive tools.

The Constructivist (Interactional) Approach

Despite the major difference between behaviorists and nativists in their understanding of the major determinant of child development (nature versus nurture), their views of child development have one point in common: They consider children to be developed rather than to develop. For behaviorists, "the individual is fabricated out of the conditioning pattern";[6] for nativists, he or she is "fabricated" out of heredity. A very important accomplishment of the constructivist approach to child development is that it overcomes the nativists' and behaviorists' view of the child as a passive object of internal or external development-generating forces.

The major representative of this approach is the theory of the great Swiss psychologist Jean Piaget. According to Piaget, children are young "research scientists," driven by innate curiosity to explore the external world. In the course of these explorations, children come across new environmental phenomena and try to assimilate them into their schemas (that is, into their existing ways of thinking). These new environmental phenomena, however, often do not fit exactly into children's schemas, which creates disequilibrium between children's schemas and the external world. Therefore, children need to accommodate their schemas to the new environmental phenomena, which leads to the elaboration of these schemas and the development of new schemas. As a result, temporary equilibrium between children's schemas and the external world is achieved, which lasts until children come across new environmental phenomena that create a new state of disequilibrium.

According to Piaget, the process of developing new schemas leads, at a certain point, to a major shift in the course of children's development: They transition from one qualitative stage of cognitive functioning to the next one. Between birth and the age of two years, children are at the *sensorimotor stage*; they solve all problems practically through a trial-and-error procedure. Between the ages of two and six or seven years (the *preoperational stage*), children develop and advance in the ability to exercise symbolic thought, which makes it possible for them to solve problems through mental trials rather than through practical trials. They, however, cannot be attentive to several aspects of the problem or situation at the same time (centration) or take into consideration another person's perspective or position (egocentrism). Children overcome these shortcomings in their thinking when they transition to the *concrete operational stage* (from 6 or 7 years until 11 or 12 years); however their thinking at this point still has one major limitation: They are not able to solve theoretical problems, that is, to exercise formal logical thought. The ability to exercise formal logical thought appears in children around the age of 11 or 12 years, when they transition to the *formal operational stage*, which is the last stage of child development in Piaget's theoretical model.

While viewing children as active constructors of their cognition, Piaget at the same time postulates that the stages of cognitive development appear in a fixed sequence and in accordance with a timetable that is universal for children in all countries and all cultures. Neither children themselves nor their parents and teachers can make any difference in this respect. That is why, the educational implications of Piaget's constructivist theory are very similar to those of nativism: leave the child alone, provide him or her with the opportunities to explore the environment, but do not interfere with the child's explorations and do not try to promote or accelerate the child's development. Many times, when Piaget addressed American audiences, the question of whether parents or teachers can do anything to speed up the development of their children would come up. When asked such a question, Piaget would reportedly smile and say, "Ah, again, the American question!"

Well, it turns out that this "American question" is not as stupid or naive as Piaget believed it was. It has been demonstrated that, indeed, children's transition to the concrete operational stage can be facilitated with just 15 hours of intervention.[7] Moreover, it has been shown that children's transition to the formal operational stage is not as natural and universal a phenomenon as Piaget believed it was; rather, this transition is a direct outcome of school instruction.[8] In this book, I discuss scientific findings that help us understand how it is possible to promote children's development at each stage.

The Vygotskian Approach as an Alternative to the Nativist, Behaviorist, and Constructivist Approaches

Lev Vygotsky was a Russian-Jewish psychologist and educator whose ideas are now becoming more and more popular all over the world. It is not an exaggeration to say that Vygotsky is a unique phenomenon in the history of science. His life was very short (he died at the age of 37) and not very cheerful: Its beginning was darkened by the anti-Semitic laws of the Russian Empire, and its end by tuberculosis and baiting from Stalin's oppressive regime. After Vygotsky's death in 1934, his ideas were banned from public consumption in Russia. In the same year, many of his closest colleagues and followers fled from Moscow to a Russian provincial city to avoid repression that would have been possible had they remained in Moscow. It was only as a result of de-Stalinization at the end of the 1950s and the beginning of the 1960s, that Vygotsky's selected works were published in Russia. In the 1970s–1980s, English translations of his major works were published, and starting in the 1980s, more than 50 years after his death, Vygotsky has been widely recognized as "the Mozart of psychology"[9] whose ideas are surprisingly up to date.

The major reason for such a broad recognition of Vygotsky's approach relates to the fact that it provides an innovative view of the processes of child learning and development, which has found strong support in recent studies conducted by American researchers. According to Vygotsky, children's learning and development are neither predetermined by heredity, as nativists hold; nor determined by conditioning, as behaviorists hold; nor the result of children's independent explorations, as constructivists hold. Rather, children's learning and development are the result of adult *mediation*, that is, the engagement of children in age-appropriate activities, in the context of which adults promote the development in children of new motives and teach them new tools of thinking, problem solving, and self-regulation. That is how (and that is why) children develop for example intrinsic learning motivation and school readiness, that is, the characteristics necessary for successful learning at school.

Using Vygotsky's theoretical ideas as the basis for their studies, his Russian followers have elaborated these ideas and extended them to the level of practical applications and instructional programs. The 50-year experience of the implementation of the Vygotskian ideas in educational practices in Russia has confirmed the validity of these ideas and has demonstrated the efficiency of Vygotskian educational practices for the promotion of children's learning and development.

The Purpose, Structure, and Content of this Book

Although, as mentioned earlier, Vygotskian ideas enjoy broad recognition in the world scientific community, English-speaking educators are much less familiar with these ideas and their practical applications. An overwhelming majority of publications on the Vygotskian approach in English are addressed to researchers in the field of child development and learning rather than to practicing educators or students in teacher education programs. Of those few publications that are addressed to educators, many present the original ideas of Vygotsky rather than the contemporary elaborations of these ideas for educational practices. Some others even misrepresent Vygotsky's ideas, insisting, for example, that Vygotsky believed "that the acquisition of new concepts is most meaningful to students when they are given an opportunity to construct their own knowledge and to discover things for themselves.[10] The remaining few publications that do provide readers with correct and up-to-date knowledge of the Vygotskian approach and practical recommendations on its use target only a certain area of application (for example, early childhood education[11] or mathematics education[12]). The purpose of this book is to describe for English-speaking educators how the contemporary Vygotskian approach to children's learning and development can be used to improve educational practices from birth through adolescence.

The book consists of two parts. Part I provides readers with a general overview of the Vygotskian ideas and practical implementations of these ideas for different developmental periods. In Chapter 1, I discuss the Vygotskian notion of mediation as the major determinant of the development of new abilities, mental processes, and motives in children. My major goal when writing this chapter was to introduce the Vygotskian ideas in a reader-friendly fashion so that they will be clear and meaningful to readers with no background in psychology (without, however, reducing the quality of the analysis). That is why I discuss these ideas in "simple words" and illustrate my discussion with many examples taken not only from scientific research but also from everyday life. Chapters 2 through 7 are devoted to the analysis of periods in children's development from birth through adolescence. When discussing children's learning and development in each of the periods, I pay special attention to how educational practices during each of these periods should be organized to facilitate children's development and to prepare them for the successful transition to the next age period. In particular, I discuss the issue of school readiness and describe special activities designed by the Vygotskians for prekindergarten and kindergarten children to promote their school readiness.

Part II focuses on the issue of school instruction. In Chapter 8, I discuss the findings of American cognitive psychologists and Russian Vygotskians about the content and process of student learning and the requirements for good teaching that follow from these findings. My further analysis (Chapters 9 and 10) makes it possible to conclude that neither traditional explicit instruction nor constructivist instruction (which is often advocated these days as a good alternative to explicit instruction) meet these requirements for good teaching or lead to good learning and developmental outcomes. Finally, in Chapter 11, I describe the Vygotskian theoretical learning approach, demonstrate its consistency with the requirements for good teaching, show its impressive learning and developmental outcomes, and provide examples of the theoretical learning instructional programs that can be readily incorporated into the "traditional" curricula in American schools.

In the concluding chapter, I revisit the nativist idea that children's development is genetically predetermined. Using from the Vygotskian findings described in the book, I defend the conclusion that, whereas genetic heredity is a factor that influences child development, it is "cultural heredity" provided to a child through mediation that determines to a great extent how the child develops.

PART I

MEDIATION FROM BIRTH THROUGH ADOLESCENCE

1   The Vygotskian Notion of Mediation as the Major Determinant of Children's Learning and Development

Everybody would agree that the obvious answer to the question "Why do we need our mental processes?" is as follows: Our mental processes serve our practical activities aimed at our adaptation to the environment. In other words, our thinking, memory, attention, and problem-solving strategies make it possible for us to function efficiently in our environment, to meet challenges and solve problems that we come across in our lives. The same is true for animals: Their mental processes serve their practical activities aimed at their adaptation to the environment. The point is, however, that animal environment and human environment are principally different.

Animals live in a natural environment, which has not changed considerably for thousands of years. In the course of evolution and natural selection, each animal species has developed adaptive mechanisms (instincts) that are genetically transmitted from one generation to the next. Animal offsprings are born with these adaptive mechanisms and they are simply adjusted through individual learning to fit the specific characteristics of the environment in which this animal lives. This means that the developmental path of any animal is genetically predetermined: It will develop into an animal of the given species even if it is separated from all the other animals of this species after birth. A wolf-cub will always develop into a wolf.

As opposed to animals, humans live in an artificial environment, the environment that is loaded with social or cultural objects and tools. And children's adaptation to this environment requires that they learn and master the use of these objects and tools. Therefore, if we separate a newborn child from the social environment, he or she will never develop into a normal human being.

This difference in animal and human adaptation to the environment becomes obvious if we compare a newborn animal offspring and a newborn human baby. What is the most striking difference between them? As opposed to an animal offspring, a human baby is extremely helpless. She is born with very few reflexes, and nerve connections in her brain are poorly developed. It may look like a handicap, but it simply reflects the fact that socially specific forms of human behavior must be learned rather than being transmitted genetically. And another phenomenon that reflects the same fact: A period of childhood in humans is much longer than in animals. It takes most animals not more than several months to develop into an adult; it takes a child many years to enter adulthood. In modern societies, children enter adulthood long after they reach physiological maturity (puberty). This phenomenon can be easily explained in light of what said before: To reach the state of adaptation to their social environment, to find their place in the world of adults, children should learn a lot!

Psychological Tools as Mediators of Human Mental Processes

Let us return to the starting point of this discussion: Mental processes serve practical activities aimed at the adaptation to the environment. If, as discussed, human and animal adaptations to the environment are principally different, then their mental processes are different as well. This statement seems trivial, but how can we characterize this difference? To answer this question, Vygotsky and his followers have drawn an analogy between human practical activity and mental processes.

The major characteristic of human practical activity is that it is mediated by tools of labor (hammers, spades, etc.) that enormously increase human physical abilities: Even a very weak man who has a spade will dig a hole in the ground faster than a very strong man who is digging with his hands. The same is true about human mental processes: They are also mediated by tools that enormously increase their power. But these are special, psychological tools such as language, scientific concepts, signs, and symbols.

Human babies are not born with tools of labor in their hands; these tools are invented by human society, and children acquire and master them. The same is true of psychological tools: Rather than being born with such tools, children acquire and master them. Having been mastered by children, these psychological tools come to mediate their mental processes. Specifically human mental processes, which are mediated by tools, were called by Vygotsky higher mental processes to distinguish them from lower mental processes, with which children are born and which are specific to both young children and animals.

Let us continue the analogy that Vygotsky has drawn between human practical activity and mental processes. Nobody would expect a new generation to reinvent tools of labor that were invented by previous generations: Indeed, social progress, in general, comes about when every new generation receives these tools ready-made. Neither would you, probably, allow your child to learn how to use, for example, an electric saw on his own. The same is true of psychological tools that serve as mediators of human mental processes: rather than being reinvented or "discovered" by children themselves (as constructivists believe), they should be taught to children by adults.

How can we teach children psychological tools? Our psychological tools (thinking and problem-solving strategies, mnemonics, attention mechanism, etc.) are *internalized,* that is, we use them "in our heads." To teach a psychological tool to a child, we have to "exteriorize" this tool and present it to the child in the form of an external device. The child appropriates this tool and uses it initially in the same form of an external device as it was presented. Then, we have to orchestrate and monitor the process of the child's use and mastery of this tool. As the child increasingly masters the tool, it gets internalized and turns into an internal mediator of the child's mental processes.

Teaching children psychological tools, however, can hardly be accomplished in the "lecture format": "OK, son, now have a seat; I am going to teach you a new psychological tool!" Rather, adults should engage children in age-appropriate activities and in the context of these activities teach them the psychological tools needed for successful performance of these activities.

To summarize, the process of teaching the child a new psychological tool can be presented as follows. In the context of a joint age-appropriate activity with a child, an adult presents to the child a new psychological tool in the form of an external device and orchestrates and monitors the process of the child's use and mastery of this tool. As the child masters the tool, it gets internalized and turns into an internal mediator of the child's mental process. Simultaneously, the adult is getting less and less involved in the child's use and mastery of this tool. As a result, the child transits from the use of the external psychological tool under the adult's guidance to the independent use of the internal psychological tool, which indicates the completion of the development of a new higher mental process. This process of teaching children psychological tools has been called *mediation*.

Often, we mediate children without even realizing this. What follows is an example of such mediation, which results in the development in children of self-regulation.

Mediation as the Determinant of the Development of Self-Regulation in Children

Self-regulation is crucially important for our successful learning and performance. For example, you are listening to a presentation and suddenly realize that your attention has started fluctuating; immediately you give yourself a mental command and redirect your attention to the presentation. Or, you suppress a temptation to watch an interesting movie and, instead, make yourself do a project. Or, while performing a task, you come to the conclusion that you have chosen the wrong strategy and give it up in favor of a more promising strategy. In all these cases, you are taking advantage of your ability to self-regulate.

We are not born with the ability to self-regulate. Vygotsky characterized a young child as "a slave of his visual field,"[1] whose behavior is involuntary, regulated by stimuli. A new or interesting stimulus automatically draws the child's attention, and the child remains attentive to this stimulus until it loses its attractiveness. This explains why American elementary school teachers complain that "they have to 'sing, dance, or act like Big Bird' in order to teach."[2] Because elementary school students often have very poor self-regulation (we discuss the reasons for this situation in Chapter 4), teachers try to provide them with interesting stimuli, which would automatically draw the children' attention to the teacher explanation (in Chapter 8, we discuss why this strategy often does not lead to desirable learning outcomes).

The development of self-regulation in children, according to Vygotsky, is a result of adult mediation that relates to providing children with tools for self-regulation. This mediation starts in the context of an infant's unsuccessful grasping movement: The infant tries to grasp an object that is too far away, fails, and starts to cry. The mother comes to the aid of the child and gives the object to her. The importance of the mother's action, however, goes far beyond her intention to help the child get the object. She, in fact, gives the indicatory meaning to the infant's grasping movement, that is, supplies the infant with the means of nonverbal (gestural) communication that can be used to direct another person's behavior. As a result of such experiences, the infant's grasping movement transforms and reduces, and she starts to use this movement as an indicatory or pointing gesture to direct the mother's behavior. You can always tell at what point the infant's grasping movement has turned into an indicatory gesture: Instead of looking at the object, the infant shifts her gaze from the object to the mother.

Later, nonverbal means of mother-infant communication are replaced by the use of language. The mother uses language to label different objects in the child's environment and, what is especially important, to regulate the child's behavior. For example, she may say "Look" to draw the child's attention to a certain object, or she may say "No" to prevent the child from doing something dangerous or undesirable. When doing this, however, she is not only regulating the child's behavior but is also supplying the child with verbal tools of self-regulation. The child acquires these tools and starts to use them by talking aloud to himself (for example, the child says "No" to himself to overcome a temptation to do something inappropriate). Such self-addressed child's speech has been called egocentric (or private) speech.

It is interesting that, initially, to regulate their behavior, children not only repeat the exact words that their caregivers used to direct and regulate their behavior: they sometimes even imitate the caregiver' voice.[3] For example, a two-year-old girl, in her mother's absence, has climbed up on the dinner table to take a candy; she knows, however, that she is not supposed to do it, and, as the last resort to prevent herself from doing it, she says to herself: "Don't take it!", imitating not only the mother's verbal statement but the mother's voice as well.

Children also start to use egocentric (or private) speech to monitor their performance, to comprehend a situation, to find a solution to a difficult problem, or to choose a new strategy to perform a task if the old strategy does not work. For example, in one of Vygotsky's studies, a five-year-old child, when he was getting ready to draw, suddenly found out that there was no pencil of the color he needed. Immediately, the child started talking to himself: "Where's the pencil? I need a blue pencil. Never mind, I'll draw with the red one and wet it with water; it will become dark and look like blue."[4]

The preceding discussion relates to children's normal development. But what if the child is deaf and does not use egocentric (private) speech? Will it be detrimental to her ability to self-regulate? Not necessarily at all! Observations of deaf children reveal a fascinating fact: When involved in a demanding activity, these children use self-directed sign language.[5] It could be reasonably assumed that self-directed sign language plays the same self-regulatory role in their activity as egocentric speech plays in the activity of hearing children. Proceeding from the Vygotskian analysis of the development of self-regulation in hearing children, however, it can be concluded that to appropriate and master sign language as the tool of self-regulation, the deaf child should go through experiences of being regulated by sign language. This is a typical case for families in which the deaf child's parents are also deaf. Hearing parents of deaf children, however, are often much less efficient in regulating their children's behavior by the use of sign language, which, in line with Vygotsky's analysis, has been shown to be associated with substantial self-regulatory problems of their children.[6]

In addition to the use of egocentric speech to regulate their behavior, children also start to use language to regulate the behavior of others. Although such other-regulation can be directed toward parents, it is also exercised in interactions among peers in the context of their joint activities such as sociodramatic play (children's mutual regulation in the context of sociodramatic play is discussed in detail in Chapter 4).

As a result of the use by children of external verbal tools for self-regulation and for regulating the behavior of others, these tools become internalized and children develop the ability to self-regulate by the use of inner speech, that is, by giving themselves mental commands. It is interesting, however, that even adults may sometimes "regress" to ontogenetically earlier means of self-regulation by talking to themselves aloud. This is especially true if the situation is very stressful, demanding, or if we are tempted to give up what should be done in favor of indulging ourselves in immediate desires. That is why we say aloud to ourselves in the morning: "Get up! I will be late for class!" or why attacking soldiers are shouting loudly to suppress their fear and make themselves run forward.[7]

Thus, the Vygotskian ideas on the mediation of the development of self-regulation in children may be summarized as follows. Primary caregivers regulate children's behavior by using verbal tools. Children appropriate these verbal tools and start to use them in the form of egocentric (private) speech to regulate their own behavior. Also, they use these tools in the form of external speech to regulate others' behavior. As a result, children master the verbal tools, these tools become internalized, and come to mediate children's self-regulation as their new higher mental process.

The Notion of the Zone of Proximal Development of Mental Processes

The preceding analysis of the development of self-regulation illustrates Vygotsky's general idea of mediation as the major determinant of the development of new higher mental processes. As discussed, as a result of mediation, the child transits from the use of an external psychological tool under adult supervision to the independent use of what has become an internal psychological tool. Therefore, until the child has mastered and internalized a new psychological tool, and this tool has come to mediate the child's mental process, his independent use of this tool will always be below the level of his use of this tool with adult assistance. The difference between the level of independent use of a new tool by the child and his use of this tool with adult assistance has been called by Vygotsky "the zone of proximal development" (ZPD) of the child's new mental process.[8]

At first glance, Vygotsky's notion of ZPD does not add much to our understanding of child learning and development: Is it not common sense that children in many cases perform better with adult assistance than without such assistance? It turns out, however, that this notion provides us with innovative answers to such fundamental questions as how to assess children's mental development and how to teach them.

Zone of Proximal Development and Assessment. In the field of assessment, the notion of ZPD implies that it is important to assess not only what the child can do independently (the child's "mental age") but his or her ZPD as well. Vygotsky wrote:

> Most of the psychological investigations concerned with school learning measured the level of mental development of the child by making him solve certain standardized problems. The problems he was able to solve by himself were supposed to indicate the level of his mental development at the particular time.... We tried a different approach. Having found that the mental age of two children was, let us say, eight, we gave each of them harder problems than he could manage on his own and provided some slight assistance: the first step in a solution, a leading question, or some other form of help. We discovered that one child could, in cooperation, solve problems designed for twelve-year-olds, while the other could not go beyond problems intended for nine-year-olds. The discrepancy between a child's actual mental age and the level he reaches in solving problems with assistance indicates the zone of his proximal development; in our example, this zone is four for the first child and one for the second. Can we truly say that their mental development is the same? Experience has shown that the child with the larger zone of proximal development will do much better in school.[9]

Vygotsky's notion of ZPD has become one of the theoretical foundations of a new approach to the assessment of children's mental development, the so-called Dynamic Assessment (DA) approach, which is aimed at the evaluation of children's ability to benefit from adult assistance, that is, their learning ability.[10] The use of DA techniques has shown that, indeed, a child's level of independent performance as measured by IQ tests may not correlate with this child's learning ability. For example, a child may earn a very low IQ score, but when taught, learns very fast and, even more importantly, demonstrates a wide transfer of the knowledge learned (that is, is able to use this knowledge flexibly to solve new problems).[11] Any teacher will probably agree that these characteristics of the child's learning ability would inform instructional practices much better than this child's IQ score would.

Zone of Proximal Development and Instruction. In the field of instruction, Vygotsky's notion of ZPD provides us with an innovative vision of the interrelationships between instruction and development. If you look into the traditional system of school instruction, it will become obvious that it is strongly influenced by the belief that instruction should follow development; in other words, first the child should reach a certain level of development, and then we can teach him or her "developmentally appropriate" knowledge (the theoretical foundations of this belief can be found in nativist and constuctivist views on learning and development discussed in the Introduction). For example, in elementary school, children are considered incapable of abstract thinking; therefore, they are taught concrete skills through drill and practice, or verbal information through rote memorization (as I discuss later, this instructional practice is the reason, in particular, for the situation that children who come to school with a great desire to study too often lose this desire very soon).

For Vygotsky, instruction is the major avenue for mediation during the period of middle childhood. Therefore, he strongly disagreed with the view that instruction should "hobble" behind development; rather, like any other type of mediation, correctly organized instruction "marches ahead of development and leads it."[12] Thus, according to Vygotsky, we should teach children at the "ceiling" level of their ZPD, that is, the level at which they initially can perform only with a great deal of help from us. As the children develop the ability to perform more and more independently at this level, we raise the level of our teaching so that it will again target the upper threshold within their new ZPD. Such instruction "awakens and rouses to life those processes that are ready to develop, that are in the zone of proximal development."[13]

Thus, proceeding from Vygotsky's notion of ZPD, we should not wait, for example, until children develop the ability to do abstract thinking to teach them abstract knowledge. On the contrary, our teaching children abstract knowledge will promote the development of their abstract thinking. You may ask: "But how can we teach abstract knowledge to children, who are not able yet to understand it?" The answer to this question has been provided by Russian followers of Vygotsky, who used his ideas to develop the *theoretical learning* approach to instruction (I discuss this approach in Chapter 11).

The Development of New Motives

In the preceding section I presented the Vygotskian analysis of the development of mental processes in children. Vygotsky acknowledged, however, that child development cannot be reduced to the development of a child's memory, thinking, self-regulation, and so on. Another component of child development, no less important than the development of mental processes, is the development of the child's interests (or motives). Indeed, as discussed, children develop as a result of adult mediation that takes place in the context of their age-appropriate activities. But it is impossible to engage a child in a certain activity unless the child is interested in such activity – in other words, has a motive that propels him or her to engage in this activity.

As children develop, they are supposed to become engaged in more advanced types of activities; this requires that they develop new motives that will propel them to engage in these new activities. Why and how do new motives develop? When addressing this question, Vygotsky equally disagreed with those who viewed this development as the outcome of physiological maturation and those who viewed this development as a result of instilling new motives into the child by adults. He, however, never gave his explanation of this phenomenon. The credit for giving an explanation of the development of new motives in children should be granted to Russian followers of Vygotsky.

According to the Russian Vygotskians, a new motive (and, accordingly, a new activity) always ripens in the context of a current activity.[14] In other words, a child (or an adult) starts doing a new activity for the sake of something else and ends up with doing it for its own sake. This phenomenon can be illustrated with many examples from everyday life, works of fiction, and scientific observations.

One such example can be found in the novel *Gobsek* by the famous French writer Honoré de Balzak. Gobsek, a moneylender, lives on the brink of poverty. Imagine everybody's surprise, then, when after his death, tremendous wealth is found hidden in his humble apartment. Let us analyze this case in light of what I wrote earlier. For the majority of people, saving money is not an end in itself; that is, we are not propelled by the motive of saving money for its own sake. We save money to buy something, to ensure financial well-being after retirement, or, in general, to use it. Probably that was also true for Gobsek at the beginning of his moneylending career. At a certain point in his life, however, the accumulation of money has become an end in itself, that is, his new motive: saving money for the sake of having more money.

This mechanism of the development of new motives also works for the explanation of the development of alcoholism. As a rule, drinking spirits starts initially in the context of socializing or interaction with peers as one of the routines within these activities rather than for the sake of getting intoxicated. How it may later convert into an addiction has been splendidly analyzed by Jack London in his autobiographical novel, *John Barleycorn*. As London reports, initially he did not enjoy drinking alcohol at all; rather, he actually got sick after drinking. However, he had many friends, who usually met in a local bar, and he had to drink for the sake of socializing with them. Later, he caught himself going to the bar to socialize with people who were not his close friends at all; it was obvious at that point, that rather than drinking for the sake of socializing, he was socializing for the sake of drinking. Finally, London stopped even looking for excuses to drink: He started drinking at home alone, which indicated that he had developed a new pathological motive – drinking spirits for the sake of getting intoxicated.

To be sure, the mechanism of the development of new motives being discussed should not be associated with the development of only pathological motives such as saving money for the sake of having more money or drinking alcohol for the sake of getting intoxicated. For example, I often ask my graduate students, who are practicing teachers in the New York metropolitan area, to reflect on how they came to love their occupation (of course, if they have reported that they really enjoy teaching). Some of them have admitted that, when choosing education as their profession, they were driven by such factors as a decent salary, good benefits, long vacations, and so forth. It was only later, after several years of teaching, that they came to enjoy teaching for the sake of teaching – that is, developed a new motive. Some of them have reported that this motive is now so strong that they even volunteer to offer professional development workshops for their colleagues free of charge.

All the aforementioned examples of the development of new motives in humans deal with situations in which a new motive *happened* to ripen within an initial activity of the person. Of course, in each of these cases, there were certain factors (physiological, psychological, or social) that led to the development of this motive. Such an outcome, however, is not inevitable: After all, not all the people who drink alcohol for the sake of socializing are going to become alcoholics, and not all the people who choose a certain profession because of pragmatic reasons come to love their profession for its own sake. As Russian followers of Vygotsky argue, significant others can promote the development of our motives through mediation the same way as adults mediate the development of new mental processes in children.

A good example that illustrates the role of significant others in the development of our new motives has been provided by one of my former students. She was born and raised in Russia in a Jewish nonobservant family and then immigrated to the United States. In the United States, she started meeting a Jewish observant boy and began participating with him in different religious events; in particular, she took part in conversations and discussions that he had with his rabbi. Soon she became even more observant than her boyfriend was. Let us analyze this case in light of what I wrote before. Initially, the girl's participation in religious events, which included conversations and discussion with the rabbi, was likely driven by her motives to spend more time with her boyfriend and to please him. Obviously, the rabbi turned out to be a good mediator, who managed to promote the development in the girl of the new motive that propelled her to participate in Jewish religious life for its own sake.

Another example of how the development of new motives can be facilitated through mediation is the development of intrinsic learning motivation, that is, interest in learning for its own sake. As I discuss in more detail in Chapters 4 and 6, children often come to school with a great desire to study, but this can hardly be called intrinsic learning motivation; rather, the children are enjoining new "social status" and responsibilities that bring them closer to a very exciting and attractive adult world. Good teachers use this opportunity to promote the development in children of intrinsic learning motivation. In particular, they accomplish this goal by teaching the children meaningful knowledge and by praising them not for the correct answer but for the "good thinking."

Thus, according to the Vygotskians, new motives do not appear in a person "out of the blue." A new motive always ripens under the umbrella of the person's current motive, that is, within his or her current activity. To use the earlier example, a child starts studying at school driven by the motive "I am not a little boy any more: I go to school!" and may end up learning for the sake of learning, because learning itself has become interesting and exciting. But for such shift to take place, mediation of significant others (such as parents or teachers) is often a must.

Conclusion: The Vygotskian Approach to Child Learning and Development

To summarize, according to the Vygotskians, children develop within their age-appropriate activities driven by their current motives. When initially engaged in these activities, however, the children's abilities and mental processes are not advanced enough to make it possible for them to perform these activities without adult help. Therefore, at first, these activities can be performed only as joint child-adult activities. In the context of these joint activities, adults mediate the children by teaching them those psychological tools that will eventually make it possible for the children to start performing these activities independently. In addition, however, adults mediate the development of new motives in children that propel them to become engaged in new activities. But, again, these new activities require abilities and mental processes that the children have not yet developed. Therefore, again, these activities start as joint child-adult activities, in the context of which the adults provide children with mediation, and so on.

The Vygotskians used their approach to child learning and development to analyze different periods in children's development in industrialized societies and the adult mediation required during each of these periods. This analysis is presented in the following chapters.

2 First Year of Life: Infant-Caregiver Attachment as the Foundation of Further Development

Child psychologists who belong to various schools of thought are in agreement in one respect: Almost all of them argue that attachment (the establishment of infants' emotional ties to primary caregivers) is one of the most important, if not the most important, developmental accomplishments of infancy. Different researchers, however, give different explanations of the reasons for this phenomenon. Some of them believe that attachment develops as a result of the gratification by caregivers of infants' physiological needs; this belief can easily be challenged by the fact that infants develop attachment to their fathers who, as a rule, do not contribute much to the gratification of their children's physiological needs. Others believe that attachment is innately predetermined, that is, that infants are born predisposed to become attached to their primary caregivers (the findings and observations that are not consistent with this view are discussed later). The third explanation of attachment has been formulated by the Vygotskians; they argue that the roots of attachment should be sought in the history of emotional interactions of infants with primary caregivers. What follows is the Vygotskian analysis of how infant-caregiver emotional interactions develop.

The Development of Infant-Caregiver Emotional Interactions

As discussed in Chapter 1, Vygotsky emphasized newborn infants' helplessness, their inability to satisfy vital physiological needs by themselves. Indeed, in contrast to animal offsprings, human babies are born with just several reflexes serving the survival purpose, which, to make it worse, are not fully developed. For example, even such a basic reflex as sucking is so imperfect in newborn babies that they, as a matter of fact, must learn how to suck! At first glance, this "biological helplessness"[1] of human infants is their great disadvantage, especially in comparison with animal offsprings that are born much better equipped to meet the demands and challenges of the environment. This "disadvantage" of infants that results in their dependence on adults, however, is very important: It becomes the basis for the development of infant-caregiver emotional interactions.

Vygotskian observations and studies have shown that the development of infant-caregiver emotional interactions proceeds through several stages. Before I start describing these stages, however, I want to make an important reservation: All the time frames that I use when discussing these stages are very approximate. Deviations from these time frames in your infant's development should not by themselves be a reason for serious concern. With this reservation in mind, let us follow the logic of the development of infant-caregiver emotional interactions.

The First Stage: Birth to 1 Month. During the first month of life, infants do not demonstrate any positive emotional reaction toward caregivers or the external world in general. Their emotional reactions (cry, facial expressions, and body gestures) are mostly negative and triggered by physiological needs. Caregivers respond to infants' emotional reactions by determining the reason for their discomfort (whether the infant is wet, or cold, or hungry) and by gratifying their physiological needs (changing, covering, or feeding the infant). Importantly, the gratification of infants' physiological needs by itself does not result in their positive emotional reactions toward caregivers; rather, infants just relax or fall asleep.

Thus, infants' behavior during this period can hardly provide any evidence in favor of the idea that they are innately preprogrammed to develop attachment to caregivers. Just the opposite, as one researcher summarized, "it is extremely difficult to develop contact and communicate with infants during the first month of life."[2] If caregivers limit their interactions with infants to mere gratification of their physiological needs (which is often the case in orphanages), children will not develop any positive attitude toward them later on.[3] Normally, however, caregivers use the situations of feeding and changing the infants for talking to them, fondling them, and smiling at them, that is, *they take the initiative in establishing emotional contacts with infants*. As the outcome of these caregivers' initiatives, infants start responding to caregivers' emotional actions, which indicates the beginning of the second stage in the development of infant-caregiver emotional interactions.

The Second Stage: 1 to 2.5 Months. The infant's first positive emotional reaction toward caregivers can be observed at the beginning of the second month, when infants start smiling as a response to caregivers' talking to them, fondling them, and smiling at them in the context of feeding or changing. Researchers emphasize that the infant's first smiles are *evoked* through caregivers' substantial effort: "Initially, it is difficult to evoke the [infant's] smile: You should protractedly talk to the infant and to make him or her concentrate on your face[4]." By the middle of the second month, infants' smiles can be evoked outside of the context of gratification of their physiological needs, although it still requires much effort. Later, infants come to respond more and more easily with smiles at caregivers' smiles, talk, and fondling. Finally, an important shift in the development of infant-caregiver emotional interactions takes place: Infants start smiling at caregivers on their own initiative rather than merely responding to the caregivers' loving actions. This shift indicates the beginning of the third stage in the development of infant-caregiver emotional interactions.

The Third Stage: 2.5 to 6 Months. Infants' smiling at caregivers on their own initiative has been called by American researchers "social smiling." Smiling, however, is just one of the components of a very complex and intensive positive emotional reaction of infants to caregivers that starts to develop in the middle of the third month of life. The Vygotskians call this emotional reaction "the state of excitement." In addition to smiling, the state of excitement includes body gesturing and happy vocalizing. As soon as an infant notices a caregiver nearby, he or she starts smiling, vocalizing, and "expressing his joy with all the possible body gestures."[5] If caregivers respond to this infant reaction with smiling and talking, the infant expresses even more pleasure and joy. It is interesting that infants' interest in emotional interactions with caregivers may even be stronger than their physiological needs: The infant may interrupt sucking the nipple to smile at the mother. Often, the presence of a caregiver by itself is sufficient to make an infant stop crying and start demonstrating the state of excitement.

The preceding observations make it possible to conclude that, starting with the middle of the third month of life, infants *start initiating emotional interactions with caregivers*. And, they do so for the sake of emotional interactions, not because of some pragmatic reasons. As discussed in the previous chapter, when children (or adults) start doing something for its own sake, it means that they have developed a new motive; in this case, the motive that infants develop is the motive of emotional interactions with caregivers. Also, as discussed, the development of a new motive indicates the development of a new activity. Therefore, the development in infants of the *motive* of emotional interactions with caregivers indicates that the *activity* of emotional interactions with caregivers has been developed in infants as their new activity.

The further development of the activity of emotional interactions with caregivers during the discussed age periods proceeds in two main directions. First, infants' reactions toward caregivers become less global. Rather than using all means (smile, vocalization, and body gestures) to express their joy and happiness at the sight of caregivers, infants may limit their reactions, for example, to happy vocalization.

Secondly, infants are becoming more discriminating in their reactions to primary caregivers as opposed to strangers. At the beginning of the discussed age period, infants' positive reactions toward caregivers are not much different from their reactions toward strangers. Later, however, while reacting joyfully toward primary caregivers, infants start to react more neutrally and sometimes even negatively (with crying) to strangers (in American psychology, this phenomenon is called "stranger anxiety"). This difference in infant reactions toward caregivers and strangers, which may become obvious by the end of the sixth month, is one of the indicators that attachment to primary caregivers has developed.

To summarize the development of infants' emotional interactions with caregivers from birth through the age of 6 months, this activity develops in infants as a result of adult mediation, that is, involving infants in emotional interactions. Initially, this mediation (talking to infants, fondling them, and smiling at them) takes place under the umbrella of infants' current physiological motives in the context of the gratification of their physiological needs. Gradually, emotional interactions become detached from the situation of the gratification of infants' physiological needs, but are still initiated by adults. Then, the initiative for starting emotional interactions switches from adults to infants, which results later in the development of infants' attachment to their primary caregivers. Thus, as discussed, attachment is anything but innately predetermined: rather, it is the result of infant-caregiver emotional interactions that were initiated and promoted by caregivers.

Why Is Attachment Important?

As discussed earlier, not only Vygotskians but child psychologists who belong to different schools of thought view attachment as a must for normal development of children. First findings that gave strong support to this view were provided by observations of orphanage infants performed in the 1940s and 1950s.[6] All the relationships between those orphanage infants and their caregivers were limited to the gratification of the infants physiological needs, with no emotional interactions involved. Accordingly, the infants did not develop attachment to their caregivers. All those children were shown to demonstrate severe delays in their motor, cognitive, and language development as well as to suffer from various psychological disorders.

The early findings about the importance of attachment for children's successful development have been confirmed in numerous studies and observations of child and developmental psychologists. For the Vygotskians, in line with their theoretical model of child development, the most important role of attachment relates to the fact that it creates the foundation for children's transition to the next age-appropriate activity, that is, the exploration of the world of objects. As discussed later, this transition is the result of time and effort of the caregivers, who take advantage of infants' developing attachment to them to mediate them further. What follows is an analysis of how infant-caregiver attachment creates the context for mediating infants during the second half of the first year of life.

The Development of the Motive of Object Explorations. Everybody probably knows that, getting older, babies start showing more and more interest in object explorations (shaking objects, putting small objects into different holes, opening and closing boxes, etc.). Not everybody realizes, however, that the infant's interest in object explorations is initiated and promoted by caregivers rather than being spontaneous and innately predetermined.

Many caregivers start including objects and toys in the context of their emotional interactions with infants when the infants are sometimes as young as 2 months. At this age, however, infants could not care less about these objects and toys; in the Vygotskian term, play with objects is above the zone of proximal development of the infants.

Later, the baby starts playing with toys, but only if the caregiver, having engaged the infant in emotional interactions, gives a toy to the infant and encourages the infant to play with it. At this point, however, playing with a toy is not enjoyable for the infant by itself; rather, it becomes enjoyable only in the context of emotional interactions with the caregiver. This becomes especially obvious when infant-caregiver attachment has developed. A good illustration of the role of attachment as an energizer of the infant play with a toy is the situation that is familiar to everybody who has observed young infants: An infant is shaking a rattle, smiling at the mother and vocalizing happily. It is apparent that the center of this situation for the infant is the mother, not the rattle. Figuratively speaking, the infant's attitude to the rattle can be presented as follows: "Okay, if my loved and loving mother wants me to shake this stupid rattle, I will do it for her sake. In addition, it may propel her to spend a couple more minutes with me." No wonder that, as soon as the mother has left the room, the infant loses any interest in the rattle and stops shaking it, resuming shaking the rattle only when she returns.

During the second half of the first year, infants develop stronger and stronger interest in object explorations and playing with toys even without the context of emotional interactions with caregivers. As the Vygotskians explain it, it happens because attachment makes infants especially susceptible to all influences from caregivers, including the objects and toys that caregivers introduce to them in the context of emotional interactions. Therefore, "through manipulations of objects and drawing the child's attention to these manipulations, an adult can shift the child's interests and positive emotions from herself to these objects."[7] As a result of such caregiver efforts, by the end of the first year, infant interest in object explorations becomes much stronger than interest in purely emotional interactions with caregivers. Some parents may even get bitterly disappointed with such a shift in their baby's interest: Mother comes to her son, who is sitting on the floor opening and closing a box, tries to pat him, and he suddenly gets irritated – his mother is interfering with the object exploration he is deeply engaged in. Well, this reaction simply indicates that the infant's motive of emotional interactions with caregivers has been replaced by the motive of object explorations as his new dominant motive.

What happens if infants have not developed attachment? Can they still develop interest in object explorations? The answer to these questions has been provided by observations of those infants in orphanages who failed to develop attachment to caregivers. One researcher summarized her observations of such children whose age was around 1.5 years:

> In the absence of child-adult emotional bonds, the child is joyless, blank-looking, motionless, often crying. All the child's actions are centered around his own body. These actions include touching and scrutinizing his own hands, touching his body, a shirt, or a blanket, and sucking his thumb and fist.[8]

Thus, the absence of attachment is associated with infants' lack of any interest in objects within their environment.

On the other hand, even a small increase in the duration of emotional interactions with infants will subsequently result in their higher interest in object explorations. For example, it has been shown that if for two months a caregiver spends only eight extra minutes every other day on smiling at, talking to, fondling, and stroking a young infant, not only will this strengthen emotional bonds between the infant and the caregiver, but the infant will demonstrate much higher interest in the manipulation of the toys that the caregiver gives him or her later on.[9]

To conclude, the motive of object explorations develops in infants as a result of the extension of their love for primary caregivers to objects and toys that caregivers introduce to them. The development of this new motive in infants is a perfect illustration of Vygotsky's general theoretical position that "the relation of the child to the world depends on and is largely derived from his most direct and concrete relations with an adult."[10]

The Establishment of the Caregiver Role as Mediator of Infant Object-Centered Explorations. As discussed in Chapter 1, children can be provided with mediation only in the context of their joint activity with adults. Mediation cannot be successful, however, unless the child is willing to learn from this particular adult; figuratively speaking, the child should "accept" the adult as a mediator. The Vygotskians argue that attachment is crucially important for the "acceptance" by an infant of the primary caregiver as his or her mediator because it is the basis for the development in infants of the trust in caregivers as the major source of help, guidance, and support.

An important indicator of the infants' trust in their caregivers is so-called *social referencing*, the phenomenon that has been described by both the Russian Vygotskians and Western researchers. Suppose a caregiver is sitting reading a book, an infant is playing on the floor, and suddenly a stranger enters the room, or there is a strange sound. Immediately the infant will look at the caregiver for a cue: "Is it safe to continue the play?" If the caregiver looks relaxed, the infant will resume the play; if the caregiver looks concerned, the infant will cease the play and crawl to the caregiver.

The trust in caregivers has also been shown to "energize" and enrich the infant's explorations. The presence of the caregiver by itself develops in infants the feeling of a safe, supportive environment. This is why the quality of attachment to caregivers is not only associated with a higher level of infants' explorations but even predicts the quality of their exploratory behavior a year later![11]

Attachment to caregivers, however, although sufficient for providing the infant with the feeling of a safe and supportive environment, by itself is not sufficient for establishing the caregivers' role as mediators of their infants' object-centered explorations. To establish his or her new role as a mediator, the caregiver's efforts aimed at the change of focus of their interactions with infants from emotional to object-centered are crucially important.

As discussed, fortunately enough, most caregivers intuitively, often without realizing the importance of their initiatives, start modeling object-appropriate actions for their young infants and encourage them to perform these actions on their own. For example, a mother, having involved an infant in emotional interactions, puts a rattle in the infant's hand, then takes the infant's hand and shakes it, encouraging the infant to repeat this action. By doing this, the mother, in addition to increasing the infant's interest in this action, contributes to the establishment of her new role as a mediator of the infant's object-centered explorations. As a result,

> Just modeling [an object-centered action] by itself increases infants' attention to adults and the objects that they have presented. If, in addition to modeling, adults encourage infants to repeat the modeled actions and praise them for successful attempts, infants pay even more attention to adults' actions, try even harder to repeat these actions ... and express joy when praised by adults for their successful attempts.[12]

The "acceptance" by an infant of his or her primary caregiver as the mediator becomes obvious by the end of the first year, when, as discussed, infants develop a strong motive of object explorations: The infant starts taking the initiative in engaging the caregiver in joint object-centered actions. Sometimes, the infant takes this initiative in a very explicit manner by literally pushing a new toy into the caregiver's hand. The message that the infant is conveying to the caregiver is: "Help me with this toy; show me how to use it."

What will happen if caregivers fail to change the focus of their interactions with infants from emotional to object-centered? Then the infant will be just seeking caresses from them but will not be seeking their help and support with object-centered explorations. Sometimes, the infants who have already developed interest in object-centered exploration but whose caregivers have failed to establish their role as mediators of their children's explorations may even approach a stranger in seeking help with their explorations.

Infants' Mastery of the Means of Communication with Caregivers to Serve Their Joint Object-Centered Expolorations. Any joint activity requires relevant means of communication between participants, and their transition from one joint activity to another requires that the means of communication be changed.

As discussed, the earliest infant-caregiver activity is aimed at the gratification of infant physiological needs. Accordingly, infants' major "role" in this activity is to use their innate means of communication (crying, facial expressions, or body gestures) to express their physiological needs, which caregivers interpret and gratify: The baby is wet, she starts crying, the mother comes and changes her; the baby is hungry, she starts crying, mother comes and feeds the baby, etc. Many mothers even can differentiate among different types of baby crying: "I am hungry" cry, "I am wet" cry, "I am cold" cry, and so on.

Then infants become engaged in emotional interactions with caregivers. This activity requires that infants master new means of communication that, rather than expressing their distress and needs, will express their love to the caregivers and happiness when interacting with them. Accordingly, infants develop such means of communication with caregivers as smiling, vocalizing, and body gestures.

And now, infants have become engaged in a new joint activity with caregivers: their joint object-centered explorations. Obviously, such means of communication as smiling, vocalizing, and body gestures, which could successfully serve infant-caregiver emotional interactions, are not sufficient to serve their joint object-centered interactions. Indeed, your smiling is the perfect means to express your happiness to see a loved one, but it will not work as the only means of communication in the context of your doing a joint project with a colleague! Thus, infants should switch from the use of the means of emotional communication with caregivers to the use of the means of object-centered communication. What follows is the Vygotskian analysis of the development in infants of the means of object-centered communication.

The earliest type of object-centered communication is gestural communication. Vygotsky described the major means of gestural communication that 9-month-old infants start to use to direct caregivers' attention to objects in their environment: the indicatory (or pointing) gesture. As was briefly discussed in Chapter 1, Vygotsky finds the origins of the indicatory gesture in the situation in which an infant tries to grasp an object and fails because the object is too far away. The mother interprets this grasping movement as the indicatory gesture and gives the object to the infant. Thus, the mother introduces *the indicatory meaning* into the infant's unsuccessful grasping movement; figuratively speaking, she conveys the message to the infant, "If you want an object but cannot reach it, point at this object, and I will give it to you." As a result of the mother's numerous responses to the infant's grasping movement as if it were the indicatory gesture, this movement transforms, reduces, and begins to be used by the infant as a truly indicatory gesture. Thus, according to Vygotsky, the indicatory gesture is learned by infants from caregivers in the context of their object-centered interactions, and then this gesture comes to serve these interactions.

Vygotsky's followers have described some other means of gestural communication that infants use in addition to indicatory gesture. For example, even holding out a toy or another object to an adult is a means of gestural object-centered communication because, when doing it, "the child, in a way, is describing a joint action that he wishes to perform, and he uses this object or toy as an invitation addressed to the adult to become involved in the performance of this action."[13] Just as the indicatory gesture, the other means of gestural communication have also been shown to be learned by infants from caregivers in the context of their object-centered interactions.

The earliest means of gestural communication described previously, however, are sufficient to serve only very simple object-centered interactions between the infant and the caregiver (such as "give me this object" or "help me with this toy"). As infant-caregiver object-centered interactions develop and become more complex, such means of gestural communication become insufficient to serve these interactions. Therefore, by the end of the first year, infants start the mastery of a qualitatively new means of object-centered communication, that is, verbal means of communication.[14] It takes a substantial effort on the part of caregivers, however, to promote infants' transition to the use of language.

The foundation of infants' transition to verbal communication is built up by caregivers from the very beginning of their interactions with infants. Talking to infants while feeding or changing them not only develops in infants an intensive positive response to the sounds of human speech; it also makes it possible for them to establish links between objects and words. Later, caregivers name the objects that they use when playing with the infant or that the infant is paying attention to; as a result, the infant's passive vocabulary grows further. To propel infants to start using language, however, caregivers should create situations in which infants *must* use language in order to get what they want. That is why, closer to the end of the first year, many caregivers start "playing dumb" by refusing to understand the infant means of gestural communication that they understood perfectly well just yesterday. For example, the infant is pointing to the toy, but the caregiver, rather than giving this toy to the infant, keeps asking: "Do you want the ball?" trying to make the infant name the object she wants. Since verbal communication comes to serve children's object-centered interactions with caregivers during the second year, the adult role in helping the infant transit from the use of gestures to the use of words is discussed in more detail in the next chapter.

Conclusion: Mediation during the First Year of Life

As discussed, caregiver mediation is crucially important for infants' successful transitions from the activity aimed at the gratification of their physiological needs, to emotional interactions with caregivers, and finally to infant-caregiver joint object-centered explorations. It is caregivers who, in the context of infants' current activity, enrich this activity with new actions, draw the infants' interest to these actions, and mediate the development in infants of new abilities, which eventually lead to the infants' transition to the next age-appropriate activity.

To be effective, however, the mediation during the first year of life should meet both general and specific requirements. In general terms, just as any other mediation, mediation during the discussed age period should not be above the "ceiling" level of the child's zone of proximal development. For example, it is useless to push a 2-month-old infant to do object explorations, or 6-month-old infants to imitate an action of feeding a doll with a spoon modeled by a caregiver.

As for the specific requirements for mediation during the first year of life, it is important to keep in mind that overstimulation at this age is almost as bad as a lack of stimulation. Young infants need a lot of rest, and if caregivers provide an infant with excessive stimulation, she responds with irritation and distress: starts screaming or crying, or averts her gaze from the caregiver. It is certainly not a good idea to continue mediating the infant who is obviously letting you know that she wants you to leave her alone!

Inconsistent responding to a baby's requests and initiatives is another mistake that should be avoided. Clear and predictable patterns of caregiver interactions with an infant are very important for successful mediation. If today you are responsive to your baby's attempts to start emotional interactions with you, but tomorrow you ignore his initiatives, this will hardly be beneficial for the establishment of your role as a trusted and reliable mediator in the infant's life. In other words, what psychologists call *sensitive parenting* is especially important for successful mediation during the first year of life.

3 Second and Third Years: From Object-Centered Explorations to Exploration of the World of Social Roles and Relationships

As discussed, by the end of the first year of life, infants develop a strong interest in object-centered explorations. This interest, in particular, reveals itself in the fact that infants start spending much time on shaking, taking apart, and throwing different objects, putting small objects into different holes, opening and closing boxes, and so forth. To be sure, these manipulations help infants understand physical properties of objects, such as size, shape, and weight, and the ways these objects behave in different situations (e.g., a ball will roll away if kicked). The Vygotskians, however, argue that these manipulations are not those that are the most important for infant development. Indeed, when manipulating objects in accordance with their physical characteristics, children, strictly speaking, do not need adult help: Physical characteristics of objects are surface, visible, and can be revealed in the course of independent explorations. For example, children can discover by themselves that a ball rolls away if kicked, or that a rattle makes a sound if shaken. Therefore, children's independent explorations do not create a context for joint child-adult activity and, accordingly, do not provide an opportunity for adults to mediate children. In Vygotsky's terms, children engaged in independent explorations are performing at the *actual* rather than *proximal* level of development of their mental processes.

During the second and third years of life, however, infants become more and more engaged in another type of object-centered explorations: actions with objects in accordance with their social meanings, which include, but are not limited to, children's play actions with different toys. For example, whereas a younger infant would bang a spoon on the table, an older one would use a spoon to eat. Or, whereas a younger infant would shake or suck a doll, an older one would feed it. According to the Vygotskians, these are the actions that become the most important for infants' development during the second and third years of life. Indeed, when mastering actions with objects in accordance with their social meanings, children are in need of adult help: As opposed to physical characteristics of objects, their social meanings are not obvious, are not "written"[1] on objects, and, therefore, cannot be discovered by children independently.

If you believe that infants can discover on their own, for example, how to use a spoon to eat, just remember your first experience with chopsticks. Would it ever come to your mind (unless, of course, you were raised using chopsticks) that the two sticks next to your plate are used to eat? Even if you could make such a guess, would you be able to discover by yourself *how* to use these sticks to eat? Well, infants experience exactly the same type of difficulties when they start exploring the world of social objects, and they can overcome these difficulties only with adult help. Often, as discussed in the previous chapter, infants themselves approach adults for help by pushing a new toy into the caregiver's hand. Thus, learning how to use social objects inevitably takes place in the context of joint child-adult activity; the situation that, as discussed in the following sections, is used by adults to mediate children's development. First, however, let us discuss how this joint infant-adult activity develops.

The Development of Children's Object-Centered Joint Activity with Adults

Summarizing the results of Vygotskian studies, the development of child-adult object-centered activity can be presented as proceeding through the following two stages.

The First Stage: 1 Year to 2 Years. At the beginning of this stage, the number of children's nonspecific manipulations of objects (shaking, banging) gradually decreases, and more and more they imitate adult actions with objects and toys in accordance with their social meanings (for example, self-feeding or feeding a doll with a spoon). Initially, however, such imitations appear only if adults, having demonstrated appropriate actions, then encourage children to imitate them and even carry out the major component of the action for the child. For example,

> In teaching self-feeding, the caregiver has to guide the child's hand holding the spoon toward her mouth. At this point, all components of the action – from planning to execution and feedback – are carried out by the adult. Soon, the adult is able to hand over some parts of the action to the child. The child can probably soon move the spoon toward her mouth, but will still need help with picking up the food from the dish and with the final movement of actually directing the spoon into her mouth. Eventually, the entire action can be carried out by the toddler herself.[2]

Later, children imitate adult actions more and more willingly even without encouragement. These are still, however, almost exact imitations of actions with those toys and objects that adults have modeled. For example, a one-year-old girl

> always lulls and feeds only those toy-animals that her caregiver used to perform these actions. For the child of this age, it does not matter whether or not a toy resembles the object that it represents. What does matter is that this is the same toy with which an adult and the child jointly played.[3]

In the course of imitating of a new action, children constantly refer to adults to get a confirmation of the correctness of their performance, and they actively seek an adult's help if they experience difficulties with imitation of a new action.

Still later, children start to transfer the actions they have mastered in the course of joint activity with adults to new objects and situations (for example, the action of feeding a doll with a spoon is transferred to using a spoon to feed a toy dog, a toy horse, even a pillow, etc.). It is adults, however, who initially help children transfer a play action to new objects and situations ("Your baby is full now. Do you want to feed the teddy bear, I think he is hungry?").

By the end of the second year, children become able to produce a set of logically connected play actions; for example, a child feeds the doll, then takes the doll for a walk, then puts the doll to bed. And again, adults are responsible for initiating the first transitions from the performance of one play action to the performance of a set of logically connected actions ("Your baby is full now. Do you want to take her for a walk?").

Another advancement in children's play that can be observed by the end of the second year relates to children's use of object substitutes, that is, objects that stand for other objects. The use of object substitutes indicates children's transition to the second stage in the development of object-centered play.

The Second Stage: 2 Years to 3 Years. Object substitutions take place when the child realizes in the context of play that one of the objects needed to perform a play action is missing and chooses another object that can replace the missing object. For example, a child when playing with a doll suddenly realizes that she is missing a piece of soap to wash the doll's hands before supper, or a spoon to feed the doll. To be able to continue the play, she uses a stone to substitute for a piece of soap, or a stick to substitute for a spoon.

Just as with all the advancements in children's play discussed earlier, the use of object substitutes is far from being a natural and spontaneous phenomenon. Just the contrary, it is caregivers who, having engaged a child in joint play with objects, suggest that the child use a certain object instead of the missing one: "Ah, the guests are coming to our tea party soon, but we do not have tea spoons! You know, these sticks look like tea spoons, let us use them!" Or a caregiver may simply rename the object that the child is using as an object substitute without realizing it, as in the example that follows:

> Let us consider a situation in which a little girl is feeding a doll with a little ball. When an adult asks, "What is the little doll eating? An egg?," the girl smiles and, as if recognizing a familiar object in the ball, begins to unfold a whole sequence of play actions with the ball. She blows on the "egg," saying, "It's hot; soon it'll be cool," she peels it, puts some salt on it, and only after this gives it to the doll to eat with the following words, "The egg is yummy, it isn't hot anymore..." and so on. When the child renames an object during play for the first time – this usually happens when he accepts and repeats the renaming suggested by an adult – he discovers a new way of acting with objects, as it were.[4]

It is only later, as a result of their experience with object substitutions initiated and promoted by caregivers, that children start coming up with their own, sometimes very creative object substitutes. By the end of the third year, children may be able to demonstrate a high level of object substitutions, which reveals itself, in particular, in their ability to use the same object during the same play to substitute for different missing objects. For example, when performing a set of logically connected play actions (washing a doll's hands, feeding the doll, putting the doll to bed), the child may use the same stone to substitute for a piece of soap when washing the doll's hands and for an apple when feeding the doll, with a renaming of the stone in accordance with what object (a piece of soap or an apple) it is representing.

To conclude, the Vygotskians insist that advancement of children's object-centered activity during the second and third years of life is a direct outcome of adult mediation. For many years, their data on the importance of such mediation were literally ignored: Because of the popularity of Piaget's constructivist ideas, children's play in general and their use of object substitutes in particular were considered to be spontaneous natural phenomena. It is only recently that American psychologists and educators have come to acknowledge the importance of adult guidance and enrichment of children's play. To summarizing their findings,

> Maternal participation in child play lengthens play bouts, raises the level of sophistication of those bouts, and makes play more diverse, in comparison to solitary child play.... The highest level of child play occurs in direct response to maternal demonstrations and solicitations: When mothers prompt child play, child play is more sophisticated than either spontaneous child play with mother or play alone.[5]

The acknowledgment of the role of adults in children's play has come to influence educational practices as well. For example, Early Head Start home-visiting counselors and therapists are now taught how to encourage socially and economically disadvantaged parents to guide and enrich their children's play so that the children's play competence is enhanced.[6]

Why Is It Important to Guide and Enrich Children's Object-Centered Activity?

The preceding discussion answers the question why we have to guide and enrich children's object-centered activity if we want it to advance. But, why do we want it to advance? One obvious reason for this is that children's mastery of social objects is a necessary prerequisite for their growing up in the adult world. But why would we care about the quality of our children's play, in particular whether or not they use object substitutes? The point is that the mediation that we provide children within the context of guidance and enrichment of their play has been shown to result in major developmental outcomes.

The Development of the Motive of Role-Play. At first glance, a two-year-old girl and a three-year-old girl playing with their dolls are engaged in the same mother-daughter game: they feed the dolls, change them, take them for a walk, and so forth. But if you observe their play more closely, it will become obvious that the girls enjoy their play in very different ways. For the two-year-old girl, the most exciting and interesting aspects of her play relate to imitating different object-centered actions: the use of a spoon to feed the doll, or the use of a brush to comb the doll's hair. In contrast, for the three-year-old girl, the doll becomes a baby, and actions of feeding the "baby" or doing his hair are not by themselves important; rather, the girl is using these actions to imitate mother-baby relationships, such as a mother's love and tenderness toward the baby. In psychological terms, this indicates, that the girls' play is driven by different motives: the play of the two-year-old girl is driven by the motive of object-centered play, whereas the play of the three-year-old girl is driven by the motive of role-play, that is, her interest in the imitation of social roles and relationships.

The development by the child of the motive of role-play also reveals itself in explicitly assuming by her a play role and acting according to this role. Whereas the younger girl from the previous example would not accept an adult's invitation "to play at a mother" (although she would accept the invitation "to feed the baby"), the three-year-old girl would willingly accept this role and act according to it. When asked, "What are you?" she would answer with naming the play role that she is performing: "I am the mother."

As studies and observations of the Vygotskians have demonstrated, children's transition from the motive of object-centered play to the motive of role-play does not happen spontaneously. To develop such a motive, the child first should "discover" the existence of the world of social roles and relations. But for a young toddler, "the world of adults with their activities, their responsibilities, and their relationships ... is hidden under object-centered actions."[7]

Indeed, what can a child observe on her own? The child can see how different people act, but she cannot observe the reason for these actions. But social roles and relationships are not mostly about actions in and of themselves; they are about *reasons* for these actions. For example, a mother and babysitter perform the same action of feeding the baby, but they perform these actions for different reasons and these actions have different emotional "flavors" and personal meanings. Children cannot understand the reasons for adult actions by themselves. Therefore, it is the adult's responsibility to help the child "discover" the world of social roles and relations that is "hidden" under object-centered actions. The studies of the Vygotskians have made it possible to reveal two major components of adult facilitation of this "discovery."

First, adults should involve children in joint performance of *different* actions that are relevant to a certain social role. For example, if the child is playing at "feeding a baby" (that is, performing an action relevant to the role of a mother), an adult should involve the child in joint performance of other actions that are relevant to this role (washing the baby, putting the baby to bed, taking the baby for a walk, etc.). This makes it easier for the child to get detached from the performance of the specific object-centered action and look at herself as not a "feeder" but as a "mother."

Second, while children are performing play actions, an adult should explicitly refer them to the role that they are performing without realizing it. For example, observing the child washing a doll, an adult can make the comment: "Good for you! You are washing your baby *just like a mother.*" This will help the child "discover" the social role "hidden" under the object-centered play action.

To conclude, according to the Vygotskians, the development of the motive of role-play, rather than being spontaneous, is an outcome of adult mediation. This position finds stronger and stronger support among psychologists and educators around the world despite the fact that, for many years, play has been viewed as "a spontaneous and self-motivated activity."[8] For example, as some researchers have observed, children's involvement in role-play is facilitated by parents "reacting to a child who is manipulating his toys as if they were a role player: 'How is your baby today? Is she crying a lot? Did she eat her food? Did you do your shopping today?'"[9] Other researchers have reported that, when playing with a 23-month-old girl, her caregivers

> model and elicit from the child ... what mothers are responsible for providing, what they must be concerned with, and how they should act. The instruction goes beyond the little scripts for practical action such as burping, diapering, or feeding to include the attribution of internal states and the demonstration of appropriately fond or affectionate attitudes.[10]

These data and observations are highly consistent with the Vygotskian idea that "the notion of spontaneous development of role play in children is the result of adults not noticing the guidance that they, in fact, provide children with."[11] The importance of the engagement of children into role play as their new activity is discussed in detail in the next chapter.

Language Acquisition and the Development of Children's Mental Processes. One of the major features of the second and third years of life is a remarkably fast acquisition of language by children. The reason for this "language explosion"[12] is that, as the child-adult joint object-centered explorations become more and more complex, the child needs more and more elaborated help from the adult. But in order to explain to the adult his or her specific need, the child has to use more elaborated means of communication than gestural communication that successfully served child-adult interactions in the near past. The need for new means of communication with adults becomes especially strong and urgent because, as discussed in the previous chapter, by the end of the first year, many parents start "playing dumb" by refusing to understand infant gestural communication even in situations in which such means are quite sufficient. What follows is a description of a Vygotskian study that illustrates how, in the course of joint object-centered play, adults facilitate children's language acquisition.[13]

In the study, 13- to 19-month-old children became involved in joint object-centered play with an adult, in the course of which the adult named the play object. At a certain point, the adult interrupted the play and placed the object beyond the child's reach. The children's typical behavior in this situation was as follows. After several unsuccessful attempts to reach the object, the child started to use nonverbal means of communication (such as vocalizing and pointing gesture) in an attempt to have the adult give the object to him or her. The adult, however, rather than giving the object to the child, would pronounce the name of the object encouraging the child to repeat it. The child started to concentrate on the adult's articulation and tried to pronounce the word. After several attempts, the child correctly pronounced the name of the object, and the adult gave the object to the child. It is important that later, when the children came across a similar situation, they skipped all the attempts to reach an object by themselves or to influence the adult with nonverbal means of communication. Rather, they concentrated on the adult's articulation and tried to pronounce the name of the unreachable object.

The preceding observations and similar data and observations collected by child psychologists in different countries provide strong support for the following Vygotskian statement: "Nothing in the object reality would make children speak. Only adults' demands and the necessity created by them make children do the gigantic work of language acquisition."[14] In light of this statement, it becomes clear why children with certain disabilities may demonstrate language delays that are not inevitable consequences of their disabilities: Their parents "are 'too' willing to interpret and respond [which] may actually result in taking away helpful incentives and information that helps babies with disabilities to learn to talk to communicate their needs."[15]

It is important to stress that, just as with many other learning experiences of children, language acquisition should be "pushed" by adults only in the beginning. By the age of two years, children, as a rule, develop a strong interest in language, which reveals itself, in particular, in the most popular question of the children of this age: "What's that?" Children ask this question incessantly about all the new things that they come across, which make their parents sometimes get nostalgic for the near past when their children could not care less about language.

To be sure, it is difficult to overestimate the importance of the acquisition of language as the major means of social communication. For Vygotskians, however, even more important are developmental outcomes of language acquisition. As discussed in Chapter 1, Vygotsky and his followers view language as a major psychological tool that, having been mastered by children, comes to mediate their mental processes. For example, children start using verbal tools to regulate the behavior of others, as well as regulate their own behavior by the use of egocentric (or private) speech. Later, these tools become internalized, and children develop the ability to self-regulate by the use of inner speech, that is, by giving themselves mental commands.

Another major developmental outcome of language acquisition relates to the development of children's symbolic thought. The role of language acquisition in the development of symbolic thought is discussed in the next section.

Development of Symbolic Thought. It is difficult to overestimate the importance of a new ability that children start developing at the age of around two years: the ability to use symbols to represent objects and events mentally and manipulate them in their minds. This ability has been called "symbolic thought."

Before children develop symbolic thought, they can solve problems only by manual trials (Piaget called this type of performance sensorimotor). For example, if you give a child several blocks of different shapes and a board with differently shaped holes, and ask him to put each block into the hole that fits, the child will not be able to perform this task promptly and surely. Rather, he will keep trying to put the first block into each hole until he finds one that fits, then he will do the same with the second block, and so on. By contrast, a child who has developed the ability to do symbolic thought, will first solve the problem in her head and then decisively put each of the blocks directly into the hole that fits. Thus, the development of symbolic thought makes children capable of *thinking* in the colloquial meaning of this word.

In contrast to Piaget, who believed that the development of symbolic thought was a spontaneous and "natural" process, Vygotsky argued that the development of this ability is heavily determined by children's use of object substitutes. Indeed, let us consider two extreme situations: in the first one, a child is feeding a doll with a spoon, and in the second, a child is imagining himself feeding a doll with a spoon. The first situation is an example of a sensorimotor operation, which does not involve the use of symbols; the second situation is an example of pure symbolic play, which is performed mentally without any manual operations. It is easy to see that there is a huge "gap" between these two extremes; therefore, the child cannot shift directly from pure sensorimotor performance to pure symbolic performance. The use of object substitutes, however, creates a "middle ground" between these two extremes: When the child, while feeding a doll, is using a stick instead of a spoon, his performance, figuratively speaking, is 50% sensorimotor and 50% symbolic. It is 50% sensorimotor, because the child is still performing the manual operation of feeding the doll; it is 50% symbolic, because the child is imposing the meaning of a spoon on the stick and is using the stick as if it were a spoon. Thus, the use of an object substitute becomes "a pivot" for the child that helps him "detach meaning from an object"[16] and start operating symbols mentally.

Another major contributor to the development of children's symbolic thought is language, which, as discussed, children acquire amazingly fast during this age period. Language contributes to the development of symbolic thought in two ways. *First*, language helps children use object substitutes. It has been shown that the child's ability to use an object substitute significantly increases if the child is using the name of the missing object to label the object substitute. The reason for this is that

> objects used in play as substitutes for necessary but missing objects are very multifunctional and, at the same time, their resemblance to the missing objects is very relative. What, indeed, is the resemblance between a stick and a horse? A stick is not even a schematic image of a horse! The same stick can be used to substitute for a rifle, or a snake, or a tree .... The word that the child is using to name a multi-functional object substitute at a certain moment of play immediately limits the ways in which this object can be used, and determines how this object can and should be used, that is, what actions should be performed with this object. If a brick has been named "an iron," that means that it should be used for ironing; if it is named "a meatloaf," it should be eaten; and if it is named "a plate," it should be used for putting food on it and for carrying it as if it were a plate.[17]

Second, children start using words themselves as substitutes for some components of play actions. For example, when feeding a doll, the child performs several abbreviated "feeding" movements, says "had a dinner," and moves to the next episode of the play. Thus, more and more components of play actions are transferred from being performed manually to the symbolic level, which further pro-motes children's ability to operate at the level of purely symbolic thought.

Conclusion: Mediation during the Second and Third Years of Life

We have discussed developmental accomplishments that can be observed in children by the end of the third year. The significance of some of these accomplishments (language acquisition, self-regulation by means of private speech, symbolic thought) is quite obvious. The significance of some other developmental accomplishments (such as the children's new interest in the world of social roles and relations that leads to the development of the motive of role-play and children's transition to sociodramatic play as their new activity) is discussed in the next chapter. But, it is important to stress, all these developmental accomplishments, contrary to common belief, are far from being natural and spontaneous milestones in children's development. Rather, as discussed, they are the result of adult mediation.

Just as with any mediation, however, mediation during the second and third years of life should be organized in the context of joint child-adult activity rather than be mechanically imposed by an adult on a bored child. In some studies, for example, an adult modeled object substitutions in front of the child and suggested that the child imitate them.[18] The child, however, failed to show any desire to imitate the object substitutions modeled, which led the researcher to conclude that it was useless to teach a child how to use object substitutes. In light of the Vygotskian notion of mediation, however, these results were anything but surprising. As discussed before, to succeed in teaching a child object substitutions, an adult should engage him or her in joint play, create a situation in which one of the objects needed to enact the play is missing, and at this point suggest "a solution": to use a certain object instead of the missing one. Incidentally, this recommendation leads to an important conclusion: It is not a good idea if a child has all the toys that are necessary to play a certain game; this situation will not create a need to use object substitutes.

Similar recommendations can be made in regard to other adult mediational efforts during this age period. For example, it is not fruitful to teach children new words merely by making them repeat the words after you. Rather, as discussed, a situation should be created in which the child has to start using language to get what he or she wants. In general, experience of successful mediation during the second and third years provides strong support for the important Vygotskian idea that in order to develop new abilities in children, adults should engage them in the activity that requires that these abilities develop.

In addition to developmental outcomes, properly organized mediation during this age period is very beneficial in one more respect: It helps eliminate or substantially diminish the "terrible two's" negativism – the children's stubbornness, resistance, push for independence, and refusal of adult requests. Vygotskian studies have demonstrated that an important contributor to children's negativism is a delay in parents modifying their relationships with the growing child; for example, the child is two years old, but parents continue to treat him as if he were a year-and-a-half-old. In this situation, the child's negativism is a form of "rebellion" against the parents' refusal to acknowledge his new needs and abilities. Mediation at the "ceiling" level of children's zone of proximal development will substantially weaken the ground for such "rebellion."

4 Three- to Six-Year-Olds: Why Sociodramatic Play Is Important and How to Promote It

Sociodramatic play is children's joint role-play, in which they choose a plot that reflects a certain aspect of social relations (e.g., buying something in a store), distribute roles (e.g., a seller and buyers), and play together imitating the chosen aspect of social relations. The traditional view of sociodramatic play is that it is children's free and spontaneous activity, in which they do whatever they want, liberating themselves from any rules and social pressure; therefore, adults are not supposed to interfere with children's play.

The Vygotskians have developed a quite different approach to sociodramatic play. From their point of view, children play not because they want to liberate themselves from social pressure. Just the opposite; as discussed in the previous chapter, by the age of three years, children develop a strong interest in the world of adults, and they are looking forward to becoming a part of this world. In industrialized societies, however, children cannot fulfill this desire directly: They cannot be doctors or firefighters. That is why they attempt to "penetrate" the world of adults through imitating and exploring social roles and relations in the course of sociodramatic play.

But if the reason for children's play is not that they want to "have a break" from adult guidance and instructions, but rather that they want to explore adult roles and relationships, what is wrong with helping children organize and enact their play? Nothing at all, the Vygotskians argue. Moreover, without adult help, children will not become engaged in sociodramatic play at all!

Indeed, as discussed in the previous chapter, children's need to imitate social roles and relations and their ability to enact such imitation in the course of sociodramatic play do not develop spontaneously. The motive of role-play develops in three-year-old children as the result of adult efforts aimed at switching children's interest from the imitation of object-centered actions to the imitation of social roles and relationships (for example, from using of a spoon to feed a doll to playing the role of a loving mother who is nursing the baby). In addition, in order to be able to become engaged in sociodramatic play, children should be able to perform within an imaginary situation; this ability requires symbolic thought that also develops as a result of adult mediation. Finally, adult mediation has been shown to determine the development of language and rudiments of self-regulation in children, which also are necessary prerequisites for their involvement in joint play. Thus, rather than being a spontaneous and natural phenomenon, children's transition to sociodramatic play is an outcome of adult mediation during the previous period of development.

All the characteristics listed in the preceding paragraph, however, are necessary but not sufficient for children's engagement in sociodramatic play and its advancement. As has been documented by various researchers all over the world, these days many preschoolers do not participate in sociodramatic play at all. Observations on British children have led to the following conclusion:

> Much of the play in the nursery school tends to be repetitive and of a rather low level. We found that 84 percent of the play in nursery schools involved the child in only one action, e.g., swinging, or digging in the sand or perhaps running round saying, "I'm a Dalek." The kind of elaborate socio-dramatic or constructional play which involves a sequence of relatively integrated activities linked by an idea was really relatively infrequent.[1]

Observations performed in Israeli kindergarten classes and nursery schools "indicated that play was becoming extinct.... Most of the play scripts of those who were playing were dull and repetitive, showing the same roles and actions day after day and using play objects mainly at the level of object transformations."[2] American preschoolers have also been shown to demonstrate a very low level of involvement in sociodramatic play.[3] These observations, as well as similar observations collected in other Western societies, hardly support the traditional understanding of sociodramatic play as a "spontaneous" and "natural" activity as it is often viewed by parents and teachers.

Many researchers blame the extinction of sociodramatic play on children's spending their free time watching TV and playing computer or video games. According to the Vygotskians, however, these are contributors to rather than major reasons for the extinction of sociodramatic play. The major reason for this situation, in their view, is that the majority of parents and teachers, at best, believe that they should not "interfere" with children's play or, at worst, even discourage children from sociodramatic play, considering it a waste of time. From the Vygotskian perspective, as mentioned before, adult mediation of sociodramatic play is not only desirable; it is the major determinant of sociodramatic play. What kind of mediation is required to help children become engaged in sociodramatic play? The answer to this question is provided in the next section.

Adult Mediation as the Major Determinant of Sociodramatic Play

Psychologists differentiate between two major forms of mediation of sociodramatic play: explanation to children of social roles and relations, and teaching children play skills.

Explanation to Children of Social Roles and Relations. Because sociodramatic play deals with children's imitation of social roles and relations, children need to know these roles and relations to be able to imitate them. As briefly discussed in the previous chapter, however, social roles and relations cannot be discovered by children through mere observation of adult behavior. Indeed, what children can observe are adult actions. But *why* adults enact these actions and how these actions are related within the given episode of social life remain hidden from children. Therefore, the Vygotskians hold that the explanation to children of different social roles and relations, which adults already started doing during the previous stage of development, should remain the major content of adult mediation of sociodramatic play. What follows is a description of an early Vygotskian study that illustrates this point.

Five- to six-year-old kindergarten children went to a summer camp by train. Then they were given different toys (a model of the train, a model of a railroad station, etc.), and the teacher suggested that they play "railroad station." The children, however, failed to do it; they manipulated the toys but did not engage in sociodramatic play even after the teacher helped them distribute the roles (the station master, a conductor, passengers, etc.). After that, the children were taken to the railroad station again, but this time the teacher explained to them the social roles of different people at the station (this is the station master – he is the main person at the station, he receives the trains; these are passengers – they are buying tickets; this is an engineer – he is preparing a locomotive engine for a trip; this is a conductor – he is checking the passengers' tickets; etc.). The teacher also explained to the children the relationships between different episodes that they were observing (i.e., first, the passenger should buy a ticket, and then he should show it to the conductor in order to be let into the train). After returning to the kindergarten, the children assumed the roles and started to play "railroad station" enthusiastically and on their own initiative.[4]

The importance of explanation of social roles and relations to children for their engagement into sociodramatic play has been confirmed in many non-Vygotskian studies. It has been shown, in particular, that teachers and parents "can help clarify children's understanding of themes and roles by providing relevant experiences such as field trips, classroom visitations by people in different occupations, and stories about different jobs."[5] Moreover, even watching TV can be converted from an activity that interferes with children's play to an activity that benefits their play provided that adults, in the context of watching movies, explain to children the social roles and relationships presented in the movie.[6]

Teaching Children Play Skills. Some of the studies of sociodramatic play have demonstrated that it is useless merely to explain social roles and relations to children if they do not possess play skills, that is, do not know how to create the plot of a play, distribute and enact play roles, or coordinate their roles with the roles of the playmates. Without the mastery of these play skills, the knowledge of social roles and relations by itself cannot make it possible for children to play successfully, just as the knowledge of numbers will not make it possible for a child to add them if he does not know the laws of addition. Therefore, another very important avenue for adult mediational efforts relates to teaching children *how* to play.

How can we teach children play skills? Researchers have differentiated between two strategies of teaching children these skills.[7]

The first strategy relates to the teacher intervening from "outside" the play situation. For example, to help children play "hospital" such intervention includes

> questions ("How is your baby today?"), suggestions ("Let's take your baby to the clinic."), clarification of behavior ("I did the same when my baby was ill."), establishing contact between players ("Can you please help her, nurse?"), and straightforward directions ("Show the nurse where it hurts your baby. Tell her all about it.")[8]

Or, to help a child to switch from manipulating small wooden blocks to play "shoe store," the teacher may engage him in the following dialog:

TEACHER: Mr. Storekeeper, you certainly have a lot of shoes (pointing to the small blocks). Have you sold any yet?
BOBBY: No, I haven't.

TEACHER: Why don't you make some shelves out of the bigger blocks so people can see the shoes you have to sell. While you're doing that, I'll see if I can find some customers for your store.

The teacher might then approach some other children who are playing in the housekeeping corner and suggest that they make a trip to Bobby's store to buy some new shoes.[9]

The second strategy aimed at teaching children play skills relates to the teacher intervening from "inside" the play situation, that is, the teacher actually joins the children's play by assuming and enacting a role relevant to the theme of the play. For example, when playing "hospital," the teacher can

activate a whole group of children, emphasizing the missing play components for each child in her contact with the child. Thus, if she knows that Miriam, who is playing a mother, does not use make-believe with regard to objects, the teacher can say to her, from within her role as a nurse, "Here is the medicine, Mrs. Ohajon" and pretend to give her something. She can elaborate further: "Give two spoonfuls to your baby twice a day. Now call a taxi to take you home since your baby is very ill and should not go out in this cold. Here is the telephone."[10]

Or, to help Bobby engage in "shoe store" play, the teacher may assume the role of a buyer and model the desired play skills for Bobby:

TEACHER: Mr. Storekeeper, I would like to buy a pair of your shoes (pointing to the small blocks).

BOBBY: Which ones?

TEACHER: How about these nice brown ones (picks up two small blocks and pretends to put them on her feet).

BOBBY: Do you like them?

TEACHER: No, they're too tight.

BOBBY: Here, why don't you try these on? (Hands the teacher two more blocks).

The teacher might then offer to become a salesperson and help Bobby try to sell his shoes to other children.[11]

The strategies described before can also be successfully used to switch children from imitating violent or not desirable episodes from adult life that they have observed to mature and beneficial sociodramatic play. For example, having observed her mother's delivering a baby, a pre-K girl started to imitate the act of a baby delivery, with the other children standing around and enjoying the entertainment. The teacher, however, used this episode as a starting point for engaging the children, first in "hospital" play and then in "family life" play.

To conclude, adult mediation is the major determinant of children's sociodramatic play. What form of mediation should be used in any particular case, however, will depend on what exactly the limitations are of the children's knowledge that prevent them from engaging in sociodramatic play. In some cases, children may need to be trained in play skills; in others, children may need to be acquainted with social roles and relations to be imitated; in still other cases, children may need both forms of mediation.

Why Is Sociodramatic Play Important?

Thus, as shown, without adult mediation children often will not play at all or their play will remain impoverished and immature. But what is wrong with this? Why do we want children to play? Maybe the play was fine for children 70 years ago, when they did not have TV and video and computer games, but it is not needed these days, when children have so many other options to enjoy their time? Indeed, many psychologists, educators, and parents, including those who have been influenced by Piaget's writings, do not consider sociodramatic play to contribute anything important to children's development. The Vygotskians, in contrast, believe that sociodramatic play is "the leading source of development in pre-school years."[12] In Vygotsky's words, play

> creates the zone of proximal development of the child. In play a child is always above his average age, above his daily behaviour; in play it

is as though he were a head taller than himself. As in the focus of a magnifying glass, play contains developmental tendencies in a condensed form; in play it is as though the child were trying to jump above the level of his normal behaviour.[13]

Indeed, empirical studies and observations of both Vygotskian and non-Vygotskian researchers have revealed a variety of developmental outcomes of sociodramatic play. Sociodramatic play has been shown to substantially contribute to children's intellectual, cognitive, emotional, and language development, their social competence, perspective-taking skills, school achievement, and other developmental accomplishments during this period. In contrast, children who do not engage in sociodramatic play "appear to be at risk for contemporaneous difficulties and long-term maladaptive outcomes."[14] Numerous research findings have also indicated that not only does mediation of sociodramatic play lead to higher quality of children's play, but that it also results in children's development in the various domains listed earlier.

Discussing developmental outcomes of children's sociodramatic play, the Vygotskians especially stress the significance of those developmental outcomes that, in their view, are the most important for children's transition to the next period of development. In industrialized societies children start going to primary school around the age of six years, so the most significant developmental outcomes of sociodramatic play are those that contribute to the development of school readiness. Let us interrupt the discussion of sociodramatic play and discuss the notion of school readiness.

What Is School Readiness?

There is no consensus among psychologists and educators on how the term "school readiness" should be defined. Often school readiness is associated with children's mastery of such academic skills as counting, elements of reading and writing, and the like. Therefore, kindergarten teachers "face pressure to make their classrooms into scaled-down first grades with worksheets and drills. This is thought by some authorities as a way to make sure that children are prepared for first grade."[15] Many parents also pay special attention to training their children in academic skills with the hope that this training will result in their children's more successful learning at school. Initially, indeed, these children may demonstrate better success at school than their "non-trained" peers. Often, however, after several months, these children begin to demonstrate less and less interest in learning, and their learning becomes less and less successful. Proceeding from these observations, both the Vygotskians and some American researchers have come to the conclusion that the mastery of basic academic skills by itself does not make preschoolers ready for learning at school. Having analyzed the process of learning at school, the Vygotskians have identified the following major components of school readiness.

The Motive to Study at School. Sometimes teachers say about a particular student: "He is learning without interest." The fact of the matter is that learning without interest is simply impossible; as Vygotsky insightfully stated, "the problem of interest in instruction is not whether or not children learn with interest; they never learn without interest."[16] In other words, in order to study at school successfully, children should have a motive to study. As I discuss later, this should not necessarily be (and, initially, rarely is) intrinsic learning motivation, that is, an interest in learning for the sake of learning. Children should develop, however, *some* motive that propels them to study at school.

Self-Regulation. Research and observations have demonstrated that children's ability to self-regulate (to bend their behavior to school rules and regulations, to follow directions, and to attend to the teacher's explanation) is extremely important for their learning at school. Indeed, how can you teach children whose attention fluctuates, who are not able to concentrate on a task or on the teacher's explanation, or who constantly break school regulations? The results of two surveys of American teachers "clearly indicate that kindergarten teachers are concerned with children's regulatory readiness for school activities rather than with more strictly cognitive and academic aspects of readiness."[17]

Symbolic Thought. In the previous chapter, I already discussed the importance of the development of symbolic thought, that is, our ability to solve problems mentally, in our heads, rather than manually, through trial-and-error procedure. While important for successful performance even at a preschool age, this ability becomes literally a must for children's successful learning at school. Indeed, learning at school deals with the acquisition by students of scientific, theoretical knowledge, which is presented to them in the form of concepts, rules, and laws. Without symbolic thought, the acquisition of this type of knowledge is simply impossible.

Non-Egocentric Position. As briefly discussed earlier, the term "egocentrism" was introduced by Piaget to characterize the preschoolers' tendency to look at objects and events only from their own perspectives, disregarding other people's perspectives. School students' non-egocentrism is important for their successful learning in two respects. First, students come to school with many misconceptions (for example, that all birds fly, that all the heavy objects sink in water, etc.); their successful learning requires that they are ready to give up their misconceptions and start perceiving, understanding, and explaining the world from the perspective of scientific rules and laws they have been taught by the teacher. Second, classroom learning requires that children are able to work as a group, which implies that they are capable of coordinating their actions with the actions of their classmates.

Thus, although the above characteristics may not constitute the full list of components of school readiness, they certainly are the major prerequisites for children's successful learning. Let us now discuss how sociodramatic play promotes the development of these components of school readiness.

The Role of Sociodramatic Play in the Development of School Readiness

The Vygotskian general notion of the leading role of sociodramatic play in preparing children for the transition to learning at school has been supported by much empirical data and many observations. To summarize these data and observations, a correlation (sometimes "astonishingly high"[18]) has been found between the quality of sociodramatic play of kindergarteners and different aspects of their further learning at school. The Vygotskians as well as some other researchers attribute these data to the fact that sociodramatic play promotes the development of the major components of school readiness as discussed later.

The Development of the Motive to Study at School. One of the major outcomes of sociodramatic play is that by the end of the period of early childhood, children become dissatisfied with such a pseudo-penetration into the world of adults:

> [The child] looks at himself through the role he has taken, that is, through the role of an adult, emotionally compares himself with an adult, and discovers that he is not an adult yet. The realization of the fact that he is still a child comes as a result of play and leads to the development of the child's new motive to become an adult and to fulfill adult responsibilities in reality.[19]

The only "real" and "serious" role available for the child in an industrialized society, which will bring him or her nearer to an adult position in society, is the role of a school student. Therefore, the motive to fulfill adult responsibilities is concretized in children's strong desire to study at school. Often this desire is expressed directly by children's statements to the effect that they want "to go to school and start to study as soon as possible."[20] Thus, sociodramatic play leads to the development in children of the motive to study at school (in Chapters 6 and 8, I discuss how this desire to study energized by the desire to fulfill adult responsibilities can and should be converted into intrinsic learning motivation).

The Development of Self-Regulation. In contrast to the traditional view of sociodramatic play as children's free activity, Vygotsky and his followers stress that children are not free in play. In play, every child is supposed to act in accordance with his or her role. But, every role contains some implicit rules:

> If the child is playing the role of a mother, then she has rules of maternal behaviour. The role the child fulfils ... will always stem from the rules, i.e., the imaginary situation will always contain rules. In play the child is free. But this is an illusory freedom.[21]

Thus, when acting out a play role, a child follows the rule, which is "hidden ... under the role."[22]

Not all the play rules, however, are pleasant for the child. Often, playing children have to suppress their immediate desires and bend their behavior to an "unpleasant" rule in order for play to be sustained. What makes it possible for children to bend their behavior to the rules of the play? Observations of sociodramatic play have demonstrated that children who participate in play are very strictly regulating each other's behavior in regard to following the play roles. What follows is one such observation:

Six-year-old boys were playing "firefighters." They distributed the roles: One of them was "the chief firefighter," another was "the driver of the fire engine," and the others were "firefighters." The play started. The chief shouted "fire!" Everybody grasped a tool and took a seat in the fire engine. The driver "drove" the fire engine. When they got to the point of destination, the chief gave the order, and all the firefighters started to run to extinguish the fire. The first impulse of the driver was to follow everybody: After all, the most interesting part of the play was about to get started! But the other children reminded him that, according to his role, he had to stay in the engine. The child had to suppress his desire to follow everybody and, instead, he returned to the fire engine.[23]

As briefly discussed in Chapter 1, according to Vygotsky, a major determinant of children's transition to self-regulation is their use of verbal tools for regulating the behavior of others. As a result of such other-regulation, children master these verbal tools, these tools become internalized, and children develop the ability to self-regulate by the use of inner speech, that is, by giving themselves mental commands. Numerous studies and observations have demonstrated that, indeed, children's involvement in mutual regulation in play results in further development of their ability for self-regulation in non-play situations.

As discussed earlier, these days sociodramatic play is "becoming extinct."[24] Unsurprisingly, a survey of kindergarten teachers conducted by the National Center for Early Development and Learning "suggests that many children are arriving at school without effective self-regulation skills."[25] As a result, they cannot attend to the teacher's explanations, and the teacher must provide them with very strong stimulation in order to gain their attention; as teachers themselves report, "they have to 'sing, dance, or act like Big Bird' in order to teach"[26] (in Chapter 8, I discuss why this strategy does not work). Thus, not only does sociodramatic play lead to the development of children's self-regulation, but the lack of sociodramatic play is associated with deficiencies of their self-regulation as well.

Further Development of Symbolic Thought. As discussed in Chapter 3, the use by children of object substitutes (that is, objects that stand for other objects) in the context of object-centered play leads to the development of their symbolic thought. The use of object substitutes continues in the course of sociodramatic play; for example, when playing at war, children may use sticks to substitute for guns. Also, sociodramatic play itself requires that children exercise their ability to perform within an imaginary situation (develop the plot of the game, plan their play actions, make corrections in the enacting of the play roles as the play progresses, etc.). Thus, sociodramatic play leads to further development in children of symbolic thought.

Overcoming of Egocentrism. When playing, children have to treat their playmates not according to their real-life names and relations, but according to their play roles. In real life, Tom and John may have very bad relations; in play, however, they will treat each other in a collaborative and friendly manner if their roles require it. Also, playing children have to coordinate their play actions with the play actions of playmates. For example, if Phil has "shot" Steve when playing at war, Steve has to fall down and remain "dead." Finally, children have to accept the meanings their playmates have assigned to object substitutes that they are using. For example, in "doctor-patient" play, the "doctor" may decide to use a stick to stand for a syringe. For the "patient," however, the stick "may become a syringe only if he takes into account the doctor's position."[27] Thus, in sociodramatic play "the child's position towards the external world fundamentally changes ... and the ability to coordinate his point of view with other possible points of view develops."[28] From this perspective, the complaint of American kindergarten teachers that "half of their students or more have difficulty working as part of a group"[29] can be easily explained by the fact that, these days, sociodramatic play is becoming extinct.

The Vygotskian views of sociodramatic play as playing the major role in the development of school readiness, and of the importance of adult mediation of sociodramatic play, have come to exert an increasingly stronger influence on the American system of early childhood education. The Position Statement of the National Association for the Education of Young Children adopted in 2009 clearly states that "play appears to support the abilities that underlie [academic] learning and thus to promote school success," and that "active scaffolding of imaginative play is needed in early childhood settings if children are to develop the sustained, mature dramatic play."[30]

Conclusion: Sociodramatic Play – How It Develops and What It Develops

The preceding analysis makes it possible to correct two popular misconceptions in regard to sociodramatic play:

1. Often, not only the general public but child and developmental psychologists as well draw an analogy between sociodramatic play and play in animals. This analogy is only at the surface, and is simply wrong. Animal young play is natural and spontaneous, and it serves the purpose of exercising and refining some skills (for example, hunting). Sociodramatic play gratifies the need of children to imitate and explore adult roles and relationships, and it does not appear and advance without adult mediation.

2. In contrast to a popular view of sociodramatic play as a useless waste of time, "in many ways sociodramatic play means direct preparation of school behavior."[31] To be sure, there are other activities that can and should be used to prepare Pre-K and K children for school (they are discussed in the next chapter). In a way, however, sociodramatic play is unique in this respect, because it targets *all* the major components of school readiness. That is why your mediation of sociodramatic play is needed not simply for the sake of the advancement of sociodramatic play, but for the sake of making your children ready for systematic learning at school.

It is important to remember, however, that, just as with any mediation, mediation of sociodramatic play should be performed only if it is really needed, if children experience difficulties with starting or advancing their play. Your unnecessary interference with children's play may lead to just the opposite outcome: It may suppress the play rather than promoting it.

It is also important to mention that mediation of sociodramatic play should not be reduced to your only spending several minutes a day on introducing different social roles and relations to children or teaching them play skills. It is equally important that you support and promote the children's excitement and positive interest in regards to the adult world. My friend, a child psychologist from Russia, has shared with me an interesting observation: Recently, there was a period of time when Russian children's participation in sociodramatic play abruptly dropped. The reason for this situation was quite clear. The country was going through a period of economic depression. Therefore, the adults were concerned about keeping their jobs or being able to maintain their standard of living, and children could see and feel their parents' distress. As a result, the adult world lost its attractiveness to the children; they came to associate it with frustration and anxiety. Therefore, do your best to present the adult world to children in a positive light. Of course, it is often impossible (and may not even be a good idea) to hide from children all the problems that adults come across in their jobs or family relationships. Try to present these problems to them, however, as a challenge that adults proudly meet.

And the last concluding remark. The criticism of the replacement of sociodramatic play by teaching children academic skills under current educational practices should not lead to the conclusion that teaching preschoolers some of these skills should be totally abandoned. Rather, the "Vygotskians stress that preacademic activities can be beneficial in the early childhood classroom, but only if they emerge out of children's interests and only if they occur in a social context appropriate for young children."[32] Sociodramatic play creates a perfect context for teaching children such academic skills as counting, reading, and writing. For example, in the context of playing at a supermarket, teaching children how to write and read shopping lists and count the items to be bought will be a natural and meaningful component of their play and will be consistent with the children's needs to enact their roles.

5   Mediation of Preschoolers' Activities to Promote School Readiness

Although, as discussed in the previous chapter, the Vygotskians view sociodramatic play as the most important preschooler activity, preschoolers are engaged in other age-specific activities, such as constructive play with the use of building blocks, listening to and retelling fairy tales, playing with dollhouses, playing with water and sand, motor activities (such as running and jumping), and so forth. No doubt, these activities are fun and contribute somewhat to children's cognitive, social, and motor development, especially if they are performed with adult involvement. The point is, however, that these age-specific activities can be substantially modified and enriched so that they will promote children's development to a much greater extent and will specifically target the development of children's school readiness. In this chapter, I describe several such activities designed by the Vygotskians for Pre-Kindergarten and Kindergarten children.[1]

Architects, Builders, and Building Inspectors[2]

This activity begins with the teacher suggesting to children that they become architects; they will be drawing houses and castles, and other children will be using their drawings to build these houses and castles. To be sure, the children become very enthusiastic about this suggestion. But, to become an architect, one should learn first to draw what a house or castle looks like from different sides.

Figure 5.1. Three views of a cylinder.

And the children start to learn. They are given stencils (transparent templates) and different blocks (for example, a cylinder). The child should find the holes in the stencil that represent three views of this block (the front view, the side view, and the view from above) and use these holes to draw the three views of the block (Figure 5.1).

Then the assignments become more difficult: The child is given a two-block construction (for example, a house) and she has to use the stencil to draw its three views (Figure 5.2).

At this stage, it is useful to engage children in joint performance by assigning them different roles: one of them builds the house, the second one draws the three views of the house, and the third one compares the drawings against the house and corrects any mistakes found.

Figure 5.2. Three views of "a house."

Figure 5.3. An "architect" uses the stencil to draw the three views
of an imaginary castle.

Finally, the children are engaged in the following activity: One
of the children (the architect) uses the stencil to draw the front view
and the view from above of the imaginary castle she wants to be built
(Figure 5.3). Another child (the builder) builds the castle following
the architect's drawings (Figure 5.4). Then, the architect draws the
side view of the built castle.

After that, the third child (the building inspector) is checking
whether or not the castle matches the drawings (Figure 5.5). It is
important that each child is provided with an opportunity to enjoy

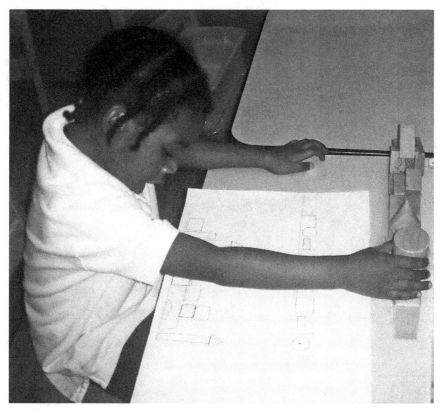

Figure 5.4. A "builder" builds the castle following the architect's drawings.[11]

each of these roles: If, today, a child is the builder, tomorrow, she will be assigned the role of the architect, and the day after tomorrow, she will be the inspector.

Look at the castle in Figure 5.5 that a Pre-Kindergarten child built following another child's drawings; not every adult would be able to perform such a task! But the described activity is not only very challenging and interesting to children; it also contributes to the development of the major components of their school readiness.

Drawings of the three views of a building are its external symbolic representations, just as object substitutes are external symbolic representations of objects that they replace. As discussed in Chapter 3,

Figure 5.5. A "building inspector" is checking to see if the castle matches the drawings.[12]

the use of object substitutes leads to the development of children's symbolic thought; similarly, drawing the three views of a building, using the drawings to construct the building, or checking whether or not the castle matches the drawings contribute to the development of children's *symbolic thought*.

When representing the building from different views (front, side, and above), children develop the ability to look at things and events from different perspectives. This experience helps them *overcome their egocentrism*.

Finally, as mentioned, this activity implies that children switch over their responsibilities (today, a child inspects the correctness of the building against the drawings, and tomorrow, another "inspector" will be evaluating the correctness of this child's building). Thus, children are engaged in mutual control, which, as discussed earlier, contributes to the development of their *self-regulation*.

Constructing Models of Fairy-Tales[3]

Young children experience serious difficulties when trying to retell a tale that has been read to them. As a rule, a child tries to memorize the tale word for word. As a result, when retelling the tale, the child retells some of the sentences word for word regardless of whether or not these sentences are important, but skips some of the major episodes of the tale. Why does this happen?

When adults read a story or an article with the goal of remembering it, they construct a mental model of the text. For example, if this is a love story, the important episodes may be: How they met, how an enemy made them separate, how they met again, how they got married, and so forth. If it is a scientific article, the model that adults construct may be as follows: the hypothesis, the study, the data, and the conclusion. Young children, for sure, cannot construct such mental models on their own. So, let us teach them how to do it.

In the beginning of this activity, children are taught how to use substitutes (sticks, paper cutouts, etc.) to represent the main characters of a tale. For example, the teacher is reading *Goldilocks and the Three Bears*, and the children should raise a yellow stick when Goldilocks is mentioned, a big brown stick when the father-bear is mentioned, a medium brown stick when the mother-bear is mentioned, and a small brown stick when their baby is mentioned.

After that, the children are taught how to use substitutes to model different episodes of a tale. For example, the teacher reads a tale about a fox, a cat, and a rooster, and the children use paper cutout substitutes (the fox – an orange circle, the cat – a gray circle, and the rooster – a red circle) to model the tale episodes on their tables with schematic pictures of a forest, the rooster's house, etc. For example, "the cat went to the forest" (a child moves the gray circle to the

Figure 5.6. A cutout model of *The Bun* tale.

"forest" on the table); "the fox went to the rooster's house" (the child moves the orange circle to the rooster's house), "caught the rooster and dragged him to the forest" (the child moves the orange and red circles to the "forest"), and so on.

Later, several children work together on the same table. One of them models a tale episode, another child evaluates the correctness of the model of this episode constructed by the first child, and the third child retells this episode following the model constructed. Then, the children switch over their roles.

At the next step, the children are taught how to use paper cut-outs to construct the model of the whole tale. With teacher's help, they use substitutes to reproduce major episodes of a new tale in a special field that consists of a set of section; the number of sections is equal to the number of the episodes in the tale. Then they use the model constructed to retell the tale. For example, the teacher reads the Russian tale *The Bun* (the Bun rolls away from home, rolls to the forest, successfully escapes from a wolf, and a bear, but then meets a witty fox, who tricks the Bun and eats it). Figure 5.6 presents the model that Pre-Kindergarten children constructed for this tale, and that they successfully used after that to retell the tale.

Later on, the children learn how to construct pictorial models of new tales. While listening to a tale, the child draws its model (a set of boxes connected with arrows) and fills in each of the boxes with symbolic drawings that represent the characters of the given episode. Then the child retells the tale following the model. For example, the teacher reads the Russian tale *A Girl and a Little Bear* (a girl goes to

Figure 5.7. A pictorial model of *A Girl and a Little Bear* tale.[13]

the forest, meets a little bear, they make friends, and the bear gives a magic mushroom to the girl). Figure 5.7 presents the model that a Kindergarten child constructed for this tale and then successfully used to retell the tale.

Still later, the children become able to retell new tales without constructing their pictorial models. This does not mean, however, that they do not construct models of new tales anymore; rather, they now construct *mental* models of new tales and stories just the same way adults do.

To be sure, learning how to construct mental models of a new story and then to retell its major episodes following this model is a very important academic accomplishment; this is the foundation for the development of reading comprehension. But, in addition, given that the children work with symbolic models of tales, this experience leads to the development of their *symbolic thought*. Also, the children's mutual control in which they are engaged at certain steps of the described activity results, as discussed, in the development of their *self-regulation*. Thus, the activity discussed in this section leads to the development of two important components of school readiness.

Constructing and Using Room Plans[4]

In this activity, children construct and use room plans for the arrangement and search of different objects. In the beginning, this activity is built around the construction and use of plans for the furniture arrangement in a dollhouse.

First, the teacher and the child arrange furniture in a dollhouse. Then the teacher says: "A friend of our doll Mary loves how Mary has arranged her furniture, and he wants to arrange his furniture the same way. He asked us to give him a plan of Mary's room. Let us help him." The teacher gives the child several cutouts, the sizes and shapes of which correspond to different pieces of furniture (a circle for a table, a small square for a chair, a long rectangle for a bed, etc.), and the child, with the teacher's help, uses these cutouts to construct a plan of the room on a special board, the size and shape of which corresponds to the size and shape of the doll's room.

Then, the teacher gives the child the opposite task: "Mary decided to rearrange the furniture in her room. She made a plan of how she wants the furniture to be arranged in her room (the teacher gives the child a plan of the furniture arrangement). Look, here is a table, here – a bed.... Let us help her arrange the furniture in her room as the plan shows." The child, with the teacher's help, uses the plan to arrange the furniture (Figure 5.8).

Later, the children are offered another task. They are provided with a "furnished" dollhouse (a picture of a beetle is hidden under one of the furniture pieces) and a plan of the furniture arrangement. The teacher says: "A beetle has flown into the room and hidden here (the teacher marks one of the furniture pieces in the plan). Mary wants to find it. Let us help her." The child should use the room plan with the mark to find the beetle in the dollhouse.

Still later, one child hides the beetle under a furniture piece and marks the corresponding piece in the plan, and another child should find the beetle following the mark in the plan.

After the children have mastered the construction and use of plans of a dollhouse, they start performing this activity in a "real" environment, for example, in their classroom. Accordingly, the plans that the children work with represent reduced models of their classroom. In the beginning, the tasks the children perform are similar to some of those that they performed with the dollhouse

Figure 5.8. A child is arranging the furniture in a dollhouse following the plan.

(for example, they use the plan to look for a "bear," who has hidden under a furniture piece). Later, the children are presented with new tasks (for example, a child is asked to find her or his friend's table in the plan of the classroom; or the teacher marks one of the tables in the plan, and the child who is sitting at this table is supposed to stand up).

Finally, an important complication is introduced to the children's activity: To perform the aforementioned tasks, they should use reversed room plans, that is, plans are shown to them upside down. This activity requires that the child, when using the plans to search for different objects, "converts" them in his or her mind.

The major contribution of the discussed activity to children's school readiness relates to the development of their *symbolic thought*. Indeed, room plans are external symbolic representations, the use of which, as already discussed, gradually leads to the development of children's ability to operate symbols in their minds. Also, some tasks involve children's joint activity with elements of mutual control; this, as also already discussed, is advantageous for the development of *self-regulation*.

Constructing and Using Models of Quantities[5]

In the beginning of this activity, children are taught to measure different objects: sticks, water, sand, and so on. In the course of measuring, they come to realize that each object has different parameters (amount, weight, length, etc.), and that each parameter of an object has to be measured with a proper measure. For example, the amount of water can be measured with a spoon or a cup, the length of a stick can be measured with a ruler or a shorter stick, and so on.

After that, the children are asked to compare a certain parameter of two different objects (for example, the amounts of water in two buckets) using a proper measure (a cup). The children enthusiastically pour water from the first bucket, then from the second bucket, but in the end fail to tell if there was more water in the first bucket or in the second bucket: They either did not count the cups they were pouring, or forgot the number of cups poured from the first bucket as soon as they started pouring water from the second bucket. Therefore, they willingly accept the suggestion of the teacher, first to construct the models of the amounts of water in both buckets, then to compare these models, and after that to tell in which bucket there was more water. The activity now looks as follows. Having poured out the first cup of water from the first bucket, the child puts a chip on the table, pouring out the second cup is marked with the second chip, and so forth. The same procedure is performed with the second bucket. As a result, the child represents the amounts of water in the buckets with their models: two sets of chips. Having then compared these sets, the child tells in which of the two buckets there was more water, and what the difference in the quantities of water in these buckets was.

Because this activity involves the construction and use by children of external symbolic representations of different quantities, it promotes the developments of their *symbolic thought*. In addition, this activity results in children's overcoming centration as the major shortcoming of their thinking at this stage (see Introduction for a brief discussion of the phenomenon of centration). Last but not least, this activity creates the foundation for children's understanding of the scientific concepts of number and quantity later on (as discussed in Chapter 9, one of the major reasons for school students' poor learning outcomes in math relates to their lack of understanding of the concepts of number and quantity).

Using Schedules of the Day[6]

In the beginning of this activity, children together with the teacher choose a symbol (a "ticket") for each of the class activities (reading, constructive play, sociodramatic play, etc.). Then, in the morning, each child is provided with a schedule of the day's activities that are presented as a set of such symbols (Figure 5.9).

The child finds his or her subgroup based on what the first activity is (in Figure 5.9 it is "reading"), goes to the teacher who is running this activity, gives his or her schedule to the teacher, and participates

Figure 5.9. A schedule of the day (the first two activities have been marked as completed).

in this activity. When the activity is over, the teacher puts a sticker under the symbol of the first activity in the child's schedule, returns the schedule to the child, the child with the teacher's help finds the next activity on his or her schedule, goes to the teacher who runs this activity, and so on.

Up to this point, the responsibility for monitoring the child's participation in the activities scheduled is divided between the teacher and the child. At the next step, the teacher passes more responsibility for such monitoring to the child: The child himself or herself puts a sticker under the completed activity, and then finds the next activity in the schedule.

Still later, putting up stickers is totally eliminated. After the completion of each activity, the child simply looks at the schedule to find his or her new activity.

Thus, the children are gradually moved from following the teacher's directions with the use of external tools (stickers) to giving directions to themselves without such tools; they come to self-monitor their switching from one activity to another. So this activity contributes to the development of children's *self-regulation*. Also, the use of symbols of different activities is advantageous for the development of children's *symbolic thought*.

Do as the Animal Does[7]

This activity begins with the teacher introducing four pictures to the children. "This is a frog, it is jumping; and this is a turtle, it is walking very slowly; and this is a rabbit, it is running fast; and this is a bear, it is sleeping." When showing each picture, the teacher models the animal's behavior.

Then the teacher says: "Let us play a game: I will be showing you a picture, we all together will say what the animal in the picture is doing, and you will do it." Then the teacher shows, for example, the rabbit, says together with the children "run!" and the children run in place. Then the teacher shows the frog, says together with the children "jump!" and the children jump in place. Then, at the picture of a turtle, the teacher says together with the children "slow!" and the children walk slowly in place. The picture of a bear is used to make children calm down; they say "sleep!" and stay still.

At the next step, the teacher just shows the pictures silently, and the children should give the commands to themselves aloud: "run!", "jump!", "slow!" "sleep!" and follow these commands.

Then, one of the children shows the pictures, and the other children should give commands to themselves and follow these commands (all the children in turn enjoy the role of the "teacher").

After that, the rules of the game become more complicated: The teacher suggests that the children should not follow what the animal does unless the teacher says "Please!"[8] This complication is very important. Before, children performed the actions without making a conscious decision, almost as a conditioned response. Now, before acting, they should make a conscious decision about whether or not the action prescribed by the picture should be performed. So, the teacher shows the pictures to the children, sometimes saying "Please!" and sometimes not. If the "Please!" is said, the children should say aloud what the act is that they should perform (for example, "jump") and then perform the act. If "Please!" is not said, the children should stay still. First the teacher gives commands, and then the children, in turn, take the role of the teacher.

Then the children perform the task without giving themselves commands aloud: If the "teacher" shows a picture and says "Please," the other children should do what the picture says; if "the teacher" does not say "Please," the other children should stay still.

Finally, another important complication is introduced: If the teacher shows a picture and says "Please," the children should perform the required action only after the teacher has counted aloud to three (still later – to ten); as before, if "Please" has not been said, children do not perform any action after the teacher has finished counting. Again, first it is the teacher who runs this activity, and then the children, in turn, take the role of the "teacher."

This activity leads to children's gradual transition from acting while regulated by others, through acting by giving themselves commands aloud, to acting by giving themselves internal commands. As discussed in Chapter 1, this is the main avenue for the development of *self-regulation*.

Conclusion: Amplification of Preschoolers' Development

When discussing the problem of mediation of preschoolers' development, the Russian Vygotskian Zaporozhets differentiated between *acceleration* and *amplification* of child development. He wrote:

> Optimal educational opportunities for a young child to reach his or her potential and to develop in a harmonious fashion are not created by accelerated ultra-early instruction aimed at shortening the childhood period – that would prematurely turn a toddler into a preschooler and a preschooler into a first-grader. What is needed is just the opposite – expansion and enrichment of the content in the activities that are uniquely "preschool."[9]

This idea is highly relevant to the problem of the promotion of school readiness in preschoolers. As already mentioned in the previous chapter, it is counterproductive to "accelerate" preschoolers' development, that is, to replace their age-specific activities by engaging them in mastery of academic skills such as counting, reading, and writing – the practice that, unfortunately, some parents and educators follow. On the other hand, leaving preschoolers to enjoy their favorite activities entirely on their own is not too beneficial for their development either. What the Vygotskians recommend is *amplification* of preschooler's development by "expansion and enrichment" of their age-specific activities so that participation in these activities will promote the development of the major components of school readiness.

To be sure, the examples described in this chapter do not constitute the full list of "amplified" activities in which preschoolers can and should be engaged by adults; some other examples of such activities can be found in the book by Bodrova and Leong.[10] Moreover, some of the favorite games in which adults have engaged children for generations are also very beneficial for their development; for example the famous game *Simon Says* promotes the development of self-regulation in children in a similar way to the Vygotskian activity *Do as the Animal Does* described earlier. It is also important to stress that if you understand the Vygotskian notions about school readiness and its promotion, you yourselves will be able to come up with your own techniques of amplification of preschoolers' activities. Let us summarize these notions.

Self-regulation develops in the context of children's mutual regulation and as a result of internalization of external tools for self-regulation. Therefore, any joint activity of children in which they are engaged in mutual regulation will promote the development of their self-regulation. Also, it is important that you provide children with external tools for self-regulation and teach them how to use these tools to plan and monitor their activity (similar to the *Schedules of the Day* described earlier). Finally, in the context of children's performance, ask them questions about what they are going to do, if the intermediate outcomes of their performance are what they expected, and if the final results are what they planned. Answering your questions will promote the children's ability to use private speech to plan, monitor, and evaluate their performance, which will lead later on to the development of their ability to do self-regulation by the use of inner speech.

Symbolic thought develops as a result of children's use of external symbolic representations such as object substitutes, drawings, plans, models, diagrams, and maps. Children can be easily provided with this experience in the context of everyday life activities. For example, before rearranging the furniture in a room, develop a new plan of the furniture arrangement together with the child, and let the child use this plan to monitor and direct your furniture rearrangement. Or, when you go shopping, make the shopping list together with the child using different symbols; each symbol will stand for an item to be bought. Then let the child check off on the list which items have been put into the shopping basket and direct you on which items are still missing. Incidentally, in both everyday life activities mentioned, children will also become engaged in monitoring and regulating your behavior, which will facilitate the development of their self-regulation.

As discussed, sociodramatic play is indispensable for overcoming preschoolers' *egocentrism* (just as it is indispensable for the development of all the other components of school readiness). In addition, however, children's engagement in *any* joint activity will be beneficial in this respect, because no joint activity can be sustained without the participants' perspective-taking and coordinating of their actions. Therefore, to help children overcome their egocentrism, they should be engaged in joint projects that they enjoy and want to sustain, but that require that they look at objects or events from another person's perspective or coordinate their actions with the actions of their peers. In the context of such activities, the teacher should help children coordinate their actions and do perspective taking (similar to how the teacher does it in the context of sociodramatic play). The teacher should also supply children with tools that make it possible for them to look at objects or events from different perspectives (similar to how it is done in the *Architects, Builders, and Building Inspectors* activity, described earlier).

To be sure, the Vygotskian activities described in this chapter are not carved in stone; they can be modified and even combined within one activity. For example, you read a pirate story to your children. Then you engage them in the construction of a model of this story, which they use to retell the story. After that, with your help, children elaborate on the plot of this story, distribute roles and organize socio-dramatic play. In the context of play, the "pirates" find a map (the classroom plan) with a mark indicating hidden "treasures," and they use the map to find the "treasures" hidden in the classroom.

It is important to note that all activities described in this chapter are most beneficial for the development of school readiness if they are performed by a group of children. Therefore, Pre-Kindergarten and Kindergarten educational setting are the best environments for the organization of these activities.

6 Learning at School: Children Not Only Learn; They Develop As Well

As briefly discussed in Chapter 1, Vygotsky and his followers view school instruction as the major avenue for mediation and, therefore, as the major contributor to children's development during the period of middle childhood. According to the Vygotskians, the major reason for the development-generating effect of school instruction relates to students' acquisition of scientific knowledge, which can be contrasted with the everyday life knowledge of preschoolers.

Everyday life knowledge is the result of generalization of children's personal experience in the absence of systematic instruction. Therefore, such knowledge is unsystematic, empirical, not conscious, and often wrong. For example, the concept of a bird that young children develop includes the ability to fly as the major characteristic of birds; therefore, preschoolers do not define a penguin as a bird. Similarly, a three-year-old child, having observed a needle, a pin, and a coin sinking in water, comes to the wrong conclusion that all small objects sink and begins to use this rule to predict the behavior of different objects in water.[1] Despite its "unscientific" nature, everyday life knowledge plays an important role in children's learning as a foundation for the acquisition of scientific knowledge. For example, learning different species by school students requires that they have some understanding what animals are and know at least several representatives of the animal kingdom.

In contrast to everyday life knowledge, scientific knowledge is the result of the generalization of the experience of humankind that is fixed in science (understood in the broadest sense of the term to include both natural and social sciences as well as the humanities), and it is acquired by students consciously and according to a certain system. In the examples given earlier, the scientific concept of a bird, rather than including the ability to fly, includes such characteristics as being a vertebrate, warm-blooded animal with feathers, which lays eggs; similarly, the scientific rule that makes it possible to predict the behavior of objects in water is Archimedes' law, not the size of an object.

According to the Vygotskians, the acquisition of scientific knowledge results in several important outcomes. First, it transforms students' everyday life knowledge; students start "rethinking" what they learned before from the perspective of the newly acquired scientific knowledge ("Wow, I thought a bat is like a pigeon; but no, it is like a mouse!). Second, students start using scientific knowledge as a tool of their thinking and problem solving; figuratively speaking, school students start looking at the world through the glasses of scientific knowledge ("What is a dolphin? Let me think … it is warm blooded, and it feeds babies milk. It is a mammal!"). And, most importantly, the acquisition of scientific knowledge "plays a decisive role in the child's cognitive development."[2] Specifically, students' thinking becomes much more independent of their personal experience; they become "theorists" rather than "practitioners." The following section provides a more detailed analysis of how school instruction promotes development.

How School Instruction Promotes Development

The first solid set of empirical data supporting the Vygotskian view of the role of school instruction in children's development was obtained in the classical cross-cultural study performed by Vygotsky's closest friend and colleague, A. Luria.[3] This study became possible because of the fact that, in the early 1930s, the system of school instruction was just established in many regions of Uzbekistan and Kirghizia, Asian republics of the former Soviet Union. This situation allowed Luria and his research team to go to remote villages of those republics and study various mental processes of adult villagers, some of whom were illiterate, while some had already enjoyed one or two years of schooling.

Luria's study was followed by many other cross-cultural studies, as well as studies evaluating developmental outcomes of school instruction within one culture.[4] By now, plenty of data about the role of school instruction in the development of children's various mental processes have been collected. Let us review these data.

Perception. Illiterate and literate adults were shown different geometric shapes (squares, circles, triangles, etc.), some of which were drawn by lines, some made up of dots, and some were solid-colored; they were asked to identify among the shapes those that looked alike. It turned out that illiterate adults when performing this task associated the shapes with objects in their environment; for example, they identified a triangle and a square made up of dots as similar because both "looked like watches." Literate adults, in contrast, identified as similar, for example, a triangle drawn by lines and a triangle made up of dots, because "both are triangles." Thus, the perception of illiterate adults was dominated by their everyday life experience, whereas the perception of their literate neighbors was dominated by abstract geometrical concepts they learned at school.[5]

Memory. If you are asked to memorize a list of words (winter, bank, girl, book, orange, etc.), you probably will try to use a strategy to make logical connections between the words. For example, you may create a story about a girl who, in the winter, went to the bank to withdraw money in order to buy a book and an orange. Or you may simply draw a mental picture of a girl, who, in the winter, sits in the bank, eating an orange and reading a book. Such strategies aimed at organizing unrelated pieces of information into a meaningful system are called mnemonics, and they have been shown to enormously expend our ability to memorize and recall. The use of mnemonics may seem natural to you, but it is not: Children master them in the context of learning at school. This is why literate people perform much better than illiterate people on memory tasks in which they are asked to memorize and recall new information.[6] Even one year of schooling results in substantial improvement of children's memory: At the end of the first grade, children demonstrate much better memory than kindergarteners of the same chronological age.[7]

Linguistic Awareness. Although preschoolers do not experience problems with the practical use of grammatically correct expressive language, their linguistic awareness remains at a very poor level. As a matter of fact, a word is often viewed by preschoolers as a property of an object just as the object's size or shape. Therefore, for a preschooler, the sentence "There are twelve chairs in the room" consists of twelve words, whereas the sentence "Katja ate all the patties" does not have any words because "she ate them all."[8] Similarly, a preschooler cannot analyze the sound components of words; therefore, the child believes that the word "cat" is longer than the word "kitten," because "cat is a grown-up, and kitten is a baby." Studies have demonstrated that linguistic awareness develops in children as a result of formal reading instruction. In particular, by the end of the first grade, children demonstrate a much better ability to analyze the sound components of words than do kindergarteners of the same chronological age.[9]

Classification. Illiterate and literate adults were shown the pictures of four objects and were asked to find an object that did not belong to the group. When solving these problems, illiterate people turned out to proceed from "concrete ideas about practical [situations] in which appropriate objects could be incorporated."[10] For example, an illiterate adult, when shown pictures of a hammer, a saw, a log, and a hatchet, said:

> They all fit here! The saw has to saw the log, the hammer has to hammer it, and the hatchet has to chop it.... You can't take any of these things away. There isn't any you don't need!"[11]

In contrast, literate adults when approaching this task applied the general category "tools" and concluded that, among all the objects, only a log did not fit this category.

Hypothetical Deductive Reasoning. According to Piaget, hypothetical deductive reasoning is an important ability that develops when children transit to the stage of formal-logical thought.[12] One of the major tools of hypothetical deductive reasoning is the *syllogism*: a logical argument in which two premises lead to a definite conclusion. For example, the premises that "cotton can grow only where it is hot and dry," and that "in England it is cold and damp," lead to the conclusion that cotton cannot grow in England. However, although such a conclusion looks obvious to literate people, it is not the case for illiterate people. What follows is an example of an illiterate adult's approach to the above syllogism:

> "Cotton can grow only where it is hot and dry. In England it is cold and damp. Can cotton grow there?"
>
> "I don't know."
>
> "Think about it."
>
> "I've only been in the Kashgar country. I don't know beyond that."
>
> "But on the basis of what I said to you, can cotton grow there?"
>
> "If the land is good, cotton will grow there, but if it is damp and poor, it won't grow. If it's like Kashgar country, it will grow there too. If the soil is loose, it can grow there too, of course."
>
> The syllogism was then repeated. "What can you conclude from my words?"
>
> "If it's cold there, it won't grow. If the soil is loose and good, it will."
>
> "But what do my words suggest?"
>
> "Well ... we're ignorant people; we've never been anywhere, so we don't know if it's hot or cold there."[13]

To summarize, in contrast to the responses obtained from literate people, the most typical responses of their illiterate neighbors

> were a complete denial of the possibility of drawing conclusions from propositions about things they had no personal experience of, and

suspicion about any logical operation of a purely theoretical nature, although there was the recognition of the possibility of drawing conclusions from one's own practical experience.[14]

Thus, schooling is instrumental in the development of hypothetical deductive reasoning.[15]

IQ. As opposed to the traditional view of IQ scores as genetically predetermined, more and more data come to indicate that children's intellectual performance is grossly determined by schooling. In particular, such data have been obtained by studying children of almost the same chronological age who, for different reasons, entered school at different ages. One study evaluated intellectual performance of children who belonged to the same age group (either 8 years old or 10 years old) but had received a year's difference in schooling. It turned out that intellectual performance of 8-year-olds with three years of schooling was closer to intellectual performance of 10-years-old with four years of schooling than to intellectual performance of 8-year-olds with two years of schooling. Similar results were obtained in another study performed with fourth, fifth, and sixth graders: Intellectual performance of children in each grade was substantially below the intellectual performance of chronologically younger children in the next higher grade.[16]

Self-Analysis. As discussed in more detail in the next chapter, by the age of early adolescence, a child in literate societies develops the ability to analyze more or less objectively his or her personality, cognition, and emotions. It turns out that the development of the ability to do self-analysis in terms of psychological traits is far from being a natural advancement; rather, it requires formal-logical thought, which, as discussed, is a direct outcome of schooling. Illiterate adults, when asked to do self-analysis, either do not grasp the question at all or describe themselves in terms of external material circumstances and everyday situations. What follows, is a self-evaluation of a barely literate 18-year-old woman:

After a lengthy conversation about people's characteristics and their individual differences, the following question was asked:
What shortcomings are you aware of in yourself, and what would you like to change about yourself?

"Everything's all right with me. I myself don't have any shortcomings, but if others do, I point them out ... As for me, I have only one dress and two robes, and those are all my shortcomings." ...

No, that's not what I'm asking you about. Tell me what kind of a person you are now and what you would like to be. Aren't there any differences?

"I would like to be good, but now I'm bad; I have few clothes, so I can't go to other villages like this." ...

And what does "be good" mean?

"To have more clothes."[17]

To conclude, numerous data have provided strong empirical support to the Vygotskian idea that school instruction greatly determines different aspects of children's development during the period of middle childhood.

The Quality of School Instruction Determines Its Developmental Outcomes

Although, as discussed, even one or two years of schooling lead to serious advancements in children's development, the depth and extent of these advancements will depend on the quality of instruction. Indeed, as discussed in Chapter 1, Vygotsky emphasized that a development-generating effect of instruction is determined by whether or not the process of instruction has been organized in the proper way: "The only good kind of instruction is that which marches ahead of development and leads it."[18] In other words, "good" instruction should target the "ceiling" level of children's zone of proximal development rather than the current level of their functioning. As an example of instruction that did not meet this requirement, Vygotsky

mentioned an instructional system that had been used in the former
Soviet Union in the 1920s:

> For a time, our schools favored the "complex" system of instruction,
> which was believed to be adapted to the child's ways of thinking. In
> offering the child problems he was able to handle without help, this
> method failed to utilize the zone of proximal development and to
> lead the child to what he could not yet do. Instruction was oriented
> to the child's weakness rather than his strength, thus encouraging
> him to remain at the preschool stage of development.[19]

To a certain extent, the preceding criticism by Vygotsky can be
addressed to the contemporary traditional system of school instruction. As briefly discussed in Chapter 1, all traditional school curricula have been influenced by the belief that instruction should follow
development, in other words, that we should teach knowledge at the
developmental level that the child has already reached. In American
education, to make it worse, the "traditional" underestimation of
the importance of instruction for children's development has been
aggravated by behaviorist ideas about teaching and learning. These
ideas continue to implicitly influence American education despite
the fact that behaviorism has not been the dominant learning theory
for more than half a century. Behaviorists understand teaching as
conditioning new responses in students, and learning as mastery of
these responses by students' by means of drill-and-practice and rote
memorization. Thus, learning outcomes are reduced by behaviorists to correct responses (answers); the idea that school instruction
should lead to certain *developmental* outcomes, such as higher-order
reasoning, is simply ignored by behaviorists.

The poor learning and developmental outcomes of American
school instruction have been the focus of attention of American
society since the publication of the 1983 report of the National
Commission on Excellence in Education with a title that speaks for
itself: *A Nation at Risk*. The report presented the results of various
studies that revealed, in particular, that among 17-year-old students

40% could not draw inferences from a written text, two-thirds could not solve several-step math problems, 80% could not write a persuasive essay, and that on many academic tests American students performed well below their peers from other industrialized societies. Reflecting on these data, the report said that the American nation was committing "an act of unthinking, unilateral educational disarmament."[20]

In 2008, the U.S. Department of Education published the report *A Nation Accountable: Twenty-Five Years after A Nation at Risk*. The goal of the report was "to review the progress we have made" over 25 years, but the general conclusion was already formulated on the first page of the report: "If we were 'at risk' in 1983, we are at even greater risk now."[21] In particular, the report indicated that "educational achievement of 17-year-old students has largely stagnated" since *A Nation at Risk* publication.[22] Studies and observations of American students' learning outcomes have led to the conclusion that

> most students have command of lower-level, rote skills, such as computation in math, recalling facts in science, decoding words in reading, and spelling, grammar, and punctuation in writing.... Many if not most students have difficulty using what they know to interpret an experiment, comprehend a text, or persuade an audience. They can't rise above the rote, factual level to think critically or creatively. They can't apply what they know flexibly and spontaneously to solve ill-structured, ambiguous problems that require interpretation.[23]

To summarize, "current curricula and teaching methods successfully impart facts and rote skills to most [American] students but fail to impart high-order reasoning and learning skills."[24] In Part II of the book, I discuss in more detail what is wrong with the traditional system of school instruction in the United States, as well as in some other countries, and present the Vygotskian *theoretical learning* approach to instruction that has been shown to result in impressive learning and developmental outcomes in school students. In particular, when learning math under this approach, elementary school students "evidenced mathematical understanding typically not found among U.S. high school and university students."[25]

How to Promote Children's Interest in Learning

Just like any mediation, school instruction can not be imposed on passive children; children will not learn if they do not want to learn. As Vygotsky noted, "the problem of interest in instruction is not whether or not children learn with interest; they never learn without interest."[26] The point is, however, that children's learning can be propelled by different interests.

As discussed in Chapter 4, when children first come to school, they are interested in performing the role of a school student, which brings them closer to the attractive adult world. This is why they are so excited about all external attributes associated with the role of a student, including such of its attributes about which in the near future they will cease to be excited. The famous Russian Vygotskian, D. Elkonin, who spent many years as an elementary school teacher, shared with us a recollection of his first day as a schoolteacher, which was also the first day of school for his students. At the end of the day, he told the children that the classes were over and they could go home. The children, however, kept sitting and looked somewhat disappointed; finally, one of them asked: "And what about the homework?" In order to not disappoint the children further, Elkonin gave them some task as homework and immediately forgot about it. The next day, however, the first thing he saw when he entered the classroom were sheets of paper in front of the children with the homework completed; all the children were waiting impatiently for him to review their homework and give them a grade. Thus, for those children, homework was still something they wanted as an important indicator of their new social roles of students, rather than being a burden to be avoided.

I myself have a similar recollection about my first year as a school student. In those days, students in Russia had to wear a school uniform, and I remember how I insisted on wearing this uniform even when going to a supermarket with my parents: I was proud that I was not a preschooler any more, and that everybody could see it.

Children's excitement about social roles of school students has been clearly demonstrated in one study with older preschoolers.[27] "Positive" and "negative" adjectives (clean – dirty, good – bad, fast – slow) were written on separate cards. In front of the child, there were two boxes with attached pictures: on one picture, there were school students with bookbags; on the other, playing children. The researcher said to the child pointing at the boxes: "These are school students, who study at school; and these are preschoolers, who are playing. I will be reading different words. You should think whether each word suits better a school student or a preschooler and put the card with this word into the proper box." After that, the experimenter read aloud the adjectives in random order. After reading an adjective, the experimenter gave the card to the child, who put it into one of the boxes. The results of this study demonstrated that almost all the children attributed the "positive" adjectives (clean, good, fast, etc.) to school students and the "negative" adjectives (dirty, bad, slow, etc.) to preschoolers.

To be sure, parents should fully support and encourage children's view of their new roles and responsibilities as students as very important and respected. For example, the time when a child is doing homework should be as respected by the family as the time when the child's father or mother is preparing an important presentation for the next day. From this perspective, it is much better to postpone a family dinner for 30 minutes to "let John finish his homework" than saying, "dinner is ready; you will finish homework after dinner." Similarly, parents should not discourage young pupils ecstatic attitude toward their teachers as "supermen" who know everything (as I discuss in Chapter 10, ironically, teachers themselves sometimes intentionally destroy this attitude in children). Therefore, the argument "the teacher knows better!" that young pupils often use in their disputes with parents should not be easily dismissed by parents or, even worse, irritate them as an indicator of a "sad" fact that there is another significant adult in their children's lives.

To be sure, by itself, children's interest in performing the role of school student cannot serve as learning motivation: After all, to enjoy this new role, it is not a must for children to learn; it is sufficient to come to school with a bookbag, sit in the classroom, and follow some simple school regulations. This interest, however, is a good foundation for the development in children of learning motivation. Traditionally, learning motivation is divided into two types: extrinsic motivation and intrinsic motivation.

Extrinsic Learning Motivation. Extrinsic learning motivation relates to learning motivated by external desirable outcomes; most commonly, by various rewards. In the Introduction, I already discussed some shortcomings of the behavior modification methodology based on the use of rewards. In the field of learning, rewards have been shown to diminish students' intrinsic interest in learning (that is, interest in learning per se). In particular, because learning outcomes are traditionally evaluated by the use of grades, rewards are often issued for good grades; this practice redirects students' attention from the importance of learning to the importance of earning good grades. Good grades, however, do not necessarily reflect good learning but may, for example, be outcomes of meaningless drill-and-practice, rote memorization, or, even worse, cheating on tests.

The problems associated with the use of rewards have led researchers to recommend that rewards should be used as little as possible; if still used, they should be as modest as possible and be withdrawn as soon as possible.[28] In other words, extrinsic learning motivation may be used as a temporary solution that helps engage students in learning, but it should not become the permanent "engine" that drives student learning.

Intrinsic Learning Motivation. Intrinsic learning motivation is defined as learning for the sake of learning, that is, because learning itself is enjoyable. As opposed to extrinsic motivation, intrinsic learning motivation leads to students' learning above and beyond the school requirements, and their selecting challenging learning tasks. Intrinsically motivated students also demonstrate greater task persistence and better learning outcomes than their extrinsically motivated classmates.

How does intrinsic learning motivation develop? To answer this question, let us remember the Vygotskian analysis of the development of new motives presented in Chapter 1. Just like any new motive, intrinsic interest in learning may sometimes develop spontaneously in the context of children's learning driven by a reward. The following example illustrates this point:

> In an effort to get my daughter to try ice skating ... I promised an ice-skating outfit for circling the rink without touching the wall. By the end of that session she accomplished the task. She was so delighted by her sense of developing competence, and intrinsically motivated to continue to develop her skills, she forgot about the promised reward.[29]

Everybody will probably agree, however, that it would not be realistic to expect such an outcome in a classroom on a regular basis. Therefore, having used children's enjoyment of their roles of school students or external rewards to engage them in learning, adults should purposefully mediate the development in children of intrinsic learning motivation.

The major role in mediating the development in children of intrinsic learning motivation should be played by teachers (see Chapter 8 for a discussion of this matter), but the role of parents in this respect should not be underestimated either. Even the kind of questions parents ask their children when they come home from school (e.g., "What grades did you get today?" or "What have you learned today?")

will make a difference in terms of what kind of attitude the children develop toward learning: learning for the sake of getting good grades, or learning for its own sake. This is not to say that the grades should be ignored; they simply should be considered one of the indicators of good learning rather than an end in itself. Similarly, if parents are checking their children's homework, they should not pay attention only to whether or not the answer is correct; rather, they should ask questions such as "How did you solve this problem?" or "How can you double check if the answer is correct?" and praise the children for their "good thinking" and efforts rather than for the correct answer. In simple words, everything parents do to redirect their children's attention from outcomes of learning, such as grades, to the process of learning as important and thrilling in itself will contribute to the development of their intrinsic learning motivation. To the contrary, a parent saying to his or her son, "Don't worry about math, I was never good in it and I make a good living"[30] will hardly be beneficial for the development of his intrinsic interest in learning math.

Conclusion: Schooling as the Major Avenue for Mediation during the Period of Middle Childhood

Today, it is impossible to deny the leading role of school instruction in children's development: Even one or two years of schooling have been shown to result in great advancement of children's cognitive abilities. But *how well* school instruction will promote children's development will depend on three major factors. One such factor was discussed earlier: To learn successfully and benefit from school instruction, children should come to school with the major components of school readiness in place. Prerequisites for success, however, by themselves do not guarantee success. In this chapter, I have discussed the other two major factors that determine the developmental outcomes of school instruction.

The first factor is *what and how* children are taught. Teaching children "correct responses" through drill-and-practice or rote memorization, which is typical of traditional elementary school curricula all over the world, and of the American traditional curricula even beyond elementary school, is not especially advantageous for their cognitive development. In Part II of the book, I discuss in more detail the major shortcomings of traditional curricula and present alternative approaches to instruction. As readers will see, some of these alternative approaches (which are very popular among educators) aggravate rather than overcome the shortcomings of the traditional curricula, whereas some others do provide teachers with a fruitful alternative to traditional school instruction.

To benefit from school instruction, however, children should be actively involved in the process of learning. Therefore, the second factor that determines the developmental outcomes of school instruction is students' learning motivation. As discussed, intrinsic learning motivation – that is, learning for the sake of learning – is more advantageous in this respect than extrinsic learning motivation, that is, learning for the sake of external rewards. As discussed in Part II, *what and how* children are taught strongly influences what kind of learning motivation, if any, children will develop. Parents, however, should also do their best to promote intrinsic interest in learning in their children by means of asking them questions and making statements aimed at redirecting their attention from outcomes of learning to the process of learning as an interesting and self-rewarding activity.

7   Understand Adolescents and Make a Difference!

Adolescence is a transitional period between childhood and adulthood. It starts with the beginning of puberty (the process of sexual maturation) and ends when adolescents gain adult status (that is, start enjoying the major privileges and responsibilities of adulthood). In modern industrialized societies, this period covers the ages from approximately 11 or 12 years until 20 or 21 years.

Just like the view of any other developmental period, the view of adolescence is greatly determined by a researcher's theoretical perspective. Piagetians associate adolescence with the development of formal-logical thought, that is, the ability to reason at the theoretical level. Freudians associate adolescence with the development of new desires that make sexual intercourse the major motive of adolescent behavior. For Erikson and his followers, the major characteristic of this period is a search for personal identity, that is, self-understanding that will provide an answer to the most important question adolescents are concerned with: "Who am I?" As for parents and teachers, their characterization of this period often reflects the major point of their concern: drastic changes in adolescents' mood state, behavior, and relationships with parents; the phenomena that seem to give a rational for calling adolescence "the period of storm and stress."

To be sure, all these characteristics reflect important aspects of adolescent development. What is missing in the views of adolescence described in the previous paragraph, however, is an integration of these characteristics into a holistic picture of this period. After all, an adolescent child is a whole person rather than being a combination of sexual desires + formal-logical thought + search for personal identity + "storm and stress," and so on.

As opposed to the views of adolescence described earlier, Vygotsky and his followers have suggested a holistic model of adolescent development that integrates in a meaningful way the major characteristics of adolescents' cognition, personality, social behavior, and sexual maturation. Briefly, this model can be presented as follows.

Physiological maturation results in the development in adolescents of sexual needs and desires. By their nature, these needs and desires direct adolescents toward their peers; in other words, adolescents develop a strong motive that propels them toward deep engagement in peer interactions.

Just like any other kind of interpersonal interactions, however, interactions within a peer group are impossible unless the members of the group use certain norms and values to regulate their relationships: what is good, and what is bad; what is acceptable, and what is not; etc. In search of such norms and values adolescents refer to the major source of social wisdom that proved to be trustworthy in the past – their parents: In the context of interactions with parents, adolescents adopt basic parental norms and values and start using them as standards for the behavior of their peers.

At the same time, to function efficiently within a peer group, adolescents should use those adopted norms and values as standards for their own behavior – that is, they should exercise self-reflection. Fortunately enough, adolescents are now equipped with the cognitive ability that is necessary to exercise self-reflection: They have developed formal-logical thought.

Thus, in the context of interactions within a peer group, adolescents use social norms and values adopted from parents as standards for the behavior of their peers and for their own behavior. As a result, they test, master, and internalize these social norms and values, which become "building blocks" of their forming identities.

The search for personal identity is not an easy process, and it may contribute to what has been called "adolescent storm and stress." "Storm and stress," however, is anything but an inevitable outcome of the search for personal identity; it can be avoided or at least greatly diminished by correct parental practices and peer support.

The Vygotskian model of adolescent development has been supported by numerous studies and observations collected by American psychologists. Let us elaborate in more detail the key points of this model and discuss from this perspective the role of adults in adolescents' lives.

Sexual Desires as Promoting the Development of the Motive of Interactions with Peers

Vygotsky's idea that sexual maturation lies "at the base of the whole change in the system of interests in the adolescent"[1] can hardly be called "exotic"; as a contemporary American psychologist points out, "as their reproductive organs reach maturity, boys and girls begin to engage in new forms of social behavior because they begin to find the opposite sex attractive."[2] The contribution of sexual needs to young adolescents' interest in interactions with peers can be masked by the fact that, initially, each peer group consists of the members of the same sex. Studies have demonstrated, however, that a key function of same-sex peer groups "is to provide a context for the transition to sexual relationships."[3] This transition tends to proceed gradually in several steps, each of which is facilitated by group leaders: from same-sex groups, to interactions between male and female groups (for example, at a skating rink), to same-sex groups with group leaders starting across-group heterosexual contacts, to heterosexual groups, and finally to heterosexual dating pairs.[4] The establishment of a dating pair also often involves group support: The arrangement of the first date by an adolescent often takes place in the presence of same-sex friends, and the first date itself is often performed in a "double-dating" format. Thus, a gradually diminishing presence of same-sex friends provides at each step a delicate balance between an adolescent's increasing need for intimacy and a decreasing need to feel safe and have friends' support when exploring the "terra incognita" of relationships with the opposite sex.

In light of this, it becomes evident that parental reprimands to the effect that "you are too young to be hanging out with girls" are totally useless: The boy's behavior is driven by his new needs and desires that cannot be suppressed. For the same reason, similarly useless are "discomfort, censored feelings, uneasiness over a daughter's interest in and attractiveness to teenage boys"[5] that fathers may start experiencing. Such reprimands and bitter feelings are not only useless; they are unproductive and even harmful. First, as we will see, parents' attempts to suppress natural desires of adolescent children will simply lead to conflicts with them. Second, although sexual needs and desires "prompt teenagers' withdrawal from adults and their increasing focus on peer relationships,"[6] it is interactions within a peer group that, as discussed later, will usually make adolescents look for parental help and guidance, that is, paradoxically, will eventually bring them closer to their parents.

Thus, parents should find a balance between supporting their children's natural interest in age-appropriate heterosexual relationships and discouraging them from engaging in premature sexual activity. The information and advice about sexual matters should not be presented to children in the format of the Big Talk, equally embarrassing for both parents and their adolescent children. Rather, parents can provide their children with this information in the context of discussing TV shows with them, or even by sharing with them "funny stories" about their own adolescence (without, however, undermining their children's understanding of their feelings as "unique"). In light of the fact that 90% of teenagers report that they would like to learn about sexual relationships from their parents rather than from another source, the parental role in shaping their adolescents' healthy relationships with members of the opposite sex can hardly be overestimated.

Adolescents as Thinkers

In addition to sexual desires and needs, there is another major factor that should be taken into account in understanding adolescents: their new cognitive abilities. As Vygotsky noted, "an adolescent appears before us primarily as a thinking being."[7] As opposed to younger children, whose thinking is "tied" to their personal experience, adolescents become "theorists" who are able to exercise formal-logical thought.

The development of formal-logical thought enormously increases adolescents' thinking and problem-solving capacities. First, they become capable of hypothetical-deductive reasoning, which results, in particular, in their ability to solve syllogisms. To use an example that I gave in Chapter 6, proceeding from the premises that "cotton can grow only where it is hot and dry," and that "in England it is cold and damp," people with formal-logical thought come to the correct conclusion that cotton cannot grow in England.

Second, in Vygotsky's words, "a whole world with its past and future, nature, history, and human life opens before the adolescent."[8] Formal-logical thought makes it possible for adolescents to operate abstract concepts and ideas; in particular, to understand those social norms and values that were "hidden" from their understanding earlier. A good example is the development of moral reasoning. Preteens' moral reasoning generally proceeds from a self-interest perspective: Behavior is defined as "good" if it leads to rewards or serves a person's interests, and as "bad" if it results in punishment or does not serve a person's interests. Adolescents who have developed formal-logical thought proceed in their moral reasoning from social expectations, norms, and rules: They associate "good" behavior with following social expectations, norms, and rules and "bad" behavior with breaking these expectations, norms, and rules.[9]

Finally, formal-logical thought also makes adolescents capable of self-analysis: reflection on their thoughts, feelings, abilities, competencies, and their place in the world, the existence of which they have just "discovered." Whereas preteens describe themselves in terms of specific skills and behaviors ("I can ride a bicycle"), adolescents do self-analysis in psychological terms ("I am an extrovert … I am curious about learning something new … I worry too much about different things").

In the following sections, I discuss multiple positive and (surprisingly enough!) a few negative outcomes of the development of new cognitive abilities in adolescents. At this point, I want simply to remind the reader that, as was discussed in Chapter 6, the development of formal-logical thought in adolescents is not spontaneous and "given," but rather is a direct outcome of school instruction. Therefore, the quality of adolescents' formal-logical thought (and, accordingly, the quality of other aspects of adolescents' development that require formal-logical though as a prerequisite) will depend on the quality of instruction. In Chapter 11, I describe the Vygotskian *theoretical learning* approach, which, in particular, facilitates the development of formal-logical thought in students.

Parents as the Source of "Social Wisdom" for Adolescents

Any kind of social interaction requires that participants use certain norms and values to regulate their relationships. When interactions with peers become the priority for adolescents, in search of such social norms and values they refer to those whom they trust, and who successfully mediated their relationships with the world in the past: their parents. No wonder that numerous studies and observations have revealed "consistent evidence of a strong congruence between parents and teenagers in political, religious, and moral values."[10]

The adoption of parental norms and values by adolescents, however, is not "given," but rather depends on parental practices. First, naturally enough, to serve as the source of "social wisdom," in their interactions with adolescents parents should provide *advanced models* of reasoning on political, social, and moral issues; in other words, parents should be "smarter" and more knowledgeable than their adolescent children.[11] Having observed that "there was a tendency for children to evidence a higher level of moral reasoning in the family session than in the interview," American researchers concluded:

> This is illustrative of Vygotsky's (1978) notion of the "zone of proximal development": the difference between the level of actual development and the level of proximal development. In this case, children's level of actual development was indicated by their independent reasoning about moral dilemmas in the interview, whereas their level of potential development was indicated by their performance in the family session, a somewhat instructional social context where parents were providing support for the child's acquisition of new moral concepts.[12]

Second, no matter how advanced parental "social wisdom" is, it is not a given that adolescents will accept it. Because of their new cognitive abilities, rather than simply appropriating new social knowledge, adolescents analyze and test it before accepting (or not accepting) it as their "'own' ... personal choices."[13] Therefore, "authoritative" parents who are open for discussions about social norms and values with their adolescent children have better chances to propel adolescents to accept and follow these norms than "authoritarian" parents who simply try to impose these norms and values on their children.

When initiating and encouraging discussions about social norms and values, parents should follow several simple rules. First, just like any mediation, these discussions should be related to the adolescent's current interests (for example, a good context to introduce social norms and values is a family discussion of a new movie or political news). Second, parents should not openly criticize the views and ideas that their adolescents formulate during these discussions; rather, parents should implicitly challenge adolescents by presenting their views and ideas supported with logical arguments. Third, parents should not become upset or irritated if adolescents aggressively and emotionally criticize their views and ideas; this does not necessarily mean that they really reject them. Often, such an antagonism to parental ideas is simply a "provocation" that adolescents use to propel parents to bring up additional arguments in favor of their position, which eventually will make it possible for them to accept the parental norms and values as their "'own' ... personal choices."[14]

Fourth, parents should not get bitterly disappointed if it seems they have simply wasted time and effort on "selling" their norms and values to their children: It takes a seed time to develop into a plant. Very often, "adolescents who rebel against parental values and norms come back in adult years to parental values and imitate the parental ways of life."[15]

And, one more important point to remember: Adolescents are very sensitive to any discrepancy between what parents say and what they do. If parents persuasively argue that, in social relationships, it is important to negotiate and compromise, but fail to follow this norm when interacting with their own children, their children will hardly accept this social norm (I return to this issue in the "storm and stress" section later).

Although, as discussed, an immediate reason for adolescents' interest in learning new social norms and values relates to the fact that they need them to regulate relationships within a peer group, the importance of this learning is much greater than that. In Vygotsky's words, "self-consciousness is social consciousness transferred within,"[16] that is, social norms and values learned and internalized by adolescents become tools that they use to analyze themselves and the "building blocks" of their "selves" (or, in Erikson's term, their "personal identities"). An American expert in the field of adolescent development wrote:

> Thus, the personal self develops in the crucible of interpersonal relationships with caregivers. One outcome is that the child adopts the opinions that significant others are perceived to hold toward the self, reflected appraisals that will define one's sense of self as a person.

Through an *internalization* process, the child comes to own these evaluations as his/her personal judgments about the self.... In addition to the incorporation of the opinions of significant others, children come to internalize the standards and values of those who are important to them, including the values of the larger society.[17]

Mastery of any tool, however, is accomplished only through its use: It is not sufficient to give a child a hammer; he or she should learn how to use it properly. The same is true of social norms and values: To master and internalize them, adolescents should use them in the context of solving social problems. As discussed next, interactions with peers create a necessary context for mastery and internalization of social norms and values adopted from parents.

Interactions within a Peer Group as the Context for Mastery and Internalization of Parental Norms and Values

For decades, adolescent peer groups were viewed by psychologists and the general public as "a unified, monolithic culture opposed to adult society"[18] that "steals" adolescent children from parents and family. Empirical data, however, have demonstrated that this view is simply wrong. In particular, when choosing their friends, "adolescents typically gravitate toward those who exhibit attitudes and values consistent with those maintained by the parents."[19] Even in those cases in which there is a certain discrepancy between parental and peers' values, adolescents' values and attitudes often remain more similar to those of their parents than of their friends; for example, adolescents "are more likely to follow adults' than peers' advice in matters affecting their long-term future."[20] As an American researcher summarized empirical data, "peers usually *reinforce* rather than contradict parental values."[21]

What is the mechanism of this "reinforcement" of parental norms and values that is provided by the peer groups? As noted previously, to master and internalize parental norms and values, adolescents should use them in the context of solving social problems. To be sure, some of such experiences adolescents enjoy when discussing social and moral issues with their parents. Even with "authoritative" parents, however, such discussions are "asymmetric," that is, they involve "individuals who differ in knowledge, authority, and/or power,"[22] and therefore, these interactions are not the best context for adolescents to express their disagreements or opinions. In contrast, interactions with peers are "symmetric," where "one is particularly likely to face challenges to one's perspective, and encounter alternative perspectives."[23] Thus, using social norms and values adopted from parents as standards for the behavior of their peers, adolescents test and master these norms and values, and accept them as their "'own' ... personal choices."[24]

The use by adolescents of parental norms and values as standards regulating their relationships with peers leads to another very important outcome. It is known that, as a rule, it is much easier to apply a certain social norm to evaluate the behavior of another person than to apply the same rule as a standard for your own behavior. But there is also another rule: Your experience with using a social norm to evaluate behavior of others will make it easier for you to eventually use this rule as a standard for your own behavior. Thus, in the context of interactions with peers, adolescents learn how to use parental norms and values as tools for self-reflection. As a result, these norms and values become internalized and used as "building blocks" for forming of adolescents' personal identities.

The preceding analysis, at first glance, is not consistent with the cases of adolescents joining such antisocial peer groups as youth gangs. A prominent American expert in the field of adolescence research has provided the following explanation of these cases:

> In cases where peer group norms are in obvious opposition to prevailing adult norms, such as in delinquent gangs, researchers have found that adolescents are not so much being pulled away from adults by the deviant crowd as driven to this crowd by parents' ineffective child-rearing practices.[25]

Of course, it would not be fair to say that incorrect parental practices is the only reason for adolescents' choice of a peer group that is in opposition to the society's norms and values. For example, if a family lives in a disadvantaged community, a bright student may become an underachiever simply to avoid been called "brain" by members of the only peer group that is accessible to him. Similarly, "aggressive children, who are readily labeled as such and rejected by most of their peers, gravitate toward one another and coalesce into cliques well before adolescence."[26] It is not an overstatement to say, however, that how parents bring up their children, and how successfully they provide their children with the norms and values of our society, will crucially determine the peer groups their adolescent children will choose.

Adolescent "Storm a Stress:" Is It Inevitable?

The traditional view of adolescence is that this is the period of "storm and stress" characterized by drastic changes in mood state, behavior, and relationships with parents. Given that according to this view, the impetus for these changes is puberty, adolescent "storm and stress" is considered inevitable and even normal (Anna Freud stated that it is even abnormal if an adolescent does not experience "storm and stress"). It was as early as in the 1920s, however, that this view of "storm and stress" was challenged by empirical data and observations. In particular, Margaret Mead, a prominent American cultural anthropologist, having observed and interviewed Samoan girls who had reached puberty, did not find any symptoms of "storm and stress" in them. Many more data and observations contradicting the view of "storm and stress" as a maturational phenomenon have been collected since then; therefore, these days, although still popular among the general public, this view is rejected by the majority of specialists in the field of adolescence research.

What are the reasons then for "storm and stress"? And are the "storm and stress" phenomena as inevitable and severe as they are believed to be? Let us analyze separately the major components of "storm and stress."

Mood Disruption. Rapid fluctuation of emotions, with dominance of negative emotions and depressed moods, is probably the most frequently observed component of "storm and stress." Some studies and observations have found that almost half of all adolescents experience, at some point, mild or moderate depression, with girls experiencing depression twice as often as boys. If, as it was found, there is "little relationship between pubertal stage and negative emotion,"[27] what factors are responsible for adolescent depression? Surprisingly enough, these are the same sociocultural and cognitive factors that we mentioned before when discussing all the "good things" that take place during this period.

Indeed, for preteens, the world is a very small place that is mostly limited to their close friends and families; they live in "today" and do not speculate much about the future. With the development of formal-logical thought, this happy life in the small familiar world is over. Adolescents in industrialized societies "discover" a huge new world of possibilities that presents them with an enormous number of different choices (which children in "traditional" societies simply do not have; a fisherman's son knows that when he grows up, he will become a fisherman too). And so they start asking themselves "what if" questions that never bothered them before: "Do I know what I want to become?" "Even if *today* this is what I want to become, am I sure that *tomorrow* I will have the same preferences about my future?" "Even if I am sure that my preferences will not change, am I sure that my abilities will make it possible for me to succeed in this field, or I had better choose for myself something less attractive but less competitive as well?" and so forth. To make it worse, adolescents sincerely believe that there is only one correct answer to each of these questions, and that this answer should be found today; tomorrow, it will be too late, they will already be on the wrong path of "no return," and their whole life will be ruined. No wonder that, as a result, adolescents may reveal anxiety and depression.

Proceeding from what was said before, it is probably quite normal for adolescents to experience a certain level of anxiety or depressed mood: After all, don't you yourself become anxious when you have to make an important decision about your future, or feel somewhat hopeless when something serious goes wrong in your life? This does not mean, however, that adolescent depression (especially severe depression) should be considered a normal and inevitable characteristic of this age period. And it is peers and parents who can often help adolescents not to develop or successfully overcome their depression. Peers provide adolescents with sympathetic listeners who they "can talk to about almost anything," and who will understand and emotionally support them. The role of parents in this respect is even more important: Parental help should be more "instrumental" than just "listening and understanding." Without "imposing" unsolicited advice on their adolescent children, and without creating an impression that they are taking their children's problems too lightly, in a nonjudgmental way parents should explain to their children the reasons for what they are going through. Parents may even share similar experiences they were going through during the period of adolescence. Or parents may mention somebody who changed several careers in her life, enjoying each of them (so "even if you make a mistake about your future today, it is not going to ruin all your life"). Unfortunately, sometimes, parents contribute to their adolescent children's depression rather than helping them overcome it by imposing on them unrealistically high expectations (for example, for school achievement) that their children cannot meet. Another point that should be remembered: To encourage their adolescent children to share their fears and concerns with them, parents have to maintain a good relationship with their children. Unfortunately, as discussed in the next subsection, this is not always the case.

Adolescent-Parent Conflicts. "Loss of the relationships" with their "rebellious and rejecting" adolescents often becomes a major parental concern. The good news is that this concern is greatly exaggerated;

as a rule, parents' relationships with adolescent children are not "lost," and adolescents are not as "rebellious and rejecting" as they may seem. It has been shown that "75% of teenagers reported having happy and pleasant relationships with their parents."[28] Even "amidst relatively high conflicts, parents and adolescents tend to report that overall their relationships are good, that they share a wide range of core values, and that they retain a considerable amount of mutual affection and attachment."[29] In those cases in which conflicts with a parent propel adolescents to "drift" from him or her, they often get even closer to the other parent rather than starting to spend more time with peers. Also, what is considered adolescent "rebellion" is often far from that. For example, as I mentioned before, sometimes aggressive and emotional criticism of parental views and ideas by adolescents is simply a "provocation" that they use to propel their parents to prove their point more convincingly. Finally, adolescents' criticism, argumentativeness, and negativism toward parents, rather than indicating their "rebellion," may be just as a safe way for them to act out anxiety and frustration with those who are loving and loved and, therefore, will not reject them no matter what (and maybe will even respond to this "cry for help").

To be sure, all of the aforementioned does not mean that the frequency of "real" conflicts with children does not increase as they reach adolescence. Indeed, preteens may do their best to avoid following parental regulations, but they generally do not think that parental regulations can be questioned. In contrast, adolescents, with their newly developed capacity of formal-logical thinking, "begin to see some of their parents' rules as capricious and arbitrary. They realize that there is no God-given reason why they need to be in by 9 or 10pm."[30] Often, parents are not ready for such "insolence" on the part of their children, and they continue using the argument that worked before: "I'm older than you are and your elder, so do what I say."[31] Well, that does not work anymore! In addition, was it not the parents who persuaded their children that in social relationships it is important to explain your position, reason on disputable issues, and sometimes look for a compromise? If so, why would they deprive their own children of the right to ask for reasons for parental regulations, to express their disagreement, and sometimes to expect a compromise?

Often, it takes just a bit of goodwill on the part of parents to avoid many of the conflicts with their adolescent children; after all, the majority of parent-adolescent conflicts take place around minor issues, such as keeping a room clean, personal appearance, curfews, doing the dishes, or wake-up time. For example, one girl "got very upset because her mother woke her up at 1pm, when she hadn't gotten home from a field trip the night before until 2:30am."[32] Adolescents do not want to be treated as children, they seek more independence in making their everyday life choices and decisions; so, parents should give them control at least over some aspects of their lives.

To conclude, parent-adolescent conflicts are often the result of parents' inability or unwillingness to modify their relationships with adolescent children to meet their new needs, abilities, and expectations. Giving more freedom to adolescents in making their own choices over minor issues will substantially reduce the frequency of their conflicts with parents. When dealing with more serious issues, parents should do their best to substantiate their regulations and, sometimes, try to find a compromise. At the same time, parents should make it clear that they have the final word, and that sometimes, their "No," after it has been explained and substantiated, will remain a "No." Indeed, authoritative parents (those who listen and respect their children, but also maintain rules, guidelines, and expectations for them) have substantially fewer conflicts with adolescents than do authoritarian parents, and almost as few conflicts as permissive parents (avoiding at the same time numerous negative consequences to which permissive parenting has been shown to lead[33]).

Deviant Behavior. The third major components of "storm and stress" relates to drastic increase in the rates of deviant behavior during the period of adolescence (such as violent and criminal actions, substance abuse, reckless driving, running away, self-injury, suicide, etc.). Rather than being an inevitable phenomenon of adolescence, however, deviant behavior may not appear at all, or it can be remediated if its causes are properly addressed.

For example, violent and criminal actions are, as a rule, performed by adolescents who belong to delinquent youth gangs. As already mentioned, however, adolescents' joining of delinquent gangs is often a result of ineffective child-rearing practices. For such adolescents, gangs become a substitute family, and this "family's" norms and values come to guide their antisocial behavior. Thus, often "parental practices set the stage for deviant peer's influence."[34] Adolescents' risky behavior, such as substance abuse, reckless driving, and so forth, often represents "an effort to allay inner anxiety, to overcome feelings of inadequacy and inferiority, and to cope with depression."[35] Depression can also lead to self-injury (cutting or burning), running away (often as "a cry for help"), or (in cases of severe depression) even to suicide. Thus, improving parenting styles and strategies and working on preventing and treating adolescents' depression (which in serious cases requires professional treatment) may eliminate or substantially reduce these cases of deviant behavior.

In comparison with the problems mentioned earlier, a loss of interest in school and a sharp decline in academic performance that are often observed during the period of adolescence may seem of secondary importance. Also, it is true that adolescents' problems at school may be of secondary origin (e.g., be caused by depression, which leads to sleep problems and concentration difficulties). The major reason for these problems, however, is more fundamental than the reasons for those certainly more troubling behavioral problems that were mentioned previously.

As already discussed, because of their new needs and desires, interactions with peers become the priority for adolescents. No wonder that their interest in all the other activities drops (especially if these activities interfere with peer interactions, which is often the case for traditional school learning). What are the possible solutions to this problem?

The first, most obvious solution, which has been adopted by many American educators, is to "tie" learning at school to adolescents' current interests; in other words, to involve them in cooperative learning that provides opportunities for interaction among students. Such cooperative learning typically takes place in the format of discovery learning, when a group of students are working on "discovering" new scientific knowledge rather than learning it from the teacher. However, as I discuss in Chapter 10, discovery learning results in poor learning outcomes.

The second approach to solving this problem has been suggested by the Vygotskians, who insist that interactions with peers in the course of learning should not be promoted at the expense of their learning outcomes. In Chapter 11, I discuss the Vygotskian *theoretical learning* approach that has been successfully used to teach students of different ages, including adolescents.

Conclusion: The Completion of the Mediational Journey

There is an Indian story about six blind men who try to determine what an elephant looks like by feeling its different parts. The one who feels a leg concludes that the elephant is like a pillar; another one who feels the tail says the elephant resembles a rope; the third one who feels the belly says the elephant is like a wall; and so on. Traditional views of adolescence remind one of this story: Adolescents are described as "theorists" who have suddenly become involved in a search for an answer to the question "Who am I?", or as riders carried by the wild horses of sexual desires, or as rebellious members of youth culture which is in opposition to adult society.

The advantage of the Vygotskian view of this period is that it integrates all the "elephant parts" into an "elephant" by presenting a holistic model of adolescence, which makes is possible to give a very different explanation of the major phenomena of this period. The Vygotskians insist that adults continue to play a crucial role as mediators in the lives of their adolescent children; that adolescent peer groups make it possible for their members to master and internalize parental norms and values, which eventually lead to the formation of adolescents' identities; and that "storm and stress" is, in large part, a result of ineffective parental practices. These and other ideas of the Vygotskians have been confirmed by numerous findings in the field of adolescent research discussed in this chapter.

To be sure, the notion of the crucial role of parental practices in adolescent development, which is stressed in this chapter, should not lead to an underestimation of the role of teachers in adolescent lives. Their role becomes especially important if parents, for whatever reason, have failed to serve their adolescent children as mediators. In this case, it is teachers who may and should take over some major parental mediational responsibilities as described in this chapter. I hope that the discussion throughout this chapter will help readers better understand the needs of adolescents, develop a new attitude toward those aspects of adolescents' behavior that puzzled or even irritated them before, and rethink and modify their educational practices. Adolescence is the last period in children's lives when adult mediation is crucially needed; this period is supposed to prepare children for successful transition to adulthood, and it is adult mediation that in large part will determine the success of this transition.

PART II

SCHOOL: WHAT TO TEACH
AND HOW TO TEACH

8 American Cognitive Psychologists and Russian Vygotskians talk about the Content and Process of Learning at School

Poor learning outcomes of American school students, which I briefly discussed in Chapter 6, have propelled many unsuccessful attempts to reform the American system of school instruction. Discussing the reasons for the failure of these reforms in her best-selling book, the former U.S. Assistant Secretary of Education Diane Ravitch emphasizes the fact that all these reforms failed to address "what teachers should teach and what students are expected to learn."[1] To remediate this situation, Ravitch suggests that a coherent curriculum should be developed that would prescribe the knowledge in various subject areas that students need to learn.

Although, of course, knowledge in different subject domains differs (knowledge in history is different from knowledge in math), knowledge in each subject domain can be classified into the same types, and the acquisition of any knowledge proceeds in accordance with some general laws. What follows is a brief analysis of findings of American cognitive psychologists and Russian Vygotskians about different types of knowledge and the process of its acquisition.

Types of Knowledge

Researchers differentiate between four types of knowledge: factual, conceptual, procedural, and metacognitive.[2]

Factual Knowledge. Factual knowledge is knowledge of concrete facts, names, dates, and so forth. The following statements represent examples of factual knowledge: George Washington was the first president of the United States; my dog is a mammal; if you put a coin into the water, it will sink; these two lines are called perpendicular.

Should subject domain factual knowledge be the major content of learning at school? Yes, said Eric Hirsch in his "Cultural Literacy," a best seller of the 1980s.[3] From his perspective, "words refer to things; knowing a lot of words means knowing a lot of things."[4] Hirsch even developed a list of about 5,000 words (names, historic events, terms, etc.) that school students should memorize.

No doubt, factual knowledge is important for understanding a text or memorizing new information. In particular, Hirsch refers to empirical findings that college students were not able to understand a written paragraph about the generals Grant and Lee only because they were lacking factual knowledge of the American Civil War. And, it has been shown that children may memorize new facts even better than adults can if these facts are from a field in which they are more knowledgeable than the adults are.

Another important role of factual knowledge is that it creates a background for our thinking and problem solving. For example, you are asked: "Was Thomas Jefferson the first president of the United States?" Suppose you do not know who Jefferson was, but you know that the first president of the United States was George Washington; so, you start thinking: "OK, Washington was the first president of the United States; there could not be two first presidents; therefore, Jefferson (whoever he was) could not be the first president of the United States." Thus, your factual knowledge about George Washington has helped you solve the problem.

It is important to stress, however, that factual knowledge by itself cannot serve as a psychological tool to think and solve problems. In the example from the previous paragraph, your factual knowledge about Washington as the first president of the United States became the starting point for your solving the problem, but it was your logical reasoning that made it possible for you to come to the correct answer.

Similarly, your knowledge of the fact that your dog is a mammal will not make it possible for you to identify another animal as belonging (or not belonging) to the class of mammals. Or your knowledge that a coin sinks in water will not by itself help you decide if another object will sink. Everybody would probably agree that a major goal of learning at school is the development in students of the ability to think and solve problems in subject domains. Therefore, Hirsch's view of factual knowledge as the major content of learning at school can hardly be substantiated.

Conceptual Knowledge. Conceptual knowledge is the knowledge of concepts, principles, theories, and the like. What follows are examples of conceptual knowledge: president – the leader of a country elected by the citizens for a set period of time; mammals – vertebrate, warm-blooded animals that feed their babies milk; objects with a density greater than the density of water will sink; two straight lines that meet at a right angle are called perpendicular. Thus, as opposed to factual knowledge, conceptual knowledge gives us descriptions of classes of objects and phenomena and, as such, is a psychological tool that can be used to think and solve problems. For example, the knowledge of the concept of mammals can be used to identify different animals as belonging or not belonging to the class of mammals.

The preceding examples of conceptual knowledge represent generalizations based on essential characteristics of objects and phenomena that belong to a given class (for example, being warm-blooded and feeding babies milk are essential characteristics of mammals). Often, however, we develop misconceptions, that is, generalizations that are based on so-called correlational characteristics – those that can often be found among representatives of a given class but that are not necessary and sufficient for belonging to this class. An example of a typical misconception that young children develop is a belief that all birds fly; proceeding from this misconception, children do not identify a penguin as a bird, but identify a bat as such. Sometimes, children may even develop misconceptions that are based on totally irrelevant characteristics. Earlier I referred to a study in which a three-year-old child, having observed a needle, a pin, and a coin sinking in water, developed a misconception that "all small objects sink," and began to use this misconception to predict the behavior of different objects in water.[5] As we know, the size of an object is irrelevant to whether or not this object will sink.

Suppose, however, students have learned correct conceptual knowledge. Will this knowledge by itself make it possible for them to solve subject domain problems? To answer this question, let us elaborate on the analogy that the Vygoskians have drawn between tools of labor and psychological tools. To be able to hammer in a nail, it is not sufficient to have a hammer; one also needs to master the proper procedure of its use. The same is true for conceptual knowledge as a psychological tool: The knowledge of a concept by itself does not guarantee that one can use this concept to solve problems. A child may know the definition of mammals by heart, but when shown a picture of a dolphin, he identifies it as a fish. And this is true not only for children. Earlier I gave the definition of perpendicular lines. Read this definition again and try to solve the following problem: "n is meeting p at a right angle. Are n and p perpendicular lines?" The answer Yes may seem obvious to you, but it is wrong.[6] Thus, just as you cannot use a hammer if you have not mastered the procedure of its use, you cannot use conceptual knowledge as a psychological tool for thinking and problem solving if you have not mastered the relevant procedural knowledge.

Procedural Knowledge. Procedural knowledge is the knowledge of skills, strategies, and techniques; in other words, it is knowledge of how to do something. In everyday life, procedural knowledge makes it possible for us to drive a car, to hammer in a nail, or to use a spoon to eat. At school, procedural knowledge makes it possible for students to solve academic problems. For example, to figure out if a given country is a presidential republic, a student will check out whether or not the country leader has been elected by the citizens for a set period of time. To find out if a given animal is a mammal, a student will check out whether or not this animal is warm-blooded and feeds its babies milk. In order to find out if a given object will sink in water, a student will check out whether or not its density is greater than the density of water. And to find out if these are two perpendicular lines, a student will check out whether or not these are two straight lines meeting at a right angle.

At first glance, the acquisition of procedural knowledge should be considered a sufficient and desirable outcome of both everyday life learning and learning at school. And, it is true that everyday life procedural knowledge serves our needs pretty well; after all, if you have learned how to drive a car well, is it not what you wanted to accomplish? It turns out, however, that, as a school learning outcome, procedural knowledge alone is not very advantageous. The problem is that by itself procedural knowledge is meaningless: Students master the procedure, but they do not understand why this procedure works and in which cases it should be used. Therefore, this procedure remains nontransferable: Students can use it to solve problems that are very similar to those that the teacher gave them when illustrating how this procedure works, but they cannot apply it in novel situations. For example, observations have shown that

> many students don't know why the math procedures they learn in school work. Students leave school having the computational skills to solve standard problems but lacking the higher-order mathematical understanding that would allow them to apply their skills widely in novel situations. Too often, math instruction produces students who can manipulate number symbols but who don't understand what the symbols mean.[7]

How can we make procedural knowledge that students learn meaningful and transferable? The answer to this question was suggested by the Vygotskians back in the 1930s: teaching students a combination of procedural and conceptual knowledge.[8] American cognitive psychologists, who came to the same idea in the 1990s, called it "marrying concepts to procedures."[9] Conceptual knowledge learned together with a subject domain procedure makes the procedure meaningful and transferable; therefore, students become able to use the procedure in novel situations to solve relevant subject domain problems.

Metacognitive Knowledge. Metacognitive knowledge is often described as our ability to self-regulate: to plan and monitor our behavior and to evaluate its outcomes.[10] In the previous chapters, I discussed how preschoolers develop the ability to suppress their impulsivity and bend their behavior to rules and regulations. School students are supposed to develop their self-regulation to an even higher level so that they become able to regulate their thinking, learning, and problems solving (researchers often refer to these processes as "thinking about thinking").

For example, a student has the task of learning about the vertebrate species. Before starting to learn, she *plans* the outcome of her learning: to learn the essential characteristics of vertebrate species and how to use these characteristics to identify the species to which a given animal belongs. Then, while learning, she *is monitoring* her comprehension of the material by asking herself questions: "OK, so what are the essential characteristics of mammals? They are warm-blooded and feed babies milk! And what if an animal is warm-blooded but it does not feed babies milk? Then, it is a bird! So, feeding babies milk is a major feature that differentiates mammals from birds! And what about the ability to fly? I always thought that this is another major feature that differentiates birds from mammals! Let me reread the sections on mammals and birds ... Wow, no, the ability to fly does not differentiate birds from mammals: Some birds cannot fly, and some mammals can! So, it looks like I now understand the material. But, let me test myself." And, to *evaluate* her knowledge in this field, the student answers the questions at the end of the chapter, or (which is even better) chooses different animals, identifies to which species each of them belongs, and then checks the correctness of her answers.

The importance of metacognitive knowledge has been revealed in studies with so-called intelligent novices, that is, people with good metacognitive knowledge but no knowledge in a given subject domain. It turned out that those people could successfully learn by themselves in an absolutely new subject domain. Thus, metacognitive knowledge can even compensate for a lack of subject domain knowledge when we start our learning in a subject domain. Unsurprisingly, it is metacognitive knowledge that has often been found to differentiate successful students from their peers whose learning is less successful.

Fortunately enough, it has been shown that not only does metacognitive knowledge seriously determine the success of student learning, but that it can also be learned by students. Therefore, just as young children should be taught how to regulate their behavior, school students should be taught how to regulate their thinking, learning, and problems solving, and such "teaching for metacognition" should be viewed as an important component of school instruction.

Knowledge Processing

To teach students successfully, it is not sufficient to provide them with the knowledge you want them to learn; you should also help them *process* (acquire, master, and memorize) this knowledge. To be able to do this, it is important to know how new knowledge is processed in our cognitive system. The studies of American cognitive scientists made it possible to construct *the model of information processing*;[11] this model is presented in simplified form in Figure 8.1. Let us discuss the consecutive steps in information processing.

Sensory Register. When reading a textbook, listening to a teacher, or following a teacher's modeling of a new problem-solving strategy, a student, in addition to this subject domain knowledge, is obtaining through her sensory organs other types of information. She is hearing voices from the street, is seeing her classmates' new dresses

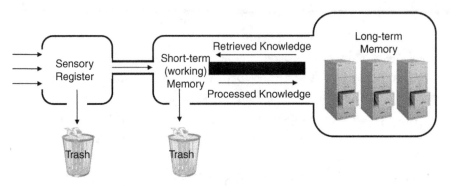

Figure 8.1. The model of information processing (in simplified form).

and a cup of coffee on the teacher's table, is feeling shoes that are too tight, is smelling a sandwich that her classmate brought to class and so on. If she is deeply engaged in learning, she may not be aware of all these different types of information, but not only does she obtain them; they are even held in her cognitive system for a short period of time. The component of human cognitive system in which all the information from sensory organs is collected and held for a short period of time (from less than a second to three or four seconds) is called the sensory register.

The following situation, which is familiar to those who use the subway, illustrates how incoming information is held in the sensory register. You are reading a book in the train and, suddenly, you "hear" the words of the conductor: "The next station is Sheepshead Bay." You realize that the present station is yours, but it is too late: The doors just closed, and the words that you "heard" were said by the conductor a couple of seconds ago. So, rather than "hearing" the conductor's announcement, you evoked them from your sensory register.

Why do we need the sensory register? Obviously, you cannot (and you do not want to) process all the information that you have obtained through your sensory organs. Holding all the incoming information in the sensory register for a brief time is necessary for the selection of those pieces of information that will be held for further processing, and those that should be trashed. And the mechanism for this selection is attention.

Attention. Sometimes attention is called "clear perception," or an analogy is drawn between attention and a flashlight beam that lights up some objects in the room leaving other objects in the dark. To elaborate on this analogy, the beam of this "flashlight" is very narrow, and the number of the "objects" it lights up is very small. As a matter of fact, we cannot attend to several things simultaneously. At first glance, this statement is not consistent with our everyday life experiences: After all, we all can "walk and chew gum at the same time." We are able to do it, however, only because we have mastered both walking and chewing gum so well that performing these activities do not require our attention. But if you distract a toddler's attention with something when he is walking, he may fall down: The process of walking still requires all of his attention. Thus, an experienced driver who is confident that he may attend simultaneously to driving a car and talking on a cellphone is wrong: He is simply switching his attention back and forth between driving and talking on the phone. While the situation on the road is stable, this works pretty well. But if an emergency happens while his attention is on the conversation, it will take him an extra second to redirect his attention to the road information held in his sensory register and to respond to the emergency, and it may be one second too late.

What factors are responsible for what we are attending to? There are two such factors. The first one relates to certain characteristics of the obtained information that automatically draw our attention. For example, a loud sound in a quiet room, an interesting announcement on TV, which happens to be on, or a smell of food when you are hungry will automatically draw your attention even if you are deeply involved in doing a project. For young children, characteristics of the obtained information constitute the only factor that determines the direction of their attention; therefore, as discussed in Chapter 1, Vygotsky characterized a young child as "a slave of his visual field" rather than being a "master" of his own attention.

It is in an attempt to provide students with information that will automatically make them attend to the lesson that, as mentioned, elementary school teachers "sing, dance, or act like Big Bird" when teaching. In light of the preceding analysis, however, it becomes clear why this teaching strategy does not work. Yes, the children's attention becomes involuntarily drawn by the teacher's "funny behavior," but they attend to just this behavior rather than to the content of the lesson. As a result, it is the teacher's "funny behavior" that will be selected for further processing, but not the knowledge that the teacher is trying to teach.

To be sure, adults' attention sometimes is also involuntary drawn by obtained information. But their attention is also determined by another factor: A voluntary decision to direct attention to certain things that do not attract attention by themselves. The ability to make ourselves be attentive to something that does not draw our attention by itself is a result of development of our self-regulation. As discussed earlier, Vygotsky provided us with an analysis of the development of self-regulation in children: They appropriate verbal tools that adults use to regulate their behavior, and start using them to self-regulate by talking aloud to themselves (so-called egocentric or private speech) and to do mutual regulation in the context of sociodramatic play. As a result, these verbal tools become internalized, and self-regulation by the use of inner speech becomes possible. Later we will discuss how self-regulation can be promoted at school.

Thus, those pieces of information in the sensory register to which a student pays attention (either involuntarily or voluntarily) will be selected for further processing, and those pieces of information to which she does not attend will be trashed. The pieces of information selected for further processing are moved into the next component of human cognitive system: short-term (or working) memory.

Short-Term (Working) Memory. The pieces of information that have been moved into short-term (working) memory are maintained there for only about 20 seconds (that is why it is called *short-term* memory). This duration can be prolonged by the use of so-called maintenance rehearsal, that is, repeating the information again and again (this is what you do when, having scheduled an appointment on the phone, you keep repeating the date and time until you have a chance to record the information).

The major function of this component of our cognitive system (which is indicated by the word *working* in its name), however, is not maintaining information but rather its deep processing (in simple words, thinking it over). It is information processing in our working memory and its quality that will determine whether or not and how well it will be remembered: the non-processed information will be trashed; the processed information will be moved to and stored in long-term memory.

The importance of information processing for successful memorization can be illustrated with a simple experiment. Three groups of students were given the same list of words but with different assignments. In the first group, for each word students had to find a word with the opposite meaning; in the second group, students had to count the number of letters in each word; and in the third group, students had to memorize the words so that they could recall them later. Then the students were asked to recall the words. It turned out that in the first group, in which students' assignment made them actively think over the word meanings, the recalls were substantially higher than in the second group, in which the assignment did not direct students toward thinking over the word meanings. Moreover, the recalls in the first group were not any worse (or were even better) than the recalls in the third group, in which students had intentionally memorized the words. Thus, for successful learning it is not even so important whether or not students are involved in intentional learning with the goal of remembering the material. It is important, however, that students are engaged in performance of a task that requires deep processing of the material; if this is the case, the material will be successfully memorized even without the conscious intention to learn.[12]

Later in this section, we will discuss information processing in working memory in more detail. Now let us move together with processed information from working memory to long-term memory.

Long-Term Memory. Cognitive psychologists often draw an analogy between long-term memory and a computer hard drive, or a set of filing cabinets that contain knowledge accumulated by a person through his or her life. New information, if successfully processed in working memory, is moved into the right "filing cabinet," the right "folder," and the right "file" of your long-term memory, so that it enriches the knowledge in this field that you have accumulated in the past. When you need to use this knowledge, you can easily retrieve it from long-term memory and transfer it into working memory.

If, however, new information has not been processed well enough, it may be stored in the wrong "file." In this case, something like "the tip-of-the-tongue phenomenon" can be observed: You know that you have certain knowledge but cannot recall it. This situation is similar to your unsuccessful attempt to find a document that you mistakenly put in the wrong file or folder in your filing cabinet. Thus, a child who cannot answer the teacher's question and is saying in despair, "But I learned it!" often tells the truth: He did learn the material, but did not process it well enough; as a result, this material has been "misfiled," and therefore he cannot find it.

Now, let us return to working memory and discuss how new information should be processed there so that it will be properly stored in long-term memory and, when needed, successfully retrieved from long-term memory.

Deep Information Processing in Working Memory. As mentioned earlier, deep information processing relates to thinking over new information. As a result, the new information becomes understood and connected with the "old" knowledge, and it can then be successfully stored in the right "file" of long-term memory. The type of learning that is based on deep information processing is often called *meaningful learning.*

To be sure, types of meaningful learning will depend on what information is supposed to be learned. To process *factual knowledge*, successful learners often use so-called mnemonics, that is, tricks that help impose an artificial meaning on the knowledge to be memorized. For example, to memorize the five Great Lakes (Huron, Ontario, Michigan, Erie, and Superior), it is helpful to make a connection between the first letter of each lake and a letter in the word HOMES.[13]

In contrast to factual knowledge, *conceptual knowledge* already exists within a certain meaningful system. For example, all the animals can be divided into vertebrates and invertebrates; in turn, vertebrates can be divided into warm-blooded and cold-blooded animals; warm-blooded animals can then be divided into mammals and birds; and so on. Learning the concepts of animal species within this system (as opposed to learning one species after another) will make it easier for children to understand the importance of those characteristics that are essential for an animal belonging to a given species. For example, the importance of the characteristic "warm-blooded" will become obvious to a student when this concept "meets" the concept of cold-blooded animals in her working memory and these concepts are processed together; this will help the student realize that the characteristic "warm-blooded" vs. "cold-blooded" makes it possible to divide all the vertebrate animals into two large groups. In addition, to learn the concepts of animal species in a meaningful way, the student should retrieve from her long-term memory the old knowledge related to the topic (for example, the knowledge of what blood is).

What kind of processing will lead to the acquisition of conceptual knowledge? As discussed earlier, the student, when reading a textbook, may ask herself questions aimed at monitoring her comprehension of the material and evaluation of the learning outcomes ("OK, so what are the essential characteristics of mammals? They are warm-blooded and feed babies milk! And what if an animal is warm-blooded but it does not feed babies milk? Then it is a bird!"). Or, as will be discussed further, she may learn this conceptual knowledge in the context of problem solving, which requires that the student also has the relevant procedural knowledge.

To process *procedural knowledge,* a student should use it to solve problems in a given subject domain: A new subject domain procedure "meets" a relevant problem in working memory and is used to solve the problem. As this procedure is used to solve the subject domain problems, it becomes mastered and stored in the appropriate "file" of long-term memory. For example, to master the procedure for identifying to which species an animal belongs, the student should use the essential characteristics of different species to analyze various animals and identify the species to which each of them belongs.

As mentioned earlier, however, pure procedural knowledge remains meaningless and, therefore, nontransferable. It is the relevant conceptual knowledge that makes a procedure meaningful. The idea of "marrying concepts to procedures" discussed earlier requires that subject domain concepts and procedures should "meet" in working memory to be processed together. Thus, it is important that while using a subject domain procedure to solve problems, the student also refers to the subject domain conceptual knowledge. To use the previous example, when applying the essential characteristics of different species to identify to which species a given animal belongs, the student should also refer to the conceptual knowledge of various species. In addition to making the given subject domain procedure meaningful, this type of learning, as noted, will also help the student process the relevant conceptual knowledge.

Finally, *metacognitive knowledge* (the ability to plan and monitor our thinking, learning, and problem solving, as well as to evaluate their outcomes) is not only, as shown, essential for learning other types of knowledge, but it itself should be learned. In the previous chapters, I have discussed Vygotsky's general idea about providing children with external tools for self-regulation and engaging them in mutual regulation with the use of these tools as instrumental for the development of their self-regulation. I have also illustrated how this idea works in relation to the development of self-regulation in preschoolers. This idea works perfectly well in relation to the facilitation of the development of school students' metacognition as well. Providing students with metacognitive tools and engaging them in collaborative subject domain learning that involves mutual planning, monitoring, and evaluation leads to the development of their ability to do self-planning, self-monitoring, and self-evaluation of their learning. A good example that illustrates this Vygotskian idea is *reciprocal teaching*: the instructional program designed by American researchers to facilitate the development of student's ability to monitor their reading comprehension.[14]

Reciprocal teaching is built around a collaborative performance of a teacher and students aimed at the analysis and understanding of a written text. At the beginning, the teacher models by "thinking aloud" and explains four strategies for comprehension monitoring: questioning, summarizing, clarifying, and predicting. The teacher uses these strategies to lead the group analysis of a text. Gradually, the role of the discussion leader is passed to the children, who take turns in leading the group discussion with the use of these strategies, while the teacher provides the students with feedback and assistance. As the students become more proficient in the use of comprehension-monitoring strategies within group discussion, the teacher withdraws himself or herself from the group activity, passing more and more responsibility for using these strategies to the students. Eventually, the students master and internalize the comprehension-monitoring strategies and become able to use them independently for self-monitoring their reading comprehension.

Learning Motivation

The preceding analysis was concentrated on what knowledge students should learn and how this knowledge should be processed in their cognitive system. There is, however, another factor that crucially determines students' learning outcomes: their learning motivation. As was already discussed in Chapter 6, learning motivation can be extrinsic (learning for the sake of external rewards) or intrinsic (taking pleasure in learning itself), and it is intrinsic learning motivation that leads to better learning. Let us now review three major factors that affect students' intrinsic learning motivation.

Students' Interest in Knowledge to Be Learned. It is no surprise that students are motivated to learn if the knowledge that they are learning is interesting to them. This is why relating students' learning new knowledge to their personal experiences or current interests will increase their motivation to learn this knowledge. There are, however, several problems associated with the implementation of this strategy in a classroom situation. First, different students may have different personal experiences and different interests, which may make certain knowledge interesting to some of them but uninteresting to others. Second, scientific knowledge always exists within a certain system, and it should be taught within this system; therefore, the teacher cannot constantly change the curriculum to adjust it to students' current interests ("We just watched 'Jurassic Park,' and we want to learn about dinosaurs, not mammals!") Third, relating teaching in a classroom to students' interests often takes a form of connecting given knowledge to solving real-life problems ("You need to learn how to count to be able to check your change in a supermarket"), which promotes extrinsic rather than intrinsic learning motivation.[15] Fourth, it is hardly possible to relate all the knowledge to be studied at school to students' experiences or interests ("Why should I learn algebra if I want to become a baseball player?"). Finally, relying on students' current interests deprives the teacher from developing new interests in students; as two American philosophers of education ask rhetorically, "Do we accept the possible consequences that ... concentration on what does interest children now will deny them the opportunity of being introduced to activities which would interest them once they had been initiated into them?"[16]

In light of the preceding analysis, a much more promising strategy to motivate students to learn is not to rely on their current interests, but rather to make new knowledge interesting to them by creating a so-called *problem situation*: A teacher asks students a question to which they think they know the answer, but they suddenly realize that their answers are wrong and may even contradict one another. For example, a teacher asks students what a tomato is; they answer with confidence that it is a vegetable, and become surprised when the teacher informs them that, scientifically speaking, a tomato is a fruit. This surprise (or, in Piaget's terms, *disequilibrium*) makes students interested in learning what characteristics make a plant belong to the class of fruits, and what characteristics make a plant belong to vegetables.

The notion that in order to foster students' intrinsic learning motivation, knowledge should be interesting to students leads to another requirement: Knowledge to be learned should not be either too difficult or too easy for students to grasp. Too difficult knowledge that a student cannot comprehend kills his or her interest in learning this knowledge; to make it worse, repeated failures to learn result in the development of so called "learned helplessness," that is, a loss by a student of any confidence in his or her ability to learn and, therefore, of any interest in learning. Knowledge that is too easy also leads to students losing interest in learning: It does not result in the development of a feeling of increasing competence in students, which is a necessary basis of intrinsic learning motivation. Therefore, to foster intrinsic learning motivation, knowledge that students learn should be challenging but achievable; in Vygotsky's terms, students should learn at the "ceiling" level of their Zone of Proximal Development (see Chapter 1 for a discussion of the concept of the Zone of Proximal Development).

Finally, one more characteristic of knowledge that makes it "interesting" or "uninteresting" relates to its meaningfulness. Meaningless knowledge, such as a procedure that is not supported with the subject domain concepts, is not only nontransferable; because students do not understand how and why this procedure works, they are not interested in learning it. In addition, meaningless knowledge propels meaningless learning, which leads us to the second factor that affects students' intrinsic learning motivation: how knowledge is learned.

How Knowledge Is Learned. How students learn new knowledge affects to a great extent their learning motivation. Drill-and-practice, in which students are engaged when mastering a new procedure that is not supported by relevant concepts, or rote memorization of new concepts that are not presented within a system and are not related to students' prior knowledge, is simply boring and hardly motivates students to learn. On the other hand, meaningful learning not only results in better learning outcomes, but also fosters students' intrinsic learning motivation.

It has also been shown that people are more interested in any activity if they enjoy a certain freedom in making their own choices and decisions within this activity. In regard to school learning, students are more intrinsically motivated to learn if their learning is not strictly controlled by the teacher. Therefore, for example, cooperative learning with classmates is more interesting to students than learning that is strictly directed by the teacher (this is especially true for adolescents, for whom, as discussed in Chapter 7, interactions with peers is one of the highest priorities).

Teacher's "Messages." Finally, whether or not students develop intrinsic learning motivation also depends on what "messages" a teacher gives to the students in the context of a lesson. In Chapter 6, I already discussed that, to facilitate children's intrinsic learning motivation, parents' questions and statements should promote in children the value of the process of learning rather than of its outcomes. Therefore, correct answers and good grades should be appreciated by parents as an indicator of children's good learning, effort, and "good thinking" but not as ends in themselves. Messages that teachers give to their students should also meet this requirement. In this respect, such a teacher's statement as, "Good, you tried hard and approached this problem the right way!" or "I don't think that you used the right strategy; think again" are much more beneficial for fostering a student's intrinsic learning motivation than praising a student for a correct answer or offering a sympathetic "Don't worry, you did the best you could."[17] Similarly, when presenting a new class of problems to students, the teacher may demonstrate different strategies of solving these problem and discuss with the class their advantages and disadvantages, at the same time conveying to the students an emotional "message" of her excitement and enthusiasm about being engaged in thinking.

Conclusion: To Learn How to Shoe Horses, It Is Useful to Read Books about Horseshoeing

These days, it is becoming fashionable to advocate a replacement of college teacher preparation programs with mastery by teachers-to-be of instructional techniques in the context of mentored teaching at school. As one of proponents of this idea wrote, "If I am learning to become a blacksmith, I … don't read a ton of books about how to shoe a horse. What I do is I show up and shoe horses."[18] Thus, successful teaching, from this perspective, requires just a mastery of "good" teaching techniques but not understanding of the process of student learning. As opposed to this "anti-theoretical" position, the discussion in this chapter leads to the conclusion that effective teaching is impossible without knowledge of the major findings about learning process that have been accumulated in the field of psychology. Therefore, it is fruitless and even dangerous to view the job of a teacher as that of a blacksmith and suggest replacing teacher education programs by vocational training.[19]

The discussed data of American cognitive psychologists and Russian Vygotskians, which partially overlap and partially supplement each other, make it possible to formulate important requirements for the content of student learning and the organization of its process. First, teachers should motivate students to learn by making a given topic interesting to students, and then foster further students' intrinsic learning motivation by engaging them in meaningful and challenging learning, giving them a certain freedom in making their own learning choices, and providing them with "messages" that stress the value of the process of learning. Second, teachers should direct students' attention to the essential characteristics of the material to be learned, and avoid a temptation to make the material "interesting" to the students by utilizing some "tricks" that may be interesting but that distract students' attention from the content of the lesson. Third, the knowledge that students learn should be meaningful: facts should be learned in relation to other relevant facts; concepts should be learned within a conceptual system and in their relationships with the relevant procedures; metacognitive knowledge should be mastered in the context of learning subject domain knowledge; and any new knowledge should be related to students' prior knowledge. Fourth, the teacher should guide students' processing new knowledge: provide them with mnemonics to memorize factual knowledge; engage them in solving problems with the use of subject domain procedures and relevant concepts that have been taught; model metacognitive strategies and organize students' collaborative learning in which they exercise mutual planning, monitoring, and evaluation; and help them relate the knowledge taught to their prior knowledge. Following these requirements will make the process of student learning intrinsically motivated and meaningful, and the knowledge learned will be easily retrievable from a student's long-term memory and broadly transferable.

At the same time, it is not easy to implement all these requirement for "good teaching" in an actual classroom. For example, how is it possible to abandon a teacher's strict control over students learning without increasing the probability of developing misconceptions by students? Or, how can we make a system of new subject domain concepts, the relevant procedures, and the "old" relevant knowledge retrieved from long-term memory "meet" in working memory to be processed together, if the capacity of working memory is too limited even to hold all this information, not to mention its processing? In the following chapters, we discuss how successfully these requirements for "good teaching" are met in traditional school instruction, the discovery learning approach (viewed by many as a promising alternative to traditional teaching), and the Vygotskian theoretical learning approach.

9   What Do Students Learn in "Traditional" Schools?

At first glance, the question in the chapter's title sounds too general: Do not "traditional schools" in different countries (and even within the same country) differ? And is it not true that learning outcomes of "traditional school" students in different countries (and even within the same country) are quite different? This objection sounds especially valid in light of the comparisons of learning outcomes of American students with those of students in some other countries, which continue to be a serious concern of Americans since 1957, when the Soviet Union launched the Sputnik satellite. This technological victory of Soviet scientists over their American counterparts was attributed to superior math and science education in the Soviet Union and sparked serious changes in math and science curricula in the United States.

These days, it is the learning outcomes of the Finnish and South Korean (hereinafter "Korean") students, not the Russians, that make American educators, policy makers and the general public concerned and envious. According to the data provided by the 2009 Program for International Student Assessment (PISA), American fifteen-year-olds rank 17th in science and 25th in math among their peers from 34 developed countries that belong to the Organization for Economic Co-Operation and Development (OECD). The highest-performing OECD countries are Korea (first rank in math and third in science) and Finland (second rank in math and first in science).[1] These results are especially alarming because, as U.S.

Secretary of Education Arne Duncan has indicated, "PISA assesses applied knowledge and the higher-order thinking skills critical to success in the information age."[2]

Can such superior performance of the Finnish and Korean students these days, as well as superior performance of Russian students at an earlier time, be attributed to the fact that, as opposed to the American school, school curricula in these countries have incorporated the requirements for "good teaching" discussed in the previous chapter? To answer this question, let us first discuss the studies of American cognitive psychologists and Russian Vygotskians aimed at the analysis of school curricula in the fields of history, science, and math in their countries.

Teaching History, Science, and Math in the United States and the Former Soviet Union

History. According to the results of the National Assessment of Educational Progress, among all the subjects that are taught at school, American students do their worst in history. "Inadequacies of the nation's school system" in the field of teaching history were addressed back in 1988 in the The Bradley Commission Report.[3] A major recommendation of the Report was that the study of history at school should reach "well beyond the acquisition of useful information" and result in achieving by students the ability to "develop judgment and perspective."[4] The Report has stimulated intensive studies of learning outcomes of students in history classes, which have led to a sad conclusion: Under current curricula, students memorize names, dates, and events but fail to develop "the critical, interpretive, and synthetic thinking abilities required for cultivating historical understanding."[5] Even Advanced Placement classes have been shown to "emphasize the memorization and regurgitation of factual material" rather than teaching students "skills necessary to arrive at conclusions on the basis of informed judgment."[6]

Unsurprising, according to recent data from the National Assessment of Educational Progress, less than one-quarter of all tested students performed at or above the Proficient level in 2010. What is even more troubling, the performance of 12th graders in history was worse relative to grade level standards than that of students in earlier grades, with only 12% of them performing at or above the Proficient level, and 55% not reaching even the Basic level. A possible interpretation of this fact is as follows: In elementary school, the students are not expected to demonstrate much historical reasoning; therefore, their knowledge of historic names, dates, and events allows them to perform relatively better than middle and high school students, who are expected (but fail) to demonstrate a somewhat deeper understanding of the material learned. For example, among American 12th graders, only 5% of students turned out to be able to successfully analyze and interpret historical information.[7]

Thus, to use the classification of the types of knowledge discussed in Chapter 8, in history classes, students usually acquire factual knowledge. Even this factual knowledge, however, they do not know very well: A survey of middle school American students demonstrated that 95% of them did not know who Churchill or Stalin were or when the Civil War or World War II were fought.[8] But can we blame students for their "ignorance"? As discussed, the major avenue for learning factual knowledge is rote memorization, the strategy that has been shown to kill the students' learning motivation. As an expert in the field of curriculum and instruction wrote, "teaching history by rote – that is, by having students memorize historical dates and then testing them on how well they can regurgitate that data on a test – is a pedagogical method guaranteed to get students to tune out."[9] It is little wonder that school students usually define history as a "boring subject."

Despite all these shortcoming of the history curriculum in American schools, the situation with teaching history in Russia has been much worse. Like their American peers, rather than developing the ability to analyze and interpret historical information, Russian students in history classes learn "many assorted facts about particular historic phenomena and events, with these facts often poorly interrelated and not representing systematized knowledge."[10] But, as opposed to American curriculum in history, in which all the factual data is more or less "stable," in Russia, the major historic "facts" have changed with every change in the country's leadership. During the period of Stalin's rule, the revision of historic facts happened so fast that history textbooks could not keep up with these changes; therefore, almost every history class in those days started with students, under the teacher's guidance, effacing from history textbooks the names and pictures of people whose role in the country's past had been reconsidered by Stalin. My mother, who went to school during that time, told me a "funny" (to those who did not go through this experience) story about her history class. The teacher started telling students about one episode from the Russian Civil War, which was to be continued next class the following week. During this week, however, the person who had played the leading role in this episode was prosecuted by Stalin. So, the teacher came to the next class deathly pale and started giving students the information about this person's role in the Civil War that was just the opposite of what she had told them in the previous class.

At a slower rate, the revisions of the country's past continued after Stalin, and are still taking place today. If, during Stalin's times, he himself was presented in the history textbooks as "the genius of all times and all people," during Khrushchev, history textbooks fairly described him as the organizer of massive repression against his own people; under Brezhnev, to be on the safe side, history teachers preferred to mention Stalin's name as rarely (and as "neutrally") as possible; under Putin, he has been called "an efficient manager." Similar revisions of Russian history have taken place in regard to political figures and events from the distant past (such as the Russian tzars Ivan the Terrible and Peter the Great). Thus, the saying that "Russia is a country with an unpredictable past" remains the best evaluation of the quality of teaching history in Russian schools.

Science. According to data from the National Assessment of Educational Progress, only 34% of American fourth graders and 21% of 12th graders performed in the field of science at or above the Proficient level in 2009. The percentage of eight graders performing at or above the Proficient level was 30% in 2009 and 32% in 2011 – "no cause for optimism," according to interim executive director of the National Science Teachers Association, who characterized these results as follows:

> Overall, the results show miniscule gains in student achievement. The majority of our eighth-grade students still fall below the proficiency level and only 16 of the 47 states that participated had higher science scores than in 2009. When you consider the importance of being scientifically literate in today's global economy, these scores are simply unacceptable.[11]

And, again, we can observe the same trend that was mentioned in the History section of this chapter: As students progress from elementary to higher school, their performance keeps decreasing against their academic expectations. The reason for this trend may be the same as the one we suggested to explain this trend in the field of teaching history: As students progress to higher grades, the expectations of their ability to do scientific thinking somewhat increase, but their learning outcomes remain basically at the same level. Let us discuss what knowledge students acquire and fail to acquire in science classes.

Analysis shows that, as opposed to history classes, American students in science classes learn not just factual scientific knowledge (for example, names of different chemical elements or organs of human body), but scientific concepts as well (for example, the concept of density or Newton's Laws). The problem is, however, that these scientific concepts are not "married" to relevant procedures and, therefore, students cannot use them to solve problems. In the physical sciences, for example, "a scientific concept is usually introduced by verbal or mathematical definitions that describe the concept by some characterizing features, but do not specify the actual procedures necessary to identify or to construct the concept."[12] As a result,

> Students are weak in applying the facts they know, interpreting data, evaluating experimental design, and using specialized scientific knowledge to draw conclusions. They are poor at reasoning scientifically, which is to say they don't really understand science.[13]

This problem, incidentally, affects the learning of science by American students not only at elementary and secondary school but at the college level as well. Even "engineering students who persevere through two semesters of college physics … couldn't apply Newton's Laws to simple problems, though they could all, no doubt, recite the laws and write equations for them".[14]

Not being able to use scientific concepts and laws learned at school to solve problems in science, students approach these problems proceeding from those concepts that they have developed in their everyday life (Vygotsky called these concepts "spontaneous"), which are often misconceptions. The "advantage" of these misconceptions over scientific concepts learned at school relates to the fact that they are supported by procedures for their use mastered by students through everyday life experience. For example, in their everyday life, children develop the misconception that "all birds fly," supported by the procedure that "if an animal flies, it is a bird," which they then use at school when encountering a problem of animal classification. Similar "naive theories or misconceptions," which "are hard to change with traditional science instruction," have been shown to dominate American students' reasoning in the field of physics.[15]

Memorization by heart of scientific concepts and laws, which turn out to be inapplicable when it comes to solving scientific problems, develops in students attitude toward science as a boring and useless subject; thus, the statement that "in science classes, students are learning to hate science"[16] may not be a gross exaggeration. A survey of more than 300,000 school students (mostly from the United States, but also from Canada, Mexico, and Australia) performed in 2007 has led to the following conclusion:

> Today's students ... see learning science largely as a means to high school graduation. Less than 40 percent see learning science as important for making informed decisions in the future. This perspective might be an outcome of how students are learning science, as curricula are still largely focused on the memorization of facts.[17]

And what about the former Soviet Union? Perhaps the science education in the country that launched the first Sputnik satellite was superior to that in the United States? Findings of Russian researchers did not support this assumption: Learning science in Soviet schools was also typically reduced to memorization of scientific concepts and laws that, in absence of relevant procedures, students could not use to solve subject domain problems.[18] For example, having memorized the essential characteristics of mammals, birds, and fish, elementary school students did not proceed from these characteristics when classifying animals. Rather, they proceeded from the misconceptions of mammals, birds, and fish that they had developed in their everyday lives. Their misconception of fish, for example, involved the shape of a body, fins, tail, and living in the water as the characteristics of fish. To identify fish, they used a procedure that incorporated these characteristics as necessary and sufficient for belonging to the class of fish, which led them to the conclusion that the whale is a fish.

Math. According to data from the National Assessment of Educational Progress, only 40% of American fourth graders and 35% of eighth graders performed in the field of math at or above the Proficient level in 2011. The 2009 data from the same source for twelfth graders are still worse: Only 26% of students performed in math at or above the Proficient level. Thus, again, the same trend that we have observed in the fields of teaching history and science is evident: As students progress from elementary to high school, their performance keeps lagging more and more behind the academic expectations that they are supposed to meet. So, what knowledge do American students learn in math classes?

Numerous studies and observations have shown that teaching math in American schools is often reduced to providing students with procedures for solving math problems without conceptual understanding of these procedures. For example, in elementary school, students master counting without understanding the concepts of number and quantity. Without this conceptual knowledge, students'

> basic number skills remain recipes, rather than rules for reasoning. If they don't understand how number concepts and structures justify and support these skills, their only alternative is to try to understand school math as a set of arbitrary procedures. Why arithmetic works is a mystery to them.[19]

Similarly, students master multi-digit subtraction without understanding the concept of multi-digit number, that is, as "a virtually meaningless procedure."[20]

The fact that school students learn math as a set of meaningless procedures becomes more understandable (although not less troubling) in light of the data that the same shortcoming is quite typical of college students from various teacher preparation programs. Although these students demonstrated a high level of procedural knowledge in the field of math, their conceptual understanding of these procedures turned out to be not particularly high. As a result, these teachers-to-be "were too dependent on algorithms and on the memorization of formulas, tips and rules, and they were unable to provide explanation or justification on how they obtained a particular answer."[21]

Not only does learning math procedures without related concepts result in students becoming capable of solving "standard problems but lacking the higher-order mathematical understanding that would allow them to apply their skills widely in novel situations,"[22] but it also leads to another negative consequence. Namely, students try to compensate for their lack of understanding of a given procedure by attempting to construct this understanding by themselves. Often, however, such attempts lead to the development of misconceptions rather than correct concepts, and these misconceptions come to mislead students in the situations in which they need to choose an appropriate problem-solving procedure. For example, having mastered computational procedures at the level of rote operations, students still have difficulty figuring out which of these operations should be applied in solving a given word problem. To overcome such difficulty, they

> look for a key word that reveals which operation to use. For exam-
> ple, "altogether" means add, "take away" means subtract, and "each"
> means multiply. Students pick an operation on the basis of the key
> word and apply it slavishly to every number in the problem, whether
> it makes sense or not.[23]

No wonder American students "hate word problems, don't understand their purpose, and see them as just another weird school task."[24]

Learning meaningless procedures by rote does not only result in poor learning outcomes, but also makes the process of learning extremely boring. In 2009, an independent panel research firm conducted a survey of the attitudes of U.S. middle school students toward math.[25] Despite the facts that 77% of the students reported that they most often get A's and B's in math, 53% believed that they would enter into a career that requires math skills, and 39% believed that math is the most important subject for their future careers, their general attitude toward math turned out to be rather negative. Of the surveyed students, 61% would prefer to take out the trash than to do math homework and 28% ranked math as their most disliked school subject (the worst rank among all school subjects!). It is especially troubling that students' attitude toward math was shown to become even more negative as students get older: Whereas only 10% of sixth graders reported that they "hated math," among eight graders such reports were provided by 20% of the respondents.

And, again, just as in the fields of history and science education, teaching math in a traditional Russian classroom has been shown to suffer from exactly the same shortcomings as those that we just discussed in relation to American math education. Just like for their American peers, performance in the field of math for Russian students is reduced to "recollection and reproduction of a solution method"[26] with no conceptual understanding of why and where this method works. As a result, the learned math procedures remain non-transferable, and "students, particularly younger ones, basically are altogether successful at solving only problems of a type that is known to them."[27] And, just as their American colleagues, Russian researchers have found that the major limitation of conceptual knowledge of students, which prevents them from successful learning of elementary math, is their lack of understanding of the concepts of number and quantity.

What Are the Reasons for Poor International Standing of American Students?

As discussed in the previous section, the impressive outcomes of school instruction in math and science in the former Soviet Union (in comparison with those in U.S. schools) can hardly be attributed to the use by Russian teachers of innovative teaching methodologies. Rather, in order to explain these outcomes, some other factors should be taken into account. First, Russian students received many more hours of instruction in mathematics and the sciences during their 10 years at school than American students received (or receive now) during their 12-year education program. In the field of math, after spending four years on taking elementary math, all Russian students took six more years of algebra, geometry, and trigonometry; the topics that are introduced in the United States in the fifth or sixth grade were introduced in the Soviet Union in the second or third grade.[28] In the field of science, Russian students spent five years on studying geography, five years on studying biology, four years on studying physics, and three years on studying chemistry.

Second, as a rule, math, geography, biology, physics, and chemistry classes in Russia were taught by teachers who had majored in these subjects (in contrast, in the United States, even now nearly a third of all secondary school teachers of math and more than 20% of all secondary school teachers of science have not majored or even minored in these subjects).[29]

Third, natural sciences were extremely prestigious occupations for young people in the Soviet Union; as a Russian poet semi-fatuously complained in those days,

> Somehow scientists are in favor,
> Somehow poets are in disgrace.
> It has not been done on purpose
> Everything has its own place.[30]

Fourth, the dream of the majority of caring Russian parents those days was to see their child with a Bachelor's degree. Children who did poorly at school had to drop it after the eighth grade and to enroll in a vocational or technical school (the threat "if you do not study well, you will go to a vocational school," was very popular among Russian parents to "motivate" their children to study). Moreover, even successful graduation from a high school did not guarantee an admission to a college, which was extremely competitive in the former Soviet Union; in order to pass the college entrance exams, applicants had to have deep knowledge of school subjects. To be admitted to a college was especially important for Russian school boys (and their parents), because this was the only way to avoid the military draft, which most wanted to avoid. Therefore, many parents would hire private tutors who prepared their children for the college entrance exams.

Might it be that the same (or similar) reasons are responsible for the tremendous outperforming of American students by their Finnish and Korean peers these days? Let us discuss the Finnish and Korean social values and school systems.

The Finnish "Lessons." The recently published book, *Finnish Lessons: What Can the World Learn from Educational Change in Finland*,[31] presents a thoughtful analysis of how the Finnish school "has progressed from mediocrity to being a model contemporary educational system and 'strong performer' over the past 3 decades."[32] Among all the contributors to the Finnish success, the author accentuates one factor that "trumps all others: the daily contribution of excellent teachers."[33] In Finland, as opposed to the United States, "teaching is a noble, prestigious profession – akin to physicians, lawyers, or economists."[34] Therefore, enrolling in teacher education programs is highly competitive: only 10% of applicants get accepted (and, as opposed to the United States, there are no alternative routes to become a teacher in Finland). Those lucky ones who get accepted graduate with master's degrees and a strong background in the subject that they teach (in American schools, as an example, 59% of middle school students and 43% of high school students are taught history by teachers who had neither a major nor a minor in history[35]). The teaching load of Finnish teachers is almost twice as low as in American schools; therefore, Finnish teachers have more time for professional development and curriculum planning, which makes their professional activity not only more successful but more self-rewarding as well. As a result, they stay in teaching; teacher turnover in Finland is extremely low, especially in comparison with that in the United States, where almost one-third of new teachers leave their teaching positions within three years, and nearly half leave after five years.[36]

The second major contributor to the success of the Finnish school has been found in the fact that, as opposed to the United States, the use of standardized tests is profoundly minimized there. As a result, "in Finland, most lower-secondary school teachers teach in order to help their students to learn, not to pass tests."[37] It is not only that this approach directs Finnish students toward learning rather than toward passing a test, but it has been shown to lead to much lower levels of student stress and anxiety; only 7% of Finnish students report that they feel anxiety when working on math tests (for comparison, 52% of Japanese students and 53% of French students report such anxiety).

Third, the process of learning of Finnish students is not negatively influenced by factors caused by poverty, such as inadequate nutrition and health problems, to the extent that these factors influence their American peers. In Finland, only 3.4% of the child population suffers from poverty, whereas in the United States more than 21% of children live in poverty.

Finally, there are references to several more contributors to the Finnish success, which include "placing responsibility and trust before accountability, and handing over school- and district-level leadership to education professionals,"[38] as well as "rethinking the theoretical and methodological foundations" of the instructional process.[39] It is claimed that this "rethinking" has

> clearly affected how teachers talk about learning and teaching. Earlier discourse that was characterized by traditional values of socialization and teaching of facts and automated ideals of mastery has been replaced by understanding, critical thinking, problem solving, and learning how to learn.[40]

It is important to note, however, that the author of *Finnish Lessons* does not provide any information in regard to how these new ideas have been practically implemented in classroom teaching other than referring to the popularity of cooperative project-based learning. He himself admits that "there is surprisingly little reliable research on how [these ideas] actually affected teaching and learning in Finnish schools."[41] In any case, based on the findings discussed in the next chapter, the Finnish success can hardly be attributed to the use by teachers of cooperative project-based learning.

The Korean "Success Story." Another example of a transformation from Cinderella to a Princess is the Korean educational system;

whereas 45 years ago Korean students "were generally considered 'dumb' among international students,"[42] these days they attract world-wide admiration for their academic excellence. One of the reasons for this transformation is the same as one in Finland: highly qualified teachers. As in Finland, the teaching profession in Korea is much more highly respected than, for example, in the United States. As opposed to the United States, where only 23% of teachers come from the top third of college graduates, in Korea, 100% of teachers are recruited from the top third of the academic pool.[43] In addition, these teachers come to school with a strong background in the subject that they teach; in contrast, the percentage of American secondary school teachers who have not majored or even minored in their academic subjects ranges from about 20 (in social studies) to more than 56 (in physical science).[44]

The other, major reason for the success of the Korean educational system, however, is much more similar to the one that contributed to the educational success in the former Soviet Union rather than in contemporary Finland: students' and their parents' dreams of a college diploma.

Although Korean "overheated zeal for education"[45] can be partially attributed to a traditional respect for learning typical of many Asian cultures, it has also a more pragmatic reason: In Korea, a correlation between an educational level and a socioeconomic status is much higher than it is in the United States. Moreover, "Koreans value education as the most reliable marker of high status."[46] A lack of respect towards people with low level of education in Korea is such that many factory girls "spend almost their entire salary on clothes so as to look like office girls or students when they are not in the factory itself."[47] Also, the level of social prestige correlates with the ranking of the university that a Korean attended. No wonder gaining admittance into a prestigious university is extremely competitive and requires high scores on university admission exams.

Deep engagement in learning by Korean students is propelled not only by the desire to succeed socially and economically but also by a strong belief that it is effort and hard work that will lead to success (this is in contrast to American culture in which good learning is often attributed to innate abilities, whereas greater effort is associated with lesser innate ability).[48] The belief in "success through hard study"[49] results not only in Korean students spending much more time on homework than their Finnish peers do (two hours versus half an hour a day), but also in their obsession with private tutoring. The total household expenditure on private tutoring reaches the amount that is equivalent to 80% of the country expenditure on primary and secondary education, and about 75% of Korean primary and secondary students participate in different types of private tutoring.[50] As a result, their "typical academic schedule begins at 8 a.m. and ends sometime from 10 p.m. to 1 a.m., depending on the ambition of the student."[51] In an effort to reduce the extent of this "educational masochism," the Korean government has even created special forces that break into cram-schools after 10 p.m. to make sure that there are no children there engaged in late-night study.[52]

To conclude, the major reason for the Korean "success story" is that "South Korean children work harder and spend more time on their studies than perhaps any other people in the world,"[53] rather than the use by Korean teachers of superior teaching methodologies. Just like in the United States, Korean "teachers 'teach to tests,'" but, as opposed to their U.S. peers, Korean "students spend an inordinate amount of time memorizing textbook material."[54] Moreover, according to some evaluations, "it appears that wide-spread private tutoring is a market response to an inadequate, imperfect, and incomplete provision of public education."[55] As an expert in the field of Korean studies summarized,

> What distinguishes South Korean students from those in other countries is not high-quality instruction ... but rather students' assiduous attention to their studies that follows from high motivation reinforced by social pressure to succeed. The means by which these motivations and pressures are turned into achievement are primarily hard

work, memorization, and repetition – and, for the most ambitious, participation in extracurricular study halls, use of private tutors, and attendance at cram schools.[56]

The educational obsession of Koreans, however, has its side effects; in particular, "three-quarters of middle and high school students consider running away from home or committing suicide, primarily because of parental pressure over lack of success at school."[57]

Conclusion: Replication of the Soviet, Finnish, or Korean "Success Stories" Is Not the Avenue to an American "Success Story"

The preceding analysis makes it possible to conclude that superior learning outcomes of school instruction in the former Soviet Union, Finland, and South Korea cannot be attributed to the use of innovative teaching methodologies in these counties. Rather, the major explanation of the fact that students in these countries perform better than their peers in the United States can be found in the quality of teacher preparation in these countries, as well as in some cultural and social factors that are specific to each particular country.

This is not to say, however, that the American system of school instruction does not have some specific deficiencies that contribute to poor learning outcomes of its students. Indeed, as was briefly discussed in Chapter 6, the underestimation of the importance of instruction for children's development, typical of all the "traditional" schools, has been aggravated in American schools by behaviorist ideas about teaching and learning that promote the idea of learning by means of drill-and-practice and rote memorization. This is why, in particular, the major means of evaluation of student knowledge in American schools are standardized tests, which evaluate the correctness of students' answers rather than their understanding of the knowledge they have learned and their use of this knowledge for higher-order reasoning.

In this connection, let us return to the trend mentioned earlier: As American students progress from elementary to high school, their performance in the fields of history, math, and science keeps lagging more and more behind the academic expectations they are supposed to meet. At the same time, there is another trend: According to data from international comparative studies, the relative international standing of U.S. students also declines as they progress through school. In general, American students perform above the international average in grade 4, close to the international average in grade 8, and below (sometimes, considerably below) the international average in grade 10. The following explanation of both trends can be suggested. Under traditional school curricula all over the world, elementary school children are considered incapable of abstract thinking; therefore, they are taught concrete skills through drill-and-practice, or verbal information through rote memorization. In this respect, American elementary school curricula are not inferior (and may even be superior) to elementary school curricula in other developed countries. However, as the students in other countries progress through school, their curricula target more and more the teaching of higher-order thinking and problem-solving skills, whereas, influenced by behaviorism, American curricula continue to stress the importance of conditioning students to give the right answers. Therefore, as they progress through school, American students keep lagging more and more behind both the national academic expectations and academic performance of their peers from other countries.

To conclude, some of the contributors to the Soviet, Finnish, and Korean educational success (such as better selection and better preparation of teachers-to-be) should indeed be attended to when reforming American schools. However, the major avenue to an American education "success story" cannot and should not go through replication of cultural and social phenomena that substantially contribute to educational successes in other countries. Rather, it seems advisable to reform American educational practices proceeding from the scientific requirements for the content of student learning and the organization of its process that were discussed in Chapter 8.

A new confirmation of this conclusion can be found in the 2012 PISA data that were published while this book was being prepared for printing. According to these data, American fifteen-year-olds have slipped to 21st rank in science and 26th rank in math among their peers from 34 OECD countries. What has caused much more surprise, however, is the fact that the Finnish students have lost their leading positions in science and, especially, math performance: Now, they are ranked 2nd in science and only 6th in math among OECD countries. The leading ranks in these fields (1st in science and 2nd in math) among OECD countries have been taken over by Japan, with Korea maintaining 1st rank in math but slipping to 4th rank in science. Does it mean that American educators should now start advocating a replication of the Japanese educational system as the avenue to reforming American education? The discussion in this chapter leads to a negative answer to this question.

10 Does Constructivist Instruction Present a Good Alternative to "Traditional" Teaching?

A broad dissatisfaction with learning outcomes of American students has resulted in rejection by many American educators of traditional *explicit* instruction, where a teacher directly teaches students the knowledge to learn, and advocacy instead of *constructivist* instruction. Strongly influenced by writings of Piaget and Dewey, the main idea of constructivist instruction is that scientific knowledge should not be taught to students directly; rather, this knowledge should be discovered by students themselves in the course of carrying out some kind of research activity. This idea has been promoted by advocates of constructivist instruction for half a century with some modifications. In the 1960s, constructivists advocated students' independent pure discovery learning. Starting in the 1990s, many of them have abandoned radical constructivism and "have argued in favor of a middle ground between didactic teaching and untrammeled discovery learning, that of 'guided discovery.'"[1] Also, influenced in particular by Vygotsky's theory wrongly understood (this issue is discussed later), they have advocated the idea of discoveries made by a group of students (often referred to as "communities of practice" or "communities of learners") rather than by individual students alone. In their view, a group of students involved in guided discovery is similar to a group of research collaborators solving a scientific problem by doing research and sharing their ideas, whereas the role of the teacher is to orchestrate students' discovery processes and "to challenge the learner's thinking – not to dictate or attempt to proceduralize that thinking."[2]

The general ideas presented in the opening paragraph have become the basis for the development of numerous constructivist instructional programs known as problem-based learning, project-based learning, inquiry-based learning, or discovery (guided discovery) learning. As a contemporary researcher has observed, "requiring students to discover knowledge rather than explicitly providing them with essential information has become a dominant teaching paradigm."[3] Does constructivist instruction resolve the problems and overcome the shortcomings of traditional direct instruction? To answer this question, let us first analyze the validity of theoretical assumptions that underlie constructivist instructional programs.

Analysis of the Theoretical Assumptions of Constructivist Instruction

Although theoretical assumptions of different advocates of constructivist instruction may vary in some details, many of them represent a set of common assumptions, which seem highly questionable.

First, the criticism by constructivists of traditional instruction for teaching students scientific knowledge, rather than letting them discover this knowledge, misses the point. As discussed in the previous chapter, in traditional classrooms students are often taught factual knowledge, or conceptual knowledge that is not supported by the relevant procedural knowledge, or procedural knowledge without related conceptual knowledge. Learning outcomes of such teaching are poor because of the nature of the knowledge that students have been taught, but not because this knowledge has been taught directly rather than having been discovered by them. Ironically, learning in a traditional classroom involves a lot of student "discoveries." In Chapter 9, I quoted an example of students who tried to compensate for their lack of understanding of computational procedures, which had been taught to them without related conceptual knowledge, by attempting to construct this understanding themselves so that they could choose the correct procedures when solving word problems. As you may recall, they did it by looking for a key word in a given word problem that would direct them to the computational procedure that should be used: "Altogether" means add, "take away" means subtract, and "each" means multiply. Needless to say, these constructions were misconceptions – a common outcome, as discussed later, of any type of discovery learning.

Second, as already mentioned, many contemporary advocates of constructivist instruction refer to Vygotsky's ideas as providing a theoretical foundation for their instructional practices, which represents a gross misunderstanding of Vygotsky's theory.[4] It is true that, as discussed in Chapter 1, Vygotsky stressed the importance of social interactions as the context for children's learning and development. He, however, insisted that social interactions should be used to teach children psychological tools rather than serving as a context for their constructing these tools by doing collaborative research and sharing their ideas within "communities of learners." In particular, Vygotsky wrote that learning scientific concepts by students is based on their "appropriation" of verbal definitions provided by adults.[5] When exercising self-regulation, children, as shown in Vygotsky-based studies, use verbal tools that they have *appropriated* from adults: It is not only that they repeat the exact words that their caregivers used to direct and regulate their behavior; they sometimes even imitate the caregiver' voice.[6] When discussing the development of adolescent personalities, Vygotsky stressed the importance of appropriation and internalization by adolescents of social norms and values of the society: "Self-consciousness is social consciousness *transferred within*" (emphasis added).[7] Incidentally, the analogy between psychological and technical tools, which is the cornerstone of Vygotsky's theory, is clearly in opposition to the ideas of constructivist instruction. Just as we provide children with an electric saw and explicitly teach them how to use it (rather them expecting them to reinvent it and learn how to use it through "collaborative research" and sharing their "ideas" with peers), we should provide children with psychological tools and teach them how to use these tools.

Third, the constructivist assumption that subject domain knowledge is acquired better if discovered rather than explicitly taught is not consistent with the model of information processing discussed in Chapter 8. As discussed, for new knowledge to be successfully moved into long-term memory and properly stored there (which is the desirable outcome of the process of learning), this knowledge should be processed in working memory. It is not only, however, that information can be maintained in working memory for only about 20 seconds, but the capacity of working memory is limited as well: Simultaneously, we can hold there no more than about seven novel elements of information and can process there no more than about four elements.[8] Under explicit instruction, "the problem schema"[9] (that is, the knowledge needed to solve problems in a given domain) is directly provided to students, and the capacity of their working memory is sufficient to process this knowledge; as a result, "the problem schema" is successfully moved to and stored in student long-term memory. In contrast, if, for example, medical students are attempting to construct "the problem schema" through solving various clinical problems, they

> must attend to the current diagnostic hypothesis, the data in the problem presented to them, and any intermediate hypothesis between the diagnosis and the patient data.... If we consider that more than one hypothesis has been generated, the cognitive resources needed for maintaining this information in working memory must be such that few cognitive resources are left for acquiring the problem schema.[10]

Thus, constructivist instruction "places a huge burden on working memory,"[11] which should inevitably create problems with knowledge processing in students under this approach.

Fourth, it is indisputable that students involved in pure-discovery methods develop misconceptions. It is true that under guided discovery learning the danger or student developing misconceptions is somewhat reduced, but this danger still exists. Advocates of constructivist instruction themselves admit that guided discovery learning is difficult to orchestrate,[12] and that "a great deal of [guided discovery] learning ... takes place as students work together (more or less) collaboratively, without the involvement of the teacher."[13] They argue, however, that "a skilled teacher circulating in the class-room will be able to provide just-in-time guidance (in the moment it is needed) to help students understand their errors or misunderstand-ings, and correct them."[14] A legitimate question can be formulated in this respect: What is the advantage of allowing students to develop misconceptions and then correcting them as opposed to teaching them correct knowledge in the first place? As a famous psychologist of the 1960s reflected on the discovery learning approach, "to expect a human being to engage in a trial-and-error procedure in discovering a concept appears to be a matter of asking him to behave like an ape."[15]

Let us even leave aside the aforementioned concern and address another important question: Is it that easy to correct errors and mis-conceptions that students have already made? Unfortunately, empir-ical data and observations lead to a negative answer to this question: Once a misconception has been stored in long-term memory, it is not at all easy to correct it. In particular, "mathematical misconceptions are almost impossible to correct."[16] It turns out that even college stu-dents in teacher education (!) programs "may disregard a professor's definitions of a concept, instead using their own (perhaps erroneous) understanding of what the concept means."[17] Some experimental data show that cooperative learning of a group of peers may even result in their rejection of the correct concept in favor of an incorrect concept that one of them has formulated.[18]

The chances that a teacher will be able to correct students' mis-conceptions are further reduced because of a very "relaxed" attitude toward scientific knowledge that constructivists convey to their stu-dents. They enthusiastically support students' rights to make errors in the course of learning (probably because errors and misconceptions are anyway a typical phenomenon under this approach): "As long as you're in my class it is okay to make a mistake."[19] Some of them even claim that "we especially want students to recognize that there is no right or wrong side in most decisions."[20] Or, as another constructivist insists, "frequently when students' responses deviate from our expectations, they possess the seeds of alternative approaches which can be compelling, historically supported and legitimate if we are willing to challenge our own assumptions."[21] The following concern can be formulated in this respect: How can the teacher lead students to give up their misconceptions in favor of correct scientific knowledge if he himself persuaded them that mistakes are fine, and, actually, that they are not mistakes but rather legitimate "alternative approaches"? And indeed, some constructivists go so far as to suggest that students should be encouraged to "construct solutions that they find acceptable given their current ways of knowing."[22]

There is one more obstacle that may interfere with the teacher's attempts to correct students' misconceptions in a constructivist classroom: the attitude toward the teacher that constructivists develop in students. The teacher in a constructivist classroom is a "fellow learner," who is claimed to learn from his students about as much as they learn from him. This is why constructivists even celebrate "precious opportunities for students to observe teachers 'not knowing the answer.'"[23] Well, if students consider their teacher to be a "fellow learner," who may make mistakes and whose knowledge is not any better than their knowledge, why would they be responsive to the teacher's attempt to challenge the misconception that they have discovered and that they are very proud of?

Finally, the constructivist idea of organization of student learning within "communities of practice" or "communities of learners" can also raise some concerns (although, as discussed later, if properly organized, learning within a group can be very beneficial for students). For example, advocates of "guided discovery in a community of learners" often use in their instructional programs the so-called

Jigsaw method.[24] The topic to be learned (e.g., changing populations) is divided into several subtopics (e.g., extinct, endangered, artificial, assisted, and urbanized populations). The class is divided into five "research groups," each studying one of the subtopics. After all the students have become "experts" in their subtopic, an "expert" in extinct population comes to the "endangered population" group and teaches this group her subtopic; in turn, an "expert" in the "endangered population" teaches the "extinct population" group his subtopic; and so on. As a result, all the students are supposed to master the whole topic.

As I noted previously, discovery learning (even guided by the teacher) may lead to students' developing misconceptions, and even by their rejection of the correct concept in favor of a misconception that one of them has formulated. Suppose, however, that it has not happened, and that the students who are learning by the Jigsaw method have become real experts in the subtopic they have studied. Does it really mean, however, that they have simultaneously become experts *in teaching this subtopic*? Indeed, expertise in a subject domain and expertise in teaching this subject domain are two different kinds of expertise! Isn't it quite obvious that a world-class expert in a certain subject domain may at the same time be a very poor teacher of this domain? Students in teacher education programs, in addition to courses in the subject domain they are preparing to teach, also take teaching methodology courses that are supposed to make them experts in teaching. Can we really expect school students to possess even remotely the kind of teaching strategies and expertise that their teachers have? Will they succeed, in particular, in what even experienced teachers often fail to accomplish: providing their students with not only factual knowledge but also with a combination of subject-domain procedural and conceptual knowledge?

To conclude, the major theoretical assumptions of constructivist instruction are highly questionable. However, of much more importance to our discussion of this approach is the analysis of empirical findings about learning outcomes of constructivist instruction. Let us review these findings.

Does Constructivist Instruction Lead to Superior Learning Outcomes?

These days, "the failure of pure discovery as a method of instruction"[25] is hardly denied by anybody except for radical constructivists. Actually, pure discovery learning "was slowly jettisoned and replaced by 'guided discovery'" just because "the full disaster of pure discovery became apparent."[26] Do learning outcomes of contemporary constructivist instructional programs provide evidence to support the efficiency of constructivist instruction?

As leading American cognitive psychologists have observed, the problem with the evaluation by constructivists of the outcomes of their instructional methods "is a failure to specify precisely the competence being tested for and a reliance on subjective judgment instead."[27] As an illustration of this observation, they refer to a paper in which constructivist researchers

> present two examples of answers that are objectively equivalent (and receive equal scores in their objective assessment scheme). However, they are uncomfortable with this equal assessment and feel a subjective component should be added so one answer would receive a higher score because it displayed greater "communication proficiency." Although the "better" answer had neater handwriting, one might well judge it as just more long-winded than the "worse" answer. "Communication proficiency" is very much in the eyes of the beholder.[28]

The extreme subjectivity that constructivists demonstrate when evaluating the outcomes of their instructional programs can be illustrated with many more examples. In one such case, a supporter of constructivist instruction reviewed paragraphs from two "What I learned about primates" essays: one written by a student from a constructivist classroom, and the other by a student from a traditional classroom. I limit myself to quoting the three first and the three last sentences from each paragraph. The "traditional classroom" student wrote:

> I know most about gorillas so that's what I'll start with. There are different types of gorillas. For instance, the mountain gorilla has much nicer, shinier fur than the low-land gorilla.... The silverback – the leader has exclusive breeding rights. The baby will sleep in the same night nest with their mother until the mother has another baby which will usually not happen until the first baby is about 4 or 5. A night nest is a big nest made of all kinds of big plants.[29]

The "constructivist classroom" student wrote:

> There is another primate which I want to talk about. I expressed great interest in learning about this one special gorilla. This gorilla's name is Koko.... I think that Koko is a warm and gentle gorilla who loves animals and people. I also want to say thank-you to Dr. Patterson who has taught Koko everything. I'm glad I did this project because I had fun doing it and I now feel that I know Koko myself.[30]

To support his view about the superiority of the paragraph written by the "constructivist" student, the reviewer referred to "independent judges" who rated this paragraph (as well as other essays of "constructivist students") higher than those of "traditional" students "on the quality of knowledge expressed and quality of organization and presentation."[31]

Interestingly enough, when I gave these two paragraphs to another group of "independent judges" (psychologists, linguists, and educators teaching at the Graduate School of Education of Touro College, as well as graduate students in teacher education programs, most of whom are already certified teachers), their evaluation of these paragraphs were just the opposite of the one presented above. They indicated that, as opposed to the paragraph of the "traditional" student, the paragraph of the "constructivist" student was very egocentric, immature, and did not match the topic of the essay. Whereas the "traditional" student demonstrated his conceptual knowledge in the field by discussing the essential characteristics of gorillas, the "constructivist" student expressed her emotions in regard to Koko and presented some facts about this particular gorilla.

A striking example of constructivists' reliance on subjective judgment when assessing learning outcomes of their teaching methods is a reflection of a constructivist elementary math teacher whose student argued that 5/5 had to be more than 4/4. To substantiate her answer, the student drew two circular cookies, divided first into five pieces and second into four pieces, and showed that with the first cookie there was enough to give a piece to each of five friends, but with the second cookie one friend would not get a piece. The teacher reflected:

> As I listened to Sheena, I knew that next year's teacher might not be charmed by Sheena's way of thinking about this. She might see Sheena as lacking mathematical skills. Was she? Sheena could complete standard fraction worksheet items correctly, (e.g., shade ¾ of a rectangle) and she got the fraction items right on the end-of-year standardized test. Yet this nonstandard part of Sheena's thinking made me wonder ... some aspects of her answer were right. But her nonstandard approach had actually changed the question. And her response to the original question was wrong. What should be the right answer for me here? To this day, that remains uncertain.[32]

I believe the reader of this book will agree with a prospective "next year's teacher" failing to be "charmed" with Sheena's "nonstandard" thinking, which simply demonstrated that she had developed the wrong concept of a fraction. To return, however, to our discussion, it is astonishing to see to what extent some contemporary constructivists are reluctant to admit their instructional failure even in cases in which such failure is obvious!

To be sure, it is not always that constructivist instruction results in such an obvious failure as the one discussed above. What follows is my analysis of the learning outcomes of a lesson that has been presented as an example of a typical and successful lesson within the guided discovery in a community of learners approach.[33] The lesson was aimed at students' mastery of the concept of an animal. A substantial part of the lesson was spent on a rather long discussion during which the children were exchanging their understandings of what animals are. Often, these understandings turned out to be very naive; for example, when asked what elephants and otters have in common, one student answered that "they both get hunted," and another one that "they both need a lot of space." The discussion ended with one of the children opening a dictionary and reading aloud the scientific definition of an animal.

The researchers who have described this lesson claim that it was a success because of the students' engaging in the discussion, keeping the discussion focused, asking for clarification when needed, and eliciting comments from their classmates. This all may be true, but the fact is that the children took the ready-made scientific concept of an animal from a dictionary rather than constructing this concept themselves by doing research and sharing their ideas. Then how can this lesson be used to support the advantages of constructivist instruction? Also, as discussed in Chapter 8, acquisition by students of conceptual knowledge cannot be considered to be a successful learning outcome unless this knowledge is supported by the relevant procedural knowledge. In the description of the lesson, however, there is no indication that the children's learning led to their mastery of the procedural knowledge relevant to the concept of an animal (for example, that they became able to apply the acquired concept to identify certain objects as belonging, or not belonging, to the class of animals).

Some constructivists, indeed, report experimental data that seem to support the effectiveness of their instructional programs; a close look, however, leads to the conclusion that the successful learning outcomes that they report were attributable to anything but constructivist teaching. In one publication, researchers have described a successful "constructivist" teaching statistics to ninth graders, which started with engaging students in inventing a statistical formula. Most students failed to perform this task but, as the authors note,

> the goal of the instruction was not for students to re-invent what took professional mathematicians many years to articulate. Rather, the goal was to prepare them to understand the formal solution created by mathematicians when it was presented in class.[34]

This goal was successfully accomplished: After the students were taught the formula, and practiced using it, they demonstrated deep understanding of the knowledge and the ability to transfer it broadly. To what factors, however, should this success be attributed? One can reasonably suggest that the initial engagement of students in attempts to invent the formula increased their learning motivation (by creating a so-called *problem situation* – see Chapter 8), and facilitated their retrieval of relevant prior knowledge from long-term memory. The point is, however, that students were explicitly taught knowledge rather than discovering it; therefore, these data can hardly be used to support the effectiveness of constructivist instruction.

Thus, the analysis of learning outcomes of contemporary constructivist instruction leads to the conclusion similar to one that was made in the 1960s in regard to pure discovery learning:

> Actual examination of the research literature allegedly supportive of learning by discovery reveals that valid evidence of this nature is virtually nonexistent. It appears that the various enthusiasts of the discovery method have been supporting each other research-wise by taking in each other's laundry, so to speak, that is, by citing each other's opinions and assertions as evidence and by generalizing wildly from equivocal and even negative findings.[35]

Critics of contemporary constructivism argue that "there is very little positive evidence for discovery learning and it is often inferior,"[36] and that many constructivists prefer to ignore experimental data that students learn better under direct instruction rather than constructivist instruction.[37] In a recent discussion between critics and advocates of constructivism, a critic of constructivism asked his opponent to "provide three examples of research studies showing that inquiry methods are more effective than direct instruction in promoting learning for mathematical problem solving";[38] this request, however, was not responded to.

Is Constructivist Instruction Effective in Ill-Structured Domains, or for Developing in Students "Scientific Reasoning"?

The lack of empirical support of effectiveness of constructivist instruction has propelled some of its advocates to look for a compromise between direct teaching and constructivist instruction. They admit that, in the fields of teaching math and science, there is "the predominance of empirical findings indicating the greater effectiveness of highly guided instruction when compared to constructivist."[39] And they "have no objections to the argument that highly guided learning and direct instruction can be maximally effective in such domains [as math and science]."[40] They argue, however, that when teaching in so-called ill-structured domains (social studies, the arts, or reading comprehension), direct instruction is not possible. In these cases, from their perspective, "constructivist approaches are not just *nice*, they are *necessary*,"[41] and "there is *no alternative, in principle,* to constructivist approaches."[42] Another argument, which is often used by more "balanced" constructivists, is that, although constructivist instruction may not result in good learning outcomes, it is instrumental in promoting students' scientific reasoning. Let us discuss the validity of the above arguments.

"*Constructivist Instruction is More Effective than Direct Teaching in Ill-Structured Domains.*" The theoretical weakness of this argument is clearly spelled out in the following quotation:

> Describing a domain as "ill structured" most often means that either domain experts do not agree or that there are no solutions to some

problems. Nearly all problems contain "multiple solution paths," many of which achieve an acceptable resolution to a problem. In this case, the best option is to teach the most direct and simple solution path to novices. In general, when experts fail to consistently solve complex problems we can hardly expect students to discover solutions during instruction. In the case where students are expected to invent a solution, the preferable instructional approach is to provide expert-based procedures for inventing solutions to problems in the domain.[43]

The correctness of the preceding theoretical suggestion has been confirmed with the following fact: Ironically enough, the only impressive example that constructivists use to support their ideas in regard to teaching in an ill-structured domain illustrates the effectiveness of direct rather than constructivist instruction. This example is the very successful *reciprocal teaching* program, developed to promote students' reading comprehension, which I briefly described in Chapter 8. In this program, indeed, students are engaged in "constructing the meaning of a text"[44] with the use of four strategies for comprehension monitoring: questioning, summarizing, clarifying, and predicting. The point is, however, that these strategies are not "constructed" by students; rather, the teacher explicitly teaches these strategies by first modeling them for the students and then arranging their activity aimed at the mastery of these strategies!

"Constructivist Instruction Promotes 'Scientific Reasoning' in Students." As critics of this constructivist notion correctly note, it

is based upon confusing teaching science *as* inquiry ... with teaching science *by* inquiry.... The error here is that no distinction is made between the behaviors and methods of the scientist – who is an expert practicing her or his profession – and those of a student who is essentially a novice.[45]

Indeed, it is not only that scientists are experts in the subject domain that they research; they are also experts in the methods of scientific inquiry. And rather than "discovering" these methods by themselves, they learned them in university courses on research design and analysis, and then refined and elaborated these methods by doing research under close supervision of their graduate school's advisors. Thus, "the strategies of discovery … apparently do not have to be learned by discovery";[46] rather than expecting school students to discover methods of scientific inquiry, it makes much more sense to directly teach them these methods!

The idea that methods of scientific inquiry should be explicitly taught to students rather than discovered by them has been confirmed in a series of studies aimed at the comparison of these two instructional approaches. In one of these studies, elementary school children learned strategies of scientific reasoning either through discovery learning or through direct teaching. It turned out

> not only that many more children learned from direct instruction than from discovery learning, but also that when asked to make broader, richer scientific judgments, the many children who learned about experimental design from direct instruction performed as well as those few children who discovered the method on their own.[47]

Similar results were obtained in other studies that were reviewed by the U.S. National Academy of Sciences; all of them "document the lack of evidence for unguided approaches and the benefits of more strongly guided instruction" in the field of science.[48]

To summarize, the speculations that constructivist instruction is the most effective (or even the only) way to teach students knowledge in ill-structured domains or to develop their scientific reasoning are neither theoretically substantiated nor empirically supported. The following statement seems quite applicable to each of these two teaching goals:

> In the case where students are expected to invent a solution, the preferable instructional approach is to provide expert-based, domain-

specific procedures for inventing solutions to problems through procedurally guided instruction. In this case the focus of the instruction shifts from students discovering solutions to students learning a protocol for discovering solutions in a domain.[49]

Conclusion: Constructivist Instruction Aggravates Rather Than Overcomes the Shortcomings of "Traditional" Teaching

The preceding analysis leads to the conclusion that the learning and developmental outcomes of constructivist instruction are even poorer than those obtained in a traditional classroom (even though, as discussed in Chapter 9, the outcomes of traditional teaching are far from excellent). In summary:

> After a half-century of advocacy associated with instruction using minimal guidance, it appears that there is no body of research supporting the technique. In so far as there is any evidence from controlled studies, it almost uniformly supports direct, strong instructional guidance rather than constructivist-based minimal guidance during the instruction of novice to intermediate learners. Even for students with considerable prior knowledge, strong guidance while learning is most often found to be equally effective as unguided approaches.[50]

These finding make understandable such demeaning references to constructivist instruction as "constructivism advocates very inefficient learning and assessment procedures";[51] or "for someone who is not already committed to a constructivist teaching approach, it can be difficult to find a theoretical or practical justification for the procedure."[52] It is even more difficult to find any justification for constructivist instruction because it is not only inefficient but very time consuming as well: "What can be taught directly in a 25-minute demonstration and discussion, followed by 15 minutes of independent practice with corrective feedback by a teacher, may take several class periods to learn" via constructivist instruction.[53]

In order not to "throw the baby out with the bath water," however, it is important to note that some techniques that constructivists use in their instructional programs may be very efficient. One of them is the creation of a *problem situation* at the beginning of the lesson by asking students to "discover" some knowledge; this, as discussed in Chapter 8, increases students' learning motivation. In addition, the creation of a problem situation results in an "activation of prior knowledge through problem discussion in a small group,"[54] which is needed for successful processing of new knowledge by students. As was also discussed in Chapter 8, people are more interested in any activity if they enjoy a certain freedom in making their own choices and decisions within this activity; to be sure, in a constructivist classroom, students enjoy much of such freedom. Cooperative learning with classmates also motivates students to learn (this is especially true for adolescents, for whom, as discussed in Chapter 7, interactions with peers is one of the highest priorities). However, as discussed in the next chapter, all these techniques can be successfully used in teaching without subscribing to constructivist instruction.

11 The Vygotskian Theoretical Learning Approach as an Alternative to "Traditional" Explicit Instruction and to Constructivist Instruction

The Theoretical Learning Approach: An Overview

The *theoretical learning* approach to instruction has been developed by Russian Vygotskians[1] on the basis of Vygotsky's notions of scientific knowledge as psychological tools, and teaching these tools as the major content of mediation at school. Proceeding from these notions, teaching scientific knowledge should be organized just as any other type of mediation: the teacher presents ready-made scientific knowledge to students in the external form; students appropriate this knowledge and then use and increasingly master it under the teacher's supervision; as a result, this knowledge becomes internalized and turns into an internal mediator of students' thinking and problem solving.

What is the scientific knowledge that we should explicitly teach to students? As discussed in Chapter 8, the answer to this question was suggested by the Vygotskians back in the 1930s (half a century before American cognitive psychologists came up with the same idea): Scientific knowledge taught to students should be a combination of subject-domain procedural and conceptual knowledge. Such "marrying concepts to procedures"[2] makes the procedural knowledge meaningful and transferable; therefore, students become able to use this knowledge in novel situations to solve relevant subject domain problems.

Another Vygotskian idea that his followers implemented when developing the theoretical learning approach was that children's ability to self-regulate (to plan and monitor their behavior and to evaluate its outcomes) is promoted by their mutual regulation. Therefore, the process of learning should include students' cooperative learning, in the context of which they take turns regulating and monitoring each other's performance.

Finally, Russian Vygotskians have elaborated on another idea of Vygotsky: that "children ... never learn without interest."[3] In other words, in order for children to learn, they have to be interested in learning. The Vygotskians have suggested that meaningful and challenging learning at the "ceiling" level of students' Zone of Proximal Development will foster students' intrinsic learning motivation. Incorporation of cooperative learning into the process of classroom instruction, from their perspective, will also make the process of learning more interesting to students (especially for adolescents, for whom, as discussed in Chapter 7, interactions with peers is one of the highest priorities). To come to enjoy their learning, however, students should first become engaged in a learning process. To accomplish the initial engagement of students in learning, the Vygotskians have adopted the idea of creating a so-called *problem situation* (or, in Piaget's terms, *disequilibrium*) by starting a lesson with asking students a question to which they think they know the answer but then realize that their answers are wrong and may even contradict one another.

To summarize, theoretical learning in a classroom includes the following steps:

1. Promoting students' learning motivation in relation to the given topic by creating a problem situation.
2. Providing the students with the subject domain concepts related to the topic to be learned. These concepts are presented to the students in the form of written definitions so that the students do not need to memorize these concepts: They are always available for references.
3. Providing the students with a general procedure for solving subject domain problems. The procedure is presented to the students in the form of a chart: a symbolic and graphic model that prescribes all the steps one should undertake to solve a

given subject domain problem. As an alternative, sometimes this procedure is not provided to the students ready-made; rather, the teacher and the students work together using the subject domain concepts to develop a problem-solving procedure.

4. Providing the students with the subject domain problems. The students solve these problems using the step-by-step procedure. Initially, the students verbalize each step in their problem solving, and the teacher closely monitors their problem solving to make sure that they use the procedure correctly. Then the students become engaged in cooperative learning in small groups. For example, the first student might be solving a problem using the procedural chart, the second one would be monitoring the correctness of the use of the procedural chart by the first student, whereas the third student would evaluate the correctness of the final answer by referring to the list of subject domain concepts. Or the first student designs a subject domain problem, the second one solves the problem using the procedural chart, and the third one monitors the correctness of the use of the procedural chart by the second student. All the students within a learning group take turns performing each of the roles. As the students use the subject domain knowledge for problem solving, they master and internalize this knowledge, which reveals itself in their not looking anymore at the charts and written definitions while working on new problems. At this point, these external tools can be gradually removed.

Theoretical learning instructional programs have been used by Russian Vygotskains for more than 40 years to teach students of different ages (from five-year-old children through college students) a variety of subjects. What follows are three examples of theoretical learning programs that I have developed and that have been used to teach American school students.

Examples of Theoretical Learning Programs

The examples in this section represent the use of theoretical learning to teach three academic subjects (science, math, and history) in which, as discussed in Chapter 9, the performance of American school students is especially troubling. In each of these three academic subjects I chose one topic: in science – "How to identify what kind of vertebrate animal this is"; in math – "How to identify what kind of quadrilateral this is"; and in history – "How to identify what form of government this is." Then I developed theoretical learning lesson plans aimed at teaching school students each of these topics and trained my graduate students, most of whom were public school teachers, in the use of these lesson plans. After training, they had to use one of these lesson plans to teach their students the selected topic, and then to submit a report on the lesson taught.[4] What follows is a description of model lessons that were taught by my graduate students.

Model Lesson 1: Teaching Fifth Grade Students "How to Identify What Kind of Vertebrate Animal This Is." To motivate the students, the teacher showed them pictures of a dolphin, a penguin, and a bat and asked them to tell to which species each of these animals belonged. As was expected, the students mistakenly identified a dolphin as a fish, a bat as a bird, and a penguin as a mammal, and were very surprised when the teacher provided them with the correct answers. As a result, they developed an interest in the topic, which was expressed by one of them in the form of a question: "What then makes a bird a bird?"

As if responding to this question, the teacher provided the students with the subject domain concepts in the form of written definitions (Figure 11.1). Then the teacher asked the students to help her use these definitions to develop a step-by-step procedure to be used to tell to which vertebrate species a given animal belongs (of course, the teacher led the student discussion so that it would end up with the

---

Vertebrate Animals: Concepts and Definitions

Vertebrates are animals with backbones.

Warm-blooded animals are those that try to keep the inside of their bodies at a constant temperature.

Mammals are vertebrate, warm-blooded animals that feed their babies milk.

Birds are vertebrate, warm-blooded animals that lay eggs.

Cold-blooded animals are those that take on the temperature of their surroundings.

Amphibians are vertebrate, cold-blooded animals that change from a babyish, water breathing form to an adult, air-breathing form.

Reptiles are vertebrate, cold-blooded animals that have lungs.

Fish are vertebrate, cold-blooded animals that have gills.

Gills are respiration organs that extract oxygen from water.

Lungs are respiration organs in air-breathing animals.

Figure 11.1. Concepts for the lesson on "How to identify what kind of vertebrate animal this is."

proper procedure). The procedure was then presented in the form of a chart (Figure 11.2).

After that, the students were provided with the subject domain problems. The problems were pictures of different animals with their descriptions (for example, a picture of a frog with the following description: "Frogs eat insects and are cold blooded. They have backbones. They are born with gills, but the gills are replaced by lungs as they reach adulthood. They can be of many different colors"). Using the chart, each child analyzed a given animal and identified the species to which that animal belonged; the teacher monitored the

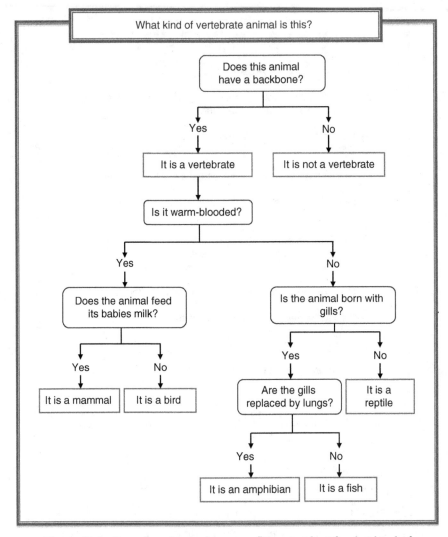

Figure 11.2. Procedure for the lesson on "How to identify what kind of vertebrate animal this is."

students' following of the step-by-step procedure when solving the problems.

Then the students worked together within small groups: In each group, one student used the chart to identify the species to which a given animal belonged, another one monitored the classmate's performance, and the third student used the conceptual list to evaluate the correctness of the answer suggested by the first student.

In her reflection on the lesson, the teacher reported that all the students solved almost all the problems correctly (on several occasions, the students made errors, but corrected these errors themselves as soon as the teacher asked them to recheck the answer). The students could defend, explain, and substantiate their answers. For example, the teacher reported how on several occasions she tried to provoke students to give the wrong answer; for example, when showing the picture of a whale, she said: "Well, to solve this problem we do not need to use the chart. This animal is obviously a fish." The students, however, would typically answer: "It may look like a fish but let us check." And, having used the chart to solve the problem, students would conclude: "It only looks like a fish, but it is a mammal!" Also the students were very interested in the lesson. As one of them said happily after the lesson, "Now I understand how it works." The teacher also noted that some of the stronger students seemed not to look at the chart and the written definitions at the end of the lesson, which could be used as an indicator that they had already mastered and internalized the new knowledge.

Model Lesson 2: Teaching Seventh Grade Students "How to Identify What Kind of Quadrilateral This Is." To motivate the students, the teacher drew a square on a board and asked them to name it. After the students correctly identified this shape, the teacher asked if this shape can be called a rhombus, or a parallelogram, or a quadrilateral. These questions initiated a heated discussion among the students, in which different points of view were presented. Many students, for example, argued that the square could not be called a rhombus because "it has right angles," or it could not be called a parallelogram because "all sides are equal." The teacher used this opportunity to introduce the subject domain concepts to the students (Figure 11.3) and then suggested that the students with his

---

Quadrilaterals: Concepts and Definitions

A **quadrilateral** – a four-sided polygon.

A **parallelogram** – a quadrilateral in which both pairs of opposite sides are parallel.

A **rhombus** – a parallelogram in which all four sides are of equal length.

A **square** – a rhombus in which each angle is 90 degrees.

A **rectangle** – a parallelogram in which each angle is 90 degrees.

A **trapezoid** – a quadrilateral in which one pair of opposite sides is parallel.

An **isosceles trapezoid** – a trapezoid in which two opposite non-parallel sides are of equal length.

Figure 11.3. Concepts for the lesson on "How to identify what kind of quadrilateral this is."

help use these concepts to develop a chart that would make it possible for anybody to identify correctly any quadrilateral. To his surprise, even those students who in the past were not excited at all about math class started enthusiastically discussing what questions in what order should be posed to identify correctly a given quadrilateral. The teacher managed to lead the discussion in such a way that it ended up with the proper procedure (Figure 11.4).

After that, the teacher suggested to the class "to test how the chart works." The students were provided with the subject domain problems (either drawn geometric shapes or their word descriptions) and solved them following the step-by-step procedure under the teacher's supervision.

Then the students solved problems within groups of two: In each group, one student used the chart to identify to what kind of

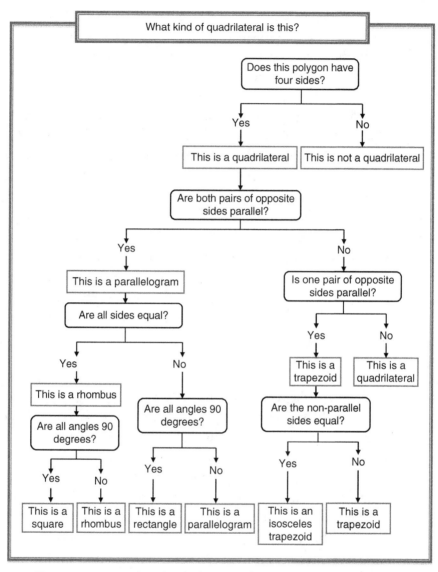

Figure 11.4. Procedure for the lesson on "How to identify what kind of quadrilateral this is."

quadrilateral a given shape belonged, whereas the other student monitored the performance of the first student using the same chart. Then they switched roles (the second student solved the next problem, with the first one monitoring his or her performance).

In his summary report, the teacher wrote that he was especially impressed not only with the almost errorless performance of his students, which they had never demonstrated before, but also with the enthusiasm and interest they demonstrated during the lesson. The teacher reported that it was almost visible how the confidence and certainty of even the weakest students grew during the lesson. Some of the students said that they wished other topics to be taught with the use of "charts." The teacher also observed that, at the end of the lesson, several strong students occasionally performed problem-solving steps without referring to the chart and written definitions; this is an indicator that those students had already started internalizing the new knowledge.

Model Lesson 3: Teaching Ninth Grade Students "How to Identify What Form of Government This Is." To motivate the students, the teacher asked them to answer the following question: "In a survey performed in one country in 1985, 21% of the population said that a particular government that ruled their country was the best they had seen in the last 60 years; they believed that this government returned economic prosperity to their country.[5] What kind of government was this?" The students unanimously decided that this government was a democracy, and some even suggested that the results of the survey referred to Franklin Delano Roosevelt. Then the teacher asked them a new question: "This country was ruled by a very religious person. His father had also ruled this country. What kind of government was this?" The students came to the conclusion that it was a monarchy. To their great surprise, it turned out that, in the first scenario, the teacher referred to the military dictatorship of General Franco in Spain, and, in the second, to the presidency of George W. Bush. The students' reactions were a mixture of

---
Governments: Concepts and Definitions

Democracy: A form of government in which the political power is held by a leader or a political party freely elected by the citizens. The following forms of government are democratic:

> **Presidential Republic:** The leader of the country (often called president) is elected by the citizens for a set period of time. Elections are held at scheduled times.

> **Parliamentary Republic:** The citizens elect members of the legislature (parliament). Each is chosen as a member of a political party. The political party that has a majority in the legislature appoints its leader as the head of the government (usually called a prime minister). The head of the government remains in power as long as his/her party does.

> **Constitutional Monarchy:** The formal head of the state is a hereditary monarch, but he or she retains only minor power or even no power at all and his or her role is mostly ceremonial. The citizens elect members of the legislature (parliament). Each is chosen as a member of a political party. The political party that has a majority in the legislature appoints its leader as the head of the government (usually called a prime minister). The head of the government remains in power as long as his/her party does. (PLEASE NOTE: If the monarch retains real power, even if it is restrained to a certain extent by a constitutionally organized government, this constitutional monarchy is a form of Authoritarianism.)

Authoritarianism: The country is ruled by a leader or small elite that governs without consent of the citizens. The following forms of government are authoritarian:

> **Monarchy:** The country is officially ruled by a single person whose right to rule is passed along through the family. The monarch (usually called the king or queen) is empowered to rule for life.

>> **Absolute Monarchy:** The monarch holds all power and rules his or her country and its citizens with no legally-organized direct opposition in force.

>> **Constitutional Monarchy:** The power of the monarch is restrained to a certain extent by a constitutionally organized government. (PLEASE NOTE: If the monarch retains only minor power or even no power at all and his or her role is mostly ceremonial, this constitutional monarchy is a form of Democracy.)

> **Theocracy:** Means literally "the rule of God." A God or a deity is recognized as the supreme civil ruler. The leaders claim to be ruling as direct agents of a deity or a God, or on behalf of a set of religious ideas.

> **Totalitarianism:** The power in the state is taken over and held by a single political party. The party has a monopoly over the police, military, economic, and education systems and uses an official all-embracing ideology and propaganda disseminated through the state-controlled mass media to maintain itself in power. Dissent is suppressed.

> **Dictatorship:** Absolute rule by a self-appointed leader or group of leaders who may use force to maintain control. In a military dictatorship, the army is in control.

Figure 11.5. Concepts for the lesson on "How to identify what form of government this is."

embarrassment and self-defense, especially in regard to the second scenario: "But you didn't tell us that he was elected!", to which the teacher said: "But you didn't ask me this! If you do not have enough information, you should not make a judgment! Let us learn what

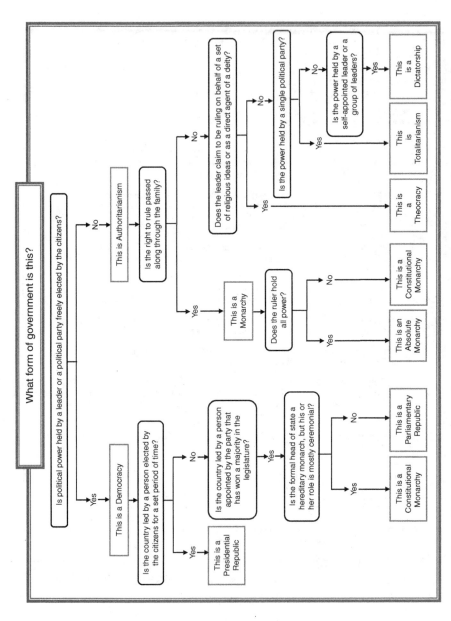

Figure 11.6. Procedure for the lesson on "How to identify what form of government this is."

we should pay attention to when attempting to answer these types of questions."

The teacher then provided the students with the subject-domain concepts in the form of written definitions (Figure 11.5), and with a step-by-step procedure to be used to tell to which form of government a given government belongs (Figure. 11.6).

After that the students were provided with the subject domain problems: descriptions of different governments, in which essential characteristics were mixed up with irrelevant ones. Using the chart, under the teacher's supervision, the students analyzed the problems and identified which form of government was described in the problem. Monitoring by the teacher of the students' following of the step-by-step procedure was especially important because answering some of the questions specified by the procedure required deeper thinking than might seem to be the case. For example, in a problem that described the current Syrian government, there was a statement that "the country is ruled by a son of its former ruler," which propelled a student to answer Yes to the question "Is the right to rule passed along through the family?" and to suggest that the described government is a monarchy. The teacher, however, challenged the correctness of the student's solution by indicating that "passing along the right to rule through the family" refers to the major mechanism of succession of power specific to a given country rather than to incidents in which a son of the former ruler has happened to be appointed as the country leader by the ruling party (which is the case in Syria).

As homework, each student was asked to bring for the next class a description of one government, which his or her classmate would have to analyze and identify for which form of government it was. The students were very interested in the assignment and spent time and effort to present a scenario as confusing as possible. What follows is an example of one of them: "There is a country where members of the cabinet served at the pleasure of the leader. Many people became dissatisfied with the leader, and they were very happy when he ended the set period of time for which he had been elected by them." In this example, the student creatively used the statements "members of the cabinet served at the pleasure of the leader," and "many people became dissatisfied with the leader" to confuse a classmate and make her believe that this was a nondemocratic government, although the key-words "the set period of time for which he had been elected by them" clearly indicate that this was a presidential democracy (specifically, the student referred to the presidency of George W. Bush).

Summarizing her lesson, the teacher reflected on how different it was from "traditional" lessons on the same topic that she had taught before. In the past, she would give definitions of different govern-ments, illustrate her explanation with examples of governments in different countries, and require that students memorize the defini-tions. The students were bored, did not show much interest in the topic, and could not use this information to identify the form of gov-ernment in a specific country. Now, the students were really interested in the topic. At the first class session, all the students solved almost all the problems correctly with the use of the chart (sometimes the students made errors, but corrected these errors themselves as soon as the teacher asked them to recheck the answer). All the students did the homework described above (which, as the teacher reported, had never happened in this class before). At the second class session, stu-dents enjoyed exchanging their scenarios and working with the chart to solve their classmates' problems. Several students told the teacher with joy that they had given "government" problems to their parents, and they could not solve them.

Evaluation of the Theoretical Learning Approach

The positive teacher reports on the outcomes of the theoretical learning lessons presented in the previous section are totally con-sistent with the results of numerous studies performed to evaluate the outcomes of the theoretical learning programs. What follows is a summary of these results.

As opposed to the "common wisdom" belief that the process of learning inevitably involves students' making many errors in the beginning of this process and then gradually improving their performance, theoretical learning proceeds almost faultlessly from the very beginning. Mistakes usually do not exceed 5–6%, and as a rule they are corrected by students themselves.[6] The reasons for this are quite understandable. From the very beginning, students are provided with all the knowledge they need to correctly solve problems in a given subject domain. Also, this knowledge is presented to students in the form of external tools (written definitions and charts) so that they do not need to stretch their short-term memory beyond its limit to hold the new knowledge, the relevant old knowledge retrieved from long-term memory, and the problem to be solved, while simultaneously doing the problem solving. In addition, because the student problem solving is initially exteriorized (a student proceeds from one step prescribed in the chart to the next one by reading questions and answering them aloud), the teacher can monitor this process and move students to the next level of problem solving only after they have mastered the previous level.

The evaluation studies of theoretical learning programs make it possible to challenge another "common wisdom" belief: that in order to make it possible for students to learn new subject domain knowledge, it should be divided into pieces and taught to them piece by piece. For example, it is believed that when teaching vertebrate species, the teacher should teach one species after another: first mammals, then birds, and so on. Indeed, under traditional instruction, such piece-by-piece teaching is often the only option: Students simply cannot memorize the characteristics of all the species simultaneously. However, because under theoretical learning new conceptual and procedural knowledge is presented to students in the form of external tools, which students do not need to memorize, it becomes possible to teach students the whole subject-domain unit rather than dividing it into pieces. Such teaching has two important advantages. First, as discussed in Chapter 8, it makes student learning more meaningful; for example, student *understanding* (as opposed to simply memorizing) the importance of such a characteristic of mammals and birds as "warm-blooded" is promoted by contrasting these species to cold-blooded species. Second, teaching the whole subject domain unit as opposed to a piece-by-piece teaching results in saving a lot of classroom time; under theoretical learning, an average reduction (against "traditional" teaching) of classroom time spent on teaching a new subject domain unit is as much as 1.5 to 2 times.[7]

As also discussed in Chapter 8, teaching students a combination of procedural and conceptual knowledge, and their deep processing of this knowledge in the course of problem solving, make the knowledge learned meaningful and broadly transferable. And, this is exactly what happens under theoretical learning! An American researcher, who studied Russian elementary school students after they had been taught mathematics for three years under the theoretical learning approach, reported that they

> evidenced mathematical understanding typically not found among U.S. high school and university students. ... [It was] refreshing to observe the degree to which ... children ... understood mathematics concepts at their most abstract level and were likewise able to generalize them to new and unfamiliar situations.[8]

Meaningful learning makes it possible for students to answer *why* questions, to substantiate the way in which they have solved a problem, and to defend their ways of solving a problem and the results obtained (e.g., see a student's response to a teacher's "provocation" in the earlier description of Model lesson 1).[9]

Another outcome of the use of theoretical learning is the development in students of interest in learning.[10] As was reported in many instances, students who came home after a theoretical learning lesson, in addition to their homework would do "extra" projects related to the learned material. An extended use of theoretical learning has been shown to result in the development in students of intrinsic learning motivation by the age of around nine years (that is, at the age when many students in "traditional" classrooms completely lose any interest in learning). Proceeding from our analysis in Chapter 8, the following reasons for the "motivational" outcome of theoretical learning can be suggested. First, as already discussed, students under this approach are engaged in meaningful learning at a challenging but achievable level, without repeated failures and multiple errors. Second, the presentation of new knowledge in the form of external tools (written definition and procedural chart) makes it possible to substantially reduce rote memorization that has been shown to literally kill learning motivation: Students acquire, master, and internalize this knowledge in the context of its use to solve problems. So, the memorization of new knowledge becomes, so to speak, a collateral product of an interesting problem-solving activity. Third, the incorporation of collaborative learning in the theoretical learning programs is also beneficial for the development of students' (especially, adolescent students') interest in learning. Finally, by its nature, the theoretical learning programs (and "messages" of a theoretical learning teacher) redirect students' attention from getting correct answers and good grades to the processes of learning and problem solving; this also contributes to the development of students' learning motivation.

In light of the preceding discussion, it seems quite understandable that learning anxiety of third graders who had been taught under the theoretical learning approach from the first grade was 2 to 2.5 times lower than learning anxiety of their peers from "traditional" schools.[11] Indeed, why would students develop learning anxiety if they enjoy learning and do not have a "history" of repeated failures and multiple errors?

Finally, evaluation studies have revealed another important (probably, the most important) outcome of theoretical learning: Its systematic use promotes students' cognitive and metacognitive development.[12] In particular, students develop a general ability to plan and reflect on their learning and problem solving, and to evaluate their outcomes; when encountering a new problem, rather than rushing to solve it, they first thoroughly analyze it to find a general principle, which they then use to solve the problem.[13] These developmental outcomes of theoretical learning are quite understandable. As a result of engagement in theoretical learning, a student

> starts to realize that essential characteristics of objects do not necessarily lie on the surface but should be uncovered. This is an important lesson for understanding scientific truth, where the lack of coincidence between empirical appearance and theoretical essence is the norm, and not an exception.[14]

Thus, the "scientific" approach to problem solving that children engaged in theoretical learning are taught to implement when dealing with particular problems eventually becomes their general cognitive approach to solving any new problem. Also, mutual planning, monitoring, and evaluation, in which students are engaged in the context of a theoretical learning lesson, promote their ability to do self-planning, self-monitoring, and self-evaluation of their learning and problem solving. Thus, the theoretical learning approach can serve as a good illustration of Vygotsky's notion of correctly organized instruction that "marches ahead of development and leads it."[15]

Conclusion: The Theoretical Learning Approach in Light of Findings of Contemporary Psychology

As was discussed in Chapters 9 and 10, neither "traditional" direct teaching nor constructivist instruction meets all the major requirements for "good teaching" formulated in contemporary psychology (see Chapter 8 for the description of these requirements). In contrast, the theoretical learning approach completely meets these requirements.

Before engaging students in theoretical learning of a new topic, the teacher generates interest in this topic by creating a problem situation (which also facilitates students' retrieval of relevant prior knowledge from long-term memory).

Knowledge that the teacher provides to students is a combination of subject domain concepts (which are presented within a system) and a general problem-solving procedure; this makes the new knowledge meaningful and broadly transferable. Providing students with ready-made knowledge and the teacher's strict control of student learning during the first stages of the learning process also prevent them from developing misconceptions.

The knowledge is provided to students in the form of external tools: written definitions and procedural charts. This makes it possible to fulfill the most difficult requirement for "good teaching": To make new subject domain concepts, the procedure, and the "old" relevant knowledge retrieved from long-term memory "meet" in working memory to be processed there (without, however, overloading working memory).

Students process new knowledge not via rote memorization and drill, but in the course of its use for problem solving. This makes their learning meaningful and promotes (rather than kills) their intrinsic learning motivation.

Elements of cooperative learning that are incorporated into a theoretical learning lesson at the later stages of student learning contribute to their interest in learning and create a context for the development of their ability to self-regulate.

It is interesting that many of the ideas used in the theoretical learning approach were formulated by Vygotsky more than half a century before they were "rediscovered" by American cognitive psychologists. In Chapter 8 I already wrote about "anti-theoretical" sentiments that are becoming fashionable among many educators these days. One such educator referred specifically to Vygotsky's theory: "I can study Vygotsky later.... Right now ... my kids need to learn how to read."[16] The impressive learning and developmental outcomes of the implementation of the theoretical learning programs make it possible to conclude that "studying Vygotsky" can really help teachers better understand how to promote their students' learning.

Conclusion: Don't Blame It on Genes!

As discussed in this book, the Vygotskians view children's development as a process determined by adult mediation: Adults engage children in age-appropriate activities, and in the context of these activities
they promote the development in children of new motives and teach
them new psychological tools. The development of new motives leads
to children's engagement in new activities, whereas the acquisition,
mastery, and internalization of new psychological tools leads to the
conversion of children's lower mental processes (with which they are
born) into specifically human higher mental processes.

Thus, according to the Vygotskians, it is "cultural heredity" (that
is, cultural experience provided to a child through mediation) that
determines how the child develops. Therefore, from their perspective, no matter what genetic predispositions there are (of course, with
the exception of genetically caused developmental delays and other
genetically based disorders), their contribution to children's development is negligible in comparison to the contribution made by
mediation.[1]

Such a conclusion, although it may sound too extreme, is supported by empirical data, some of which have already been discussed
in this book. For example, in Chapter 6, I described empirical findings that demonstrated the dominant role of schooling in the development of children's various mental processes. In particular, Luria's
study with illiterate and literate adults revealed that it was schooling (rather than individual differences in heredity) that determined

whether or not a given adult had developed the ability to exercise hypothetical deductive reasoning. Luria also performed another study, which is even more important for our understanding of the role of heredity in children's development; let us discuss it.[2]

Participants in this study were twins who belonged to two age groups: five- to seven-year-olds and eleven- to thirteen-year-olds. Within each of these groups there was the same number of identical (monozygotic) and fraternal (heterozygotic) twins. All the children were given two memory tasks.

The first task was aimed at the evaluation of the children's ability to do visual recognition, that is, to recognize images seen previously. They were shown nine geometrical shapes and then were asked to find these shapes among a set of 34 geometrical shapes presented to them. The comparison of the children's recall within each twin pair showed that, in both age groups, the identical twins performed three times more similarly than the fraternal twins did. Since identical twins have the same genotype, whereas fraternal twins average a 50% genetic similarity, the data obtained lead to the conclusion that the ability to do visual recognition is determined primarily by heredity.

In the second task, the children were read aloud a list of 15 words to be memorized and recalled. They were also offered cards with different pictures (for example, a plane in the sky, a crab on the beach, etc.) and instructed to choose a picture for each of the words so that this picture would help them remember and recall the word. Thus, the pictures were supposed to be used by the children as external memory tools. The children's results on this task were as follows.

Most of the five- to seven-year-old children had significant difficulties with the use of the pictures as external memory tools: They could not make a connection between a given word and one of the pictures. The comparison of recall within each twin pair showed that the identical twins performed 2.3 times more similarly than the fraternal twins did. Thus, in this age group, the children's recalls were still determined primarily by heredity.

In contrast to the younger children, the eleven- to thirteen-year-old children, when performing the second task, successfully invented logical links between the words to be memorized and the pictures, and later used these links to recall the words. For example, to memorize the word "theater," a child might choose the picture of a crab on the beach and give the following explanation for this choice: "The crab is sitting on the beach and is looking at the beautiful stones under the water. To him, this is like a theater." The comparison of recall within each twin pair showed that the difference between scores of the identical twins was the same as the difference between scores of the fraternal twins. Thus, in this age group, the children's success when performing the memory task was not determined by heredity.

Now let us analyze Luria's findings. Visual recognition is, in Vygotsky's terms, a lower mental process, with which we are born and which we share with some animals (even dogs are able to recognize things that they have seen before!). So the children's results on the first task have simply demonstrated that the quality of a lower mental process is strongly determined by heredity.

When performing the second task, the younger children, as discussed, could not use the pictures as external memory tools; therefore, their recall also reflected the quality of their memory as a lower mental process, which was proven to be determined primarily by heredity. The older children, however, could successfully use pictures to memorize and recall words. Thus, although their memory was not a higher mental process yet (they could not yet efficiently memorize using internal memory tools, that is, mnemonics), they could already use external memory tools provided to them. And differences in heredity were nor shown to determine their success in recalling the words.

These findings lead to a very important conclusion: Heredity, indeed, primarily determines the development of lower mental processes, with which we are born; it does not determine, however, the quality of mental processes that develop as a result of mastery by children of psychological tools provided to them through mediation.

This conclusion is in opposition to the views of development advocated by contemporary nativists. As I briefly discussed in the Introduction, nativists see heredity as the major (if not the only) determinant of children's development and the reason for individual differences in development. Let us discuss major nativist findings and arguments in more detail.

Revisiting Nativism

Although nativists are inclined to explain practically all individual differences as a result of differences in genotype, their most popular idea concerns the role of genotype in children's intellectual development. This idea seems to enjoy much empirical support obtained in studies aimed at the comparison of intellectual development of genetically related and unrelated individuals with the use of standardized intelligence tests. Although data obtained in these studies somewhat vary, the general tendency is rather consistent: The correlation of IQ test scores of genetically related individuals is much higher than that of genetically unrelated individuals irrespective of whether or not these individuals have shared the same environment. As a summary of several such studies indicates, the correlation of IQ test scores of identical twins was .86 if they had been reared together and .76 if they had been reared apart, whereas for fraternal twins reared together this correlation was .55, and for adopted children reared together it was 0.[3] According to nativists, this data make "it difficult to escape the conclusion that heredity importantly influences individual differences in IQ scores."[4]

It is important to note, however, that other data have been collected that demonstrate a substantial contribution of family environment to children's IQ.[5] For example, it has been shown that IQs of children adopted by high socioeconomic status parents are 12 points higher than IQs of children adopted by low-SES parents regardless of whether the biological mothers of the children were of low or high

SES. According to another observation, if one of two lower-SES siblings has been adopted into an upper-middle-class family, his or her IQ will be 12 to 16 points higher than the IQ of the other sibling who has not been adopted. To explain these data, it is important to know that middle-class parents have been shown to mediate their children to a much greater extent than lower-class parents. Thus, it is possible to conclude that "the low IQs expected for children born to lower-class parents can be greatly increased if their environment is sufficiently rich cognitively."[6]

Even if, however, we fully accept the nativist claim that it is heredity that primarily determines our IQ scores, another question can be raised: What do intelligence tests actually measure? Surprisingly enough, the answer to this question is not at all clear. Twice in the history of psychology, in 1921 and 1986, prominent psychologists were asked to give their views on the nature of intelligence, and their definitions of intelligence turned out to be very different.[7] Many contemporary proponents of the notion of genetically predetermined intelligence, for example, concordantly associate intelligence with an individual's speed of information processing.[8] They argue that different people process information in their brains with different speed, which is a result of differences in neurophysiological characteristics of their brains determined by heredity. Those of us lucky enough to have been born

> with greater speed of information processing, acquire more cognitively integrated knowledge and skills per unit of time that they interact with the environment. Seemingly small individual differences in speed of information processing, amounting to only a few milliseconds per bit of information, when multiplied by months or years of interaction with the environment can account in part for the relatively large differences observed between individuals in vocabulary, general information, and the other developed cognitive skills assessed by IQ tests.[9]

And indeed, experimental studies have reported a significant correlation between an individual's IQ score and such behavioral and
electrophysiological measures of speed of information processing as
choice reaction time, inspection time, and characteristics of electro-
encephalogram, which have been shown to be highly heritable.

Thus, many contemporary nativists reduce intelligence to speed
of information processing as determined by neurophysiological factors, whereas the Vygotskians stress the role of adult mediation in children's mental development. These positions, however,
are not mutually exclusive. Some cognitive psychologists have suggested that a sharp distinction should be made between intelligence
on the one hand and cognition and metacognition on the other.[10]
Intelligence, in their terms, relates to individual speed of information processing, which is genetically predetermined and difficult to
modify. In contrast, cognition and metacognition are not genetically
predetermined, are highly modifiable, and relate to children's mastery of cognitive and metacognitive tools of thinking, learning, and
problem solving.

Proceeding from this distinction, it is mediation but not innate
speed of information processing that primarily determines the
development of children's cognition and metacognition. Indeed,
irrespective of children's speed of information processing, in order
to develop their memory, an adult has to mediate their mastery of
memory tools; in order to promote their self-regulation, an adult
has to mediate their mastery of verbal means of communication; in
order to promote children's reading comprehension, an adult has to
mediate their mastery of such strategies as questioning, summarizing, clarifying, and predicting; and in order to make it possible for
children to predict the behavior of different objects in water, an adult
has to mediate their mastery of Archimedes' law.

The following objection may follow: "But, aren't nativist right
when arguing that speed of information processing will still influence

children's success in thinking and problem solving by making some of them 'fast thinkers and problem solvers' and others 'slow thinkers and problem solvers'?" To address this possible objection, let us remember the insightful analogy between tools of labor and psychological tools drawn by Vygotsky. Tools of labor, which mediate human practical activity, enormously increase our physical abilities: Even a very weak man with a spade will dig a hole in the ground faster than a very strong man who is digging with his hands. You may say: "But a strong man with a spade will still do a better job than a weak man with a spade; therefore, if you provide them both with spades, the physical strength (which is obviously influenced by genetics) still matters!" Yes, for this example, such an objection will be quite legitimate. But if instead of giving these two men spades, you give them excavators, the difference in their physical strength will become negligible; their productivity will rather depend on the level of their mastery of an excavator as a tool of labor.

The same conclusion can be suggested when discussing the role of innately predetermined speed of information processing in our thinking and problem solving: The more cognitively or metacognitevely demanding a task, the less the contribution of the speed of information processing to the successful performance of this task. This conclusion is totally consistent with the data of Luria's study discussed earlier. That study showed that heredity determined the development of such lower mental processes as visual recognition or memorizing without the use of memory tools; however, it did not determine children's memorization when they used cards with pictures as their memory tools. A study by German researchers has provided us with even more direct confirmation of the above conclusion; it has demonstrated that those university students who perform better on IQ tests "are faster than the less able on easy items, and this difference in speed decreases, overall, with item difficulty, until the more able people end up spending a similar amount of time [to the less able people] on the most difficult items."[11] Actually, more "intelligent" students in this study turned out to be even *slower* thinkers than their less "intelligent" peers on the most difficult items!

Another nativist objection to my analysis might be as follows: "But, will not the speed of information processing influence *how fast* a given child will learn a new psychological tool?" This objection seems quite legitimate. Let us, however, remember the results of a study that was discussed in Chapter 1: Some children with low IQ scores (which, as discussed, many nativists associate with a low speed of information processing) may learn very fast and demonstrate a wide transfer of the learned knowledge. Thus, the speed of information processing is not the only (and even not the major) factor determining children's learning. Indeed, in Chapter 8 we discussed findings of American cognitive psychologists and Russian Vygotskians that, if implemented in teaching, make it possible to greatly improve the process of learning and its outcomes. In particular, as discussed in Chapter 11, theoretical learning makes it possible to reduce the time that students spend on learning a new subject domain unit by 1.5 to 2 times.

To conclude, it would be wrong to deny a contribution of the inherited speed of information processing to children's thinking, learning, and problem solving. This contribution, however, seems to become more and more negligible as we increase the quality of cognitive tools that we teach our children and improve the quality of our teaching. Figuratively speaking, heredity matters a lot if we make a child dig a hole in the ground with his hands; it matters less if we equip the child with a spade and teach him how to use it; and it matters still less if we provide him with an excavator as well as with efficient training in how to operate it.

The same conclusion, in my view, can be made in regard to the development of children's noncognitive characteristics, such as their social values and moral standards. In the Introduction, I mentioned nativist studies that seem to have found a genetic contribution, in particular, to individuals' violent crime. These findings are far from being indisputable: Some researchers argue that the studies were methodologically flawed.[12] But even if we take these findings at face value and agree that heredity *contributes* to criminal behavior, it still does not mean that it *predetermines* it.

An interesting "life experiment" in this respect was performed as a result of the collapse of the Soviet Union. In the Soviet Union, amateur sports was, for all intents and purposes, professional sports. Russian leaders at different levels of government took special pride in the performance of "their" sports teams, and the members of various sports teams, while officially listed as "students," "workers," or "military men," were actually paid for their athletic performance. After the collapse of the Soviet Union, spending on sports in the country abruptly diminished. As a result, to make their living, many of the state-level sportsmen and sportswomen joined professional sports teams or became trainers overseas. As for many lower-level sportsmen (especially boxers, wrestlers, or target shooters), they joined criminal gangs that came to terrorize Russian businessmen in the 1990s.

Thus, it is quite possible that heredity may make a person gravitate toward a certain range of activities: For example, in order to become a sportsman, a soldier, or a criminal, one must possess such a characteristic as aggressiveness, which is partially predetermined by heredity. But heredity does not determine whether a person with this characteristic will choose to become a sportsman, a soldier, or a criminal. Rather, his choice is prepared in the course of identity formation, which, as discussed in Chapter 7, is strongly determined by parental mediation.

To conclude, the "hard" nativist assertion that our development is *genetically predetermined* is highly arguable. A "softer" nativist idea that our thinking, learning, social values, and moral standards are *influenced by heredity* can be, with certain reservations, accepted. But even if we fully accept this nativist idea, it is still mediation that has been shown to be instrumental in the development of the afore-mentioned cognitive and noncognitive characteristics. And even if nativists are right that some children suffer from disadvantageous heredity, it makes it even more important to provide these children with mediation that will compensate for their "bad genes."

Notes

Introduction

1 Toffler, A. (1970). *Future shock* (pp. 137–138). New York: Random House.
2 Scarr, S. (1992). Developmental theories for the 1990s: Development and individual differences. *Child Development, 63*, p. 15.
3 *Ibid.*
4 Watson, J. B. (1925). *Behaviorism* (p. 82). New York: W. W. Norton & Co.
5 Bruer, J. T. (1993). *Schools for thought: A science of learning in the classroom* (p. 8). Cambridge, MA: MIT Press.
6 Gesell, A. (1933). Maturation and the patterning of behavior. In C. Murchison (Ed.), *A handbook of child psychology* (p. 230). Worcester, MA: Clark University Press.
7 Burmenskaya, G. V. (1976). Ponyatie invariantnosti i problema psikhicheskogo razvitiya rebenka [The notion of conservation and the problem of child's mental development]. *Voprosy Psikhologii* [Questions in Psychology], *4*, 103–113; Burmenskaya, G. V. (1978). *Vozmozhnosti planomernogo razvitiya poznavatelnykh protsessov doshkolnika* [The possible ways of organized development of preschoolers' cognitive processes]. Unpublished doctoral dissertation, Moscow, Russia; Obukhova, L. F. (1972). *Etapy razvitiya detskogo myshleniya* [Stages in the development of children's thinking]. Moscow: Izdatelstvo MGU. For a review in English, see Karpov, Y. (2006). Neo-Vygotskian activity theory: Merging Vygotsky's and Piaget's theories of cognitive development. In M. A. Vanchevsky (Ed.), *Frontiers in cognitive psychology* (pp. 31–51). Hauppauge, NY: Nova Science.
8 A fact that Piaget eventually seemed to acknowledge.
9 Toulmin, S. (1978, September). The Mozart of psychology. *New York Review of Books, 28*, pp. 51–57.

10 Wink, J., & Putney, L. G. (2002). *A vision of Vygotsky* (p. 21). Boston, MA: Allyn & Bacon.

11 Bodrova, E., & Leong, D. J. (2007). *Tools of the mind: The Vygotskian approach to early childhood education* (2nd ed.). Columbus, OH: Merrill/ Prentice Hall.

12 Schmittau, J. (1993). Vygotskian scientific concepts: Implications for mathematics education. *Focus on Learning Problems in Mathematics*, **15**(2–3), 29–39; Schmittau, J. (2003). Cultural-historical theory and mathematics education. In A. Kozulin, B. Gindis, V. S. Ageev, & S. Miller (Eds.), *Vygotsky's educational theory in cultural context* (pp. 225–245). Cambridge: Cambridge University Press.

1 The Vygotskian Notion of Mediation as the Major Determinant of Children's Learning and Development

1 Vygotsky, L. S. (1998). R. W. Rieber (Ed.), *The collected works of L. S. Vygotsky, Vol. 5: Child psychology* (p. 103). New York: Plenum. (Original work published 1984).

2 Bodrova, E., & Leong, D. J. (2007). *Tools of the mind: The Vygotskian approach to early childhood education* (2nd ed.) (p. 5). Columbus, OH: Merrill/Prentice Hall.

3 Luria, A. R. (1961). *The role of speech in the regulation of normal and abnormal behavior.* Oxford: Pergamon Press.

4 Vygotsky, L. S. (1986). *Thought and language* (p. 30). Cambridge, MA: MIT Press. (Original work published 1934).

5 Jamieson, J. R. (1995). Visible thought: Deaf children's use of signed and spoken private speech. *Sign Language Studies*, **86**, 63–80.

6 Harris, R. I. (1978). Impulse control in deaf children. In L. S. Liben (Ed.), *Deaf children: Developmental perspectives* (pp. 137–156). New York: Academic Press.

7 Such an "exteriorization" of the psychological tools also takes place in the fields other than self-regulation. For example, although we, adults, have mastered mnemonics (internal tools for memorization and recall), we may still use a string around a finger in order not to forget to mail a letter or to buy bread on the way home. Similarly, we are able to count in our minds, but sometimes, if it is important to not make a mistake, we may use fingers to count, for example, how many days we have left to complete an important project.

 8 Harris, R. I. (1978). Impulse control in deaf children. In L. S. Liben (Ed.), *Deaf children: Developmental perspectives* (pp. 137–156). New York: Academic Press.

 9 Vygotsky, L. S. (1986). *Thought and language* (pp. 186–187). Cambridge, MA: MIT Press. (Original work published 1934).

10 For a practitioner-oriented description of this approach, see Haywood, H. C., & Lidz, C. S. (2007). *Dynamic assessment in practice: Clinical and educational applications.* Cambridge: Cambridge University Press.

11 Brown, A.L., & Ferrara, R.A. (1985). Diagnosing zones of proximal development. In J. V. Wertsch (Ed.), *Culture, communication, and cognition* (pp. 273–305). Cambridge: Cambridge University Press.

12 Vygotsky, L. S. (1986). *Thought and language* (p. 188). Cambridge, MA: MIT Press. (Original work published 1934).

13 Vygotsky, L. S. (1956). *Izbrannye psikhologicheskie issledovaniya* [Selected psychological works] (p. 278). Moscow: Izdatelstvo APN PSFSR.

14 Leontiev, A. N. (1959). *Problemy razvitiya psikhiki* [Problems of mental development]. Moscow: Izdatelstvo APN RSFSR.

2 First Year of Life

 1 Vygotsky, L. S. (1998). R. W. Rieber (Ed.), *The collected works of L. S. Vygotsky, Vol. 5: Child psychology* (p. 215). New York: Plenum. (Original work published 1984).

 2 Rozengard-Pupko, G. L. (1948). *Rech i razvitie vospriyatiya v rannem vozraste* [Language and the development of perception in early age] (p. 15). Moscow: Izdatelstvo AMN SSSR.

 3 Kistyakovskaya, M. U. (1970). *Razvitie dvizheniay u detei pervogo goda zhizni* [The development of motor skills in infants during first year of life]. Moscow: Pedagogika. These data are consistent with observations reported in: Spitz, R. A. (1945). Hospitalism: An inquiry into the genesis of psychiatric conditions in early childhood. *Psychoanalytic Study of the Child,* 1, 53–74. Spitz, R. A. (1946). Hospitalism: A follow-up report on investigation described in Volume 1, 1945. *Psychoanalytic Study of the Child,* 2, 113–117.

 4 Figurin, N. L., & Denisova, M. P. (1949). *Etapy razvitiya povedeniya detei v vozraste ot rozhdeniya do odnogo goda* [The stages of development of children's behavior from birth to one year] (p. 14). Moscow: Medgiz.

5 Rozengard-Pupko, G. L. (1948). *Rech i razvitie vospriyatiya v rannem vozraste* [Language and the development of perception in early age] (p. 22). Moscow: Izdatelstvo AMN SSSR.

6 Bowlby, J. (1951). *Maternal care and mental health*. Geneva: World Health Organization; Spitz, R. A. (1945). Hospitalism: An inquiry into the genesis of psychiatric conditions in early childhood. *Psychoanalytic Study of the Child*, **1**, 53–74; Spitz, R. A. (1946). Hospitalism: A follow-up report on investigation described in Volume 1, 1945. *Psychoanalytic Study of the Child*, **2**, 113–117.

7 Zaporozhets, A. V., & Lisina, M. I. (Eds.), (1974). *Razvitie obscheniya u doshkolnikov* [The development of communication in preschoolers] (p. **67**). Moscow: Pedagogika.

8 Rozengard-Pupko, G. L. (1948). *Rech i razvitie vospriyatiya v rannem vozraste* [Language and the development of perception in early age] (p. 21). Moscow: Izdatelstvo AMN SSSR.

9 Lisina, M. I. (1986). *Problemy ontogeneza obscheniya* [Problems of the ontogenesis of communication]. Moscow: Pedagogica; Zaporozhets, A. V., & Lisina, M. I. (Eds.), (1974). *Razvitie obscheniya u doshkolnikov* [The development of communication in preschoolers]. Moscow: Pedagogika.

10 Vygotsky, L. S. (1998). R. W. Rieber (Ed.), *The collected works of L. S. Vygotsky, Vol. 5: Child psychology* (p. 231). New York: Plenum. (Original work published 1984).

11 Frankel, K. A., & Bates, J. E. (1990). Mother-toddler problem solving: Antecedents in attachment, home behavior, and temperament. *Child Development*, **61**, 810–819; Main, M. (1983). Exploration, play, and cognitive functioning related to infant-mother attachment. *Infant Behavior and Development*, **6**, 167–174; Matas, L., Arend, R., & Sroufe, L. A. (1978). Continuity of adaptation in the second year: The relationship between quality of attachment and later competence. *Child Development*, **49**, 547–556.

12 Zaporozhets, A. V., & Lisina, M. I. (Eds.), (1974). *Razvitie obscheniya u doshkolnikov* [The development of communication in preschoolers] (p. 145). Moscow: Pedagogika.

13 Lisina, M. I. (1986). *Problemy ontogeneza obscheniya* [Problems of the ontogenesis of communication] (p. 61). Moscow: Pedagogika.

14 Alternatively, deaf children may start the mastery of more elaborated means of gestural communication, that is, sign language.

3 Second and Third Years

1 Elkonin, D. B. (1989). *Izbrannye psikhologicheskie trudy* [Selected psychological works] (p. 48). Moscow: Pedagogika.

2 Bodrova, E., & Leong, D. J. (2007). *Tools of the mind: The Vygotskian approach to early childhood education* (2nd ed.) (p. **108**). Columbus, OH: Merrill/Prentice Hall.

3 Elkonin, D. B. (1978). *Psikhologiya igry* [Psychology of play] (p. 162). Moscow: Pedagogika.

4 Bugrimenko, E., & Smirnova, E. (1994). Paradoxes of children's play in Vygotsky's theory. In G. Cupchick & J. Laszlo (Eds.), *Emerging visions of the aesthetic process* (pp. 292–293). Cambridge: Cambridge University Press.

5 O'Reilly, A. W., & Bornstein, M. N. (1993). Caregiver-child interaction in play. In M. N. Bornstein & A. Watson O'Reilly (Eds.), *The role of play in the development of thought* (p. 58). San Francisco: Jossey-Bass.

6 Welteroth, S. (2002). Increasing play competence for very young children: How two early head start home visitors conceptualize and actualize their roles. In J. L. Roopnarine (Ed.), *Conceptual, social-cognitive, and contextual issues in the fields of play* (pp. 183–207). Westport, CT: Ablex.

7 Elkonin, D. B. (1978). *Psikhologiya igry* [Psychology of play] (pp. 275–276). Moscow: Pedagogika.

8 Bondioli, A. (2001). The adult as a tutor in fostering children's symbolic play. In A. Gőncű & E. Klein (Eds.), *Children in play, story, and school* (p. 111). New York: Guilford Press.

9 Smilansky, S., & Shefatya, L. (1990). *Facilitating play: A medium for promoting cognitive, socio-emotional, and academic development in young children* (p. 130). Gaithersburg, MD: Psychosocial & Educational Publications.

10 Miller, P., & Garvey, C. (1984). Mother-baby role play: Its origins in social support. In I. Bretherton (Ed.), *Symbolic play: The development of social understanding* (p. 128). Orlando, FL: Academic Press.

11 Elkonin, D. B. (1978). *Psikhologiya igry* [Psychology of play] (p. **187**). Moscow: Pedagogika.

12 Siegler, R. S. (1991). *Children's thinking* (p. 146). Englewood Cliffs, NJ: Prentice Hall.

13 Elagina, M. G. (1977) Vliyanie nekotorykh osobennostei obscheniya na vozniknovenie aktivnoi rechi v rannem bozraste [The influence of some characteristics of communication on the emergence of active speech in early childhood]. *Voprosy Psikhologii* [Questions in Psychology], **2**, 135–142.

14 Lisina, M. I. (1986). *Problemy ontogeneza obscheniya* [Problems of the ontogenesis of communication] (p. **26**). Moscow: Pedagogika.

15 Yoder, P. (1992). Communication intervention with children who have disabilities. *Kennedy Center News*, **21**, p. 1.

16 Vygotsky, L. S. (1978). M. Cole, V. John-Steiner, S. Scribner & E. Souberman (Eds.), *Mind in society: The development of higher psychological processes* (pp. 98–99). Cambridge, MA: Harvard University Press.

17 Elkonin, D. B. (1978). *Psikhologiya igry* [Psychology of play] (pp. 244–245). Moscow: Pedagogika.

18 Fein, G. (1975). A trasformational analysis of pretending. *Developmental Psychology*, **1**(3), 291–296.

4 Three- to Six-Year-Olds

1 Tizard, B. (1977). Play: The child's way of learning? In B. Tizard & D. Harvey (Eds.), *Biology of play* (p. 206). London: Heinemann.

2 Glaubman, R., Kashi, G., & Koresh, R. (2001). Facilitating the narrative quality of sociodramatic play. In A. Göncü & E. Klein (Eds.), *Children in play, story, and school* (p. 137). New York: Guilford Press.

3 Elkind, D. (1987). *Miseducation: Preschoolers at risk.* New York: Knopf; Sylva, K., Roy, C., & Painter, M. (1980). *Childwatching at playground and nursery school.* Ypsilanti, MI: High/Scope.

4 Koroleva, 1957, reviewed in Elkonin, D. B. (1978). *Psikhologiya igry* [Psychology of play]. Moscow: Pedagogika.

5 Johnson, J. E., Christie, J. F., & Yawkey, T. D. (1987). *Play and early childhood development* (p. 29). Glenview, IL: Scott, Foresman, and Co.

6 Singer & Singer, 1976, reviewed in Johnson, J. E., Christie, J. F., & Yawkey, T. D. (1987). *Play and early childhood development.* Glenview, IL: Scott, Foresman, and Co.

7 Smilansky, S.,& Shefatya, L. (1990). *Facilitating play: A medium for promoting cognitive, socio-emotional, and academic development in young children.* Gaithersburg, MD: Psychosocial & Educational Publications.

8 *Ibid*, p. 151.

9 Johnson, J. E., Christie, J. F., & Yawkey, T. D. (1987). *Play and early child-hood development* (pp. 34–35). Glenview, IL: Scott, Foresman, and Co.

10 Smilansky, S., & Shefatya, L. (1990). *Facilitating play: A medium for pro-moting cognitive, socio-emotional, and academic development in young children* (pp. 151–152). Gaithersburg, MD: Psychosocial & Educational Publications.

11 Johnson, J. E., Christie, J. F., & Yawkey, T. D. (1987). *Play and early child-hood development* (p. 35). Glenview, IL: Scott, Foresman, and Co.

12 Vygotsky, L. S. (1976). Play and its role in the mental development of the child. In J. S. Bruner, A. Jolly, & K. Sylva (Eds.), *Play: Its role in devel-opment and evolution* (p. 537). New York: Basic Books. (Original work published 1966).

13 *Ibid*, p. 552.

14 Cheah, C. S. L., Nelson, L. J., & Rubin, K. H. (2001). Noncosial play as a risk factor in social and emotional development. In A. Gőncű & E. Klein (Eds.), *Children in play, story, and school* (p. 61). New York: Guilford Press.

15 Bodrova, E., & Leong, D. J. (2007). *Tools of the mind: The Vygotskian approach to early childhood education* (2nd ed.) (p. 162). Columbus, OH: Merrill/Prentice Hall.

16 Vygotsky, L. S. (1984). *Sobranie sochineniy, Tom 4: Detskaya psikhologiya* [The collected works, Vol. 4: Child psychology] (p. 35). Moscow: Pedagogika.

17 Blair, C. (2002). School readiness: Integrating cognition and emotion in a neurobiological conceptualization of children's functioning at school entry. *American Psychologist, 57*(2), 112.

18 Smilansky, S., & Shefatya, L. (1990). *Facilitating play: A medium for promoting cognitive, socio-emotional, and academic development in young children* (p. 44). Gaithersburg, MD: Psychosocial & Educational Publications.

19 Elkonin, D. B. (1978). *Psikhologiya igry* [Psychology of play] (p. 277). Moscow: Pedagogika.

20 Bozhovich, L. I. (1968). *Lichnost i ee formirovanie v detskom vozraste* [Personality and its development in childhood] (p. 218). Moscow: Prosveschenie.

21 Vygotsky, L. S. (1976). Play and its role in the mental development of the child. In J. S. Bruner, A. Jolly, & K. Sylva. (Eds.), *Play: Its role in*

development and evolution (p. 542). New York: Basic Books. (Original work published 1966).

22 Elkonin, D. B. (1978). *Psikhologiya igry* [Psychology of play] (p. 248). Moscow: Pedagogika.

23 *Ibid.*

24 Glaubman, R., Kashi, G., & Koresh, R. (2001). Facilitating the narrative quality of sociodramatic play. In A. Gőncű & E. Klein (Eds.), *Children in play, story, and school* (p. 137). New York: Guilford Press.

25 Blair, C. (2002). School readiness: Integrating cognition and emotion in a neurobiological conceptualization of children's functioning at school entry. *American Psychologist, 57*(2), 112.

26 Bodrova, E., & Leong, D. J. (2007). *Tools of the mind: The Vygotskian approach to early childhood education* (2nd ed.) (p. 5). Columbus, OH: Merrill/Prentice Hall.

27 Elkonin, D. B. (1978). *Psikhologiya igry* [Psychology of play] (pp. 281–282). Moscow: Pedagogika.

28 *Ibid*, p. 282.

29 La Paro, K. M., & Pianta, R. C. (2000). Predicting children's competence in the early school years: A meta-analytic review. *Review of Educational Research, 70*(4), 475.

30 NAEYC Position Statement (2009). *Developmentally Appropriate Practice in Early Childhood Programs Serving Children from Birth through Age 8* (p. 15). National Association for the Education of Young Children.

31 Smilansky, S., & Shefatya, L. (1990). *Facilitating play: A medium for promoting cognitive, socio-emotional, and academic development in young children* (p. 20). Gaithersburg, MD: Psychosocial & Educational Publications.

32 Bodrova, E., & Leong, D. J. (2007). *Tools of the mind: The Vygotskian approach to early childhood education* (2nd ed.) (p. 138). Columbus, OH: Merrill/Prentice Hall.

5 Mediation of Preschoolers' Activities to Promote School Readiness

1 The first three activities described below were designed at the Institute of Preschool Education (Moscow, Russia) under the leadership of Leonid Venger.

2 Brofman, V. V. (2001). *Arhitekturnaya shkola imeni papy Karlo* [Papa Carlo architect school]. Moscow: Linka-Press.

3 Dyachenko, O. M. (1980). Formirovanie deistvii prostranstvennogo modelirovaniya v protsesse oznakomleniya doshkolnikov s detskoi khudozhestvennoi literaturoi [Formation of the actions of spatial modelling in the course of preschool children's becoming acquainted with children's literature]. In L. A. Venger (Ed.), *Problemy formirovaniya poznavatelnykh sposobnostei v doshkolnom vozraste* [Challenges in establish learning abilities at a preschool age] (pp. 47–55). Moscow: Izdatelstvo NIIOP APN SSSR; Dyachenko, O. M. (1986). Formirovanie sposobnosti k naglyadnomu modelirovaniyu pri oznakomlenii s detskoi khudozhestvennoi literaturoi [Formation of the ability for graphic modeling in the course of becoming acquainted with children's literature]. In L. A. Venger (Ed.), *Razvitie poznavatelnykh sposobnostei v protsesse doshkolnogo vospitaniya* [The development of learning abilities in the process of preschool upbringing.] (pp. 94–113). Moscow: Pedagogika.

4 T. V. Lavrent'eva (1986). Formirovanie sposobnosti k naglyadnomu modelirovaniyu pri oznakomlenii s prostranstvennymi otnosheniyami [Formation of the ability for graphic modeling in the course of becoming acquainted with space relationships]. In L. A. Venger (Ed.), *Razvitie poznavatelnykh sposobnostei v protsesse doshkolnogo vospitaniya* [The development of learning abilities in the process of preschool upbringing] (pp. 33–50). Moscow: Pedagogika; Venger, L. A., & Venger, A. L. (1994). *Domashnyaya shkola* [*School at home*]. Moscow: Znanie.

5 Burmenskaya, G. V. (1976). Ponyatie invariantnosti i problema psikhicheskogo razvitiya rebenka [The notion of conservation and the problem of children's mental development]. *Voprosy Psikhologii*, [Questions in Psychology] 4, 103–113; Georgiev, L. S. (1960). *Formirovanie nachalnykh matematicheskikh ponyatii u detei* [Formation of elementary mathematical concepts in children]. Unpublished doctoral dissertation. Moscow, Russia; Obukhova, L. F. (1972). *Etapy razvitiya detskogo myshleniya* [Stages in the development of children's thinking]. Moscow: Izdatelstvo MGU.

6 Venger, L. A., & Venger, A. L. (1994). *Domashnyaya shkola* [*School at home*]. Moscow: Znanie (as described in this chapter, the activity has been modified by V. Brofman, Y. Karpov, and I. Rabinovich).

7 The activity has been developed by V. Brofman, Y. Karpov, and I. Rabinovich.

8 This idea was suggested by G. A. Tsukerman.
9 Quoted in Bodrova, E., & Leong, D. J. (2007). *Tools of the mind: The Vygotskian approach to early childhood education* (2nd ed.) (p. 142). Columbus, OH: Merrill/Prentice Hall.
10 Bodrova, E., & Leong, D. J. (2007). *Tools of the mind: The Vygotskian approach to early childhood education* (2nd ed.). Columbus, OH: Merrill/ Prentice Hall
11 Reprinted from: *Touro Links* (Spring 2010), p. 41.
12 Reprinted from: *Touro Links* (Spring 2010), p. 41.
13 Reprinted from: Dyachenko, O. M. (1986). Formirovanie sposobnosti k naglyadnomu modelirovaniyu pri oznakomlenii s detskoi khudozhestvennoi literaturoi [Formation of graphic modeling in the course of becoming acquainted with children's literature]. In L. A. Venger (Ed.), *Razvitie poznavatelnykh sposobnostei v protsesse doshkolnogo vospitaniya* [The development of learning abilities in the process of preschool upbringing] (p. 108). Moscow: Pedagogika.

6 Learning at School: Children Not Only Learn; They Develop As Well

1 Zaporozhets, A. V. (1986). Razvitie myshleniya [The development of thinking]. In A. V. Zaporozhets, *Izbrannye psikhologicheskie trudy, Tom 1* [Selected psychology works, Vol. 1] (p. 207). Moscow: Pedagogika.
2 Vygotsky, L. S. (1987). R. W. Rieber (Ed.), *The collected works of L. S. Vygotsky: Vol. 1: Problems of general psychology* (p. 220). New York: Plenum. (Original work published 1982).
3 Luria, A. R. (1976). *Cognitive development: Its cultural and social foundations.* Cambridge, MA: Harvard University Press. (Original work published 1974); Luria, A. R. (1979). *The making of mind: A personal account of Soviet psychology.* Cambridge, MA: Harvard University Press.
4 For descriptions and overviews, see Ceci S. J. (1991) How much does schooling influence general intelligence and its cognitive components? A reassessment of the evidence. *Developmental Psychology, 27,* 703–722; Cole, M. (1996). *Cultural psychology: A once and future discipline.* Cambridge, MA: The Belknap Press of Harvard University Press; Morrison, F. J., Smith, L., & Dow-Ehrensberger, M. (1995). Education and cognitive development: A natural experiment. *Developmental Psychology, 31,* 789–799; Rogoff, B., & Chavajay, P. (1995). What's

become of research on the cultural basis of cognitive development. *American Psychologist*, **50**(10), 859–877.

5 Luria, A. R. (1976). *Cognitive development: Its cultural and social foundations*. Cambridge, MA: Harvard University Press. (Original work published 1974); Luria, A. R. (1979). *The making of mind: A personal account of Soviet psychology*. Cambridge, MA: Harvard University Press.

6 For overviews, see Rogoff, B., & Chavajay, P. (1995). What's become of research on the cultural basis of cognitive development. *American Psychologist*, **50**(10), 859–877.

7 Morrison, F. J., Smith, L., & Dow-Ehrensberger, M. (1995). Education and cognitive development: A natural experiment. *Developmental Psychology*, **31**(5), 789–799.

8 Luria, A. R. (1977). Foreword. In S.N. Karpova, *The realization of the verbal composition of speech by preschool children* (p. viii). The Hague: Mouton.

9 Morrison, F. J., Smith, L., & Dow-Ehrensberger, M. (1995). Education and cognitive development: A natural experiment. *Developmental Psychology*, **31**(5), 789–799.

10 Luria, A. R. (1976). *Cognitive development: Its cultural and social foundations* (p. 54). Cambridge, MA: Harvard University Press. (Original work published 1974).

11 *Ibid*, p. 58.

12 As discussed in the introduction, Piaget, in general, disregarded the role of school instruction in children's cognitive development; it was only in his latest publications that he seemed to acknowledge the fact that schooling facilitates the development of formal-logical thought.

13 Luria, A. R. (1979). *The making of mind: A personal account of Soviet psychology* (p. 78). Cambridge, MA: Harvard University Press.

14 Luria, A. R. (1976). *Cognitive development: Its cultural and social foundations* (p. 108). Cambridge, MA: Harvard University Press. (Original work published 1974).

15 This conclusion was challenged by some researchers, who believed that people in all cultures have the same basic cognitive processes or abilities; therefore, "cultural differences in cognition reside more in the situations to which particular cognitive processes are applied than in the existence of a process in one cultural group and its absence in another" (Cole, M., Gay, J., Glick, J. A., & Sharp, D. W. [1971]. *The cultural context of learning and thinking: An exploration in experimental anthropology* [p. 233]. New York: Basic Books). They assumed that schooling, rather

than leading to the development of hypothetical deductive reasoning, leads to the extension of such reasoning to solving school-content problems. This assumption, however, has been proven wrong in a study that demonstrated that "error-free solution of simple syllogistic problems … initially emerges in the sphere of school (scientific) information and is transferred only later to the everyday sphere" (see Tulviste, P. [1991]. *The cultural-historical development of verbal thinking* [p. 127]. Commack, NY: Nova Science).

16 For overviews, see Ceci S. J. (1991) How much does schooling influence general intelligence and its cognitive components? A reassessment of the evidence. *Developmental Psychology, 27*, 703–722.

17 Luria, A. R. (1976). *Cognitive development: Its cultural and social foundations* (p. 148). Cambridge, MA: Harvard University Press. (Original work published 1974).

18 Vygotsky, L. S. (1986). *Thought and language* (p. 188). Cambridge, MA: MIT Press. (Original work published 1934).

19 *Ibid*, p. 189.

20 National Commission on Excellence in Education (1983). *A Nation at Risk: The Imperative for Educational Reform.* (p. 5). U.S. Department of Education, retrieved from http://teachertenure.procon.org/sourcefiles/a-nation-at-risk-tenure-april-1983.pdf.

21 U.S. Department of Education (2008). *A Nation Accountable: Twenty-five Years After A Nation at Risk* (p. 1), http://www2.ed.gov/rschstat/research/pubs/accountable/accountable.pdf.

22 *Ibid*, p. 4.

23 Bruer, J. T. (1993). *Schools for thought: A science of learning in the classroom* (p. 5). Cambridge, MA: MIT Press.

24 Ibid.

25 Schmittau, J. (1993). Vygotskian scientific concepts: Implications for mathematics education. *Focus on Learning Problems in Mathematics,* **15**(2&3), p. 35.

26 Vygotsky, L. S. (1984). *Sobranie sochineniy, Tom 4: Detskaya psikhologiya* [The collected works, Vol. 4: Child psychology] (p. 35). Moscow: Pedagogika.

27 For an overview, see Elkonin, D. B., & Venger, A. L. (Eds.), (1988). *Osobennosti psikhicheskogo razvitiya detei 6–7-letnego vozrasta* [Characteristics of mental development of six- to seven-year-old children]. Moscow: Pedagogika.

28 Stipek, D. (2002) *Motivation to learn: Integrating theory and practice.* Boston, MA: Allyn and Bacon.

29 *Ibid,* p. 133.

30 *Ibid,* p. 146.

7 Understand Adolescents and Make a Difference!

1 Vygotsky, L. S. (1998). R. W. Rieber (Ed.), *The collected works of L. S. Vygotsky, Vol. 5: Child psychology* (p. 16). New York: Plenum. (Original work published 1984).

2 Cole, M. (1999) Culture in development. In M. H. Bornstein & M. E. Lamb (Eds.), *Developmenmtal psychology* (p. 107). Mahwah, NJ: Erlbaum.

3 Cole, M., & Cole, S. R. (2001). *The development of children* (4th ed.) (p. 626). New York: Worth.

4 Dunphy, D. C. (1963). The social structure of urban adolescent peer groups. *Sociometry,* **26**, 230–246.

5 Larson, R., & Richards, M. H. (1994). *Divergent realities: The emotional lives of mothers, fathers, and adolescents* (p. 174). New York: Basic Books.

6 Brown, B. B. (1990). Peer groups and peer cultures. In S. S. Feldman & G. R. Elliott (Eds). *At the threshold: The developing adolescent* (p. 180). Cambridge, MA: Harvard University Press.

7 Vygotsky, L. S. (1998). R. W. Rieber (Ed.), *The collected works of L. S. Vygotsky, Vol. 5: Child psychology* (p. 30). New York: Plenum. (Original work published 1984).

8 *Ibid,* p. 42.

9 As some data suggest, this pattern in the development of moral reasoning may be typical only for Western societies. There is a general consensus, however, in regard to cognitive development as instrumental in a "progression from superficial to a profound understanding of moral rightness" (Fang, G., Fang, F., Keller, M., Edelstein, W., Kehle, T., & Bray, M. [2003]. Social moral reasoning in Chinese children: A developmental study. *Psychology in the Schools,* **40**[1], p. 137).

10 Brown, B. B. (1990). Peer groups and peer cultures. In: S. S. Feldman & G. R. Elliott (Eds). *At the threshold: The developing adolescent* (p. 174). Cambridge, MA: Harvard University Press.

11 This explains why, for example, in recent immigrant or dysfunctional families, adolescents may not look to their parents as those who are able

to provide them with norms and values respected in a given society. In such cases, adolescents may choose, for example, their teachers as an alternative source of "social wisdom." This is similar to a phenomenon described earlier: Infants whose parents fail to mediate their children's object-centered explorations may refer to even a stranger for help when experiencing a problem with a new toy.

12 Walker, L. J., & Taylor, J. H. (1991). Family interactions and the development of moral reasoning. *Child Development*, **62**(2), p. 279.
13 Harter, S. (1999). *The construction of the self: A developmental perspective* (p. 79). New York: The Guilford Press.
14 *Ibid.*
15 Wolman, B. B. (1998). *Adolescence: Biological and psychological perspectives* (p. 57). Westport, CT: Greenwood.
16 Vygotsky, L. S. (1998). R. W. Rieber (Ed.), *The collected works of L. S. Vygotsky, Vol. 5: Child psychology* (p. 182). New York: Plenum. (Original work published 1984).
17 Harter, S. (1999). *The construction of the self: A developmental perspective* (pp. 12–13). New York: The Guilford Press.
18 Brown, B. B. (1990). Peer groups and peer cultures. In S. S. Feldman & G. R. Elliott (Eds). *At the threshold: The developing adolescent* (p. 172). Cambridge, MA: Harvard University Press.
19 Lerner, R. M., & Villarruel, F. A. (1996). Adolescence. In E. DeCorte & F. E. Weinert (Eds.), *International encyclopedia of developmental and instructional psychology* (p. 132). New York: Elsevier Science.
20 Brown, B. B. (1990). Peer groups and peer cultures. In S. S. Feldman & G. R. Elliott (Eds). *At the threshold: The developing adolescent* (p. 174). Cambridge, MA: Harvard University Press.
21 *Ibid.*
22 Moshman, D. (1999). *Adolescent psychological development: Rationality, morality, and identity* (p. 39). Mahwah, NJ: Erlbaum.
23 *Ibid.*
24 Harter, S. (1999). *The construction of the self: A developmental perspective* (p. 79). New York: The Guilford Press.
25 Brown, B. B. (1990). Peer groups and peer cultures. In: S. S. Feldman & G. R. Elliott (Eds). *At the threshold: The developing adolescent* (p. 174). Cambridge, MA: Harvard University Press.
26 *Ibid*, p. 193.

27 Larson, R., & Richards, M. H. (1994). *Divergent realities: The emotional lives of mothers, fathers, and adolescents* (p. 86). New York: Basic Books.

28 Bronson, P., & Merryman, A. (2009). *Nurture shock: New thinking about children* (p. 151). New York: Twelve.

29 Arnett, J. J. (1999). Adolescent storm and stress, reconsidered. *American Psychologist*, **54**(5), p. 320.

30 Larson, R., & Richards, M. H. (1994). *Divergent realities: The emotional lives of mothers, fathers, and adolescents* (p. 140). New York: Basic Books.

31 Ibid.

32 *Ibid*, pp. 139–140.

33 Nancy Darling, an expert in the field of adolescent research, wrote: "Kids who go wild and get in trouble mostly have parents who don't set rules or standards. Their parents are loving and accepting no matter what the kids do. But the kids take the lack of rules as a sign their parents don't actually care – that their parent doesn't really want this job of being the parent" (quoted in Bronson, P., & Merryman, A. [2009]. *Nurture shock: New thinking about children* [p. 139]. New York: Twelve).

34 Tolan, P. H., Gorman-Smith, D., & Henry, D. B. (2003). The developmental ecology of urban males' youth violence. *Developmental Psychology*, **39**(2), p. 276.

35 Wolman, B. B. (1998). *Adolescence: Biological and psychological perspectives* (p. 69). Westport, CT: Greenwood.

8 American Cognitive Psychologists and Russian Vygotskians talk about the Content and Process of Learning at School

1 Ravitch, D. (2010). *The death and life of the great American school system* (p. 236). New York: Basic Books.

2 Anderson, L., & Krathwohl, D. A (2001) *Taxonomy for learning, teaching and assessing: A revision of Bloom's taxonomy of educational objectives*. New York: Longman.

3 Hirsch, E. D., Jr. (1987). *Cultural Literacy*. New York: Vintage.

4 Hirsch, E. D., Jr. (1988, July/August). A postscript by E. D. Hirsch. *Change*, p. 24.

5 Zaporozhets, A. V. (1986). Razvitie myshleniya [The development of thinking]. In A. V. Zaporozhets, *Izbrannye psikhologicheskie trudy, Tom 1* [Selected works in psychology, Vol. 1] (p. 207). Moscow: Pedagogika.

6 The correct answer is: Not necessarily (the problem may refer to line *n* meeting surface *p*).

7 Bruer, J. T. (1993). *Schools for thought: A science of learning in the classroom* (p. 81). Cambridge, MA: MIT Press.

8 Leontiev, A. N. (1983). Ovladenie uchaschimisya nauchnymi poniatiyami kak problema pedagogicheskoi psikhologii [Mastering scientific concepts by students as a problem of educational psychology]. In A. N. Leontiev, *Izbrannye psikhologicheskie proizvedeniya, Tom 1* [Selected works in psychology, Vol. 1] (pp. 324–347). Moscow: Pedagogika.

9 Bruer, J. T. (1993). *Schools for thought: A science of learning in the classroom* (p. 95). Cambridge, MA: MIT Press.

10 In the broadest meaning of this word, metacognition also includes our knowledge of how our cognition works (see Flavell, J. H. [1979]. Metacognition and cognitive monitoring: A new area of cognitive-developmental inquiry. *American Psychologist, 34*, 906–911).

11 Atkinson, R. C., & Shiffrin, R. M. (1968). Human memory: A proposed system and its control processes. In K. W. Spence & J. T. Spence (Eds.). *The psychology of learning and motivation, Vol. 2* (pp. 89–195). New York: Academic Press.

12 Smirnov, A. A. (1948). *Psihologiya zapominaniya* [Psychology of memory]. Moscow: Uchpedgiz; Zinchenko, P. I. (1961). *Neproizvol'noe zapominanie* [Incidental memorization]. Moscow: Izdatelstvo APN RSFSR; Hyde, T. S., & Jenkins, J. J. (1973). Recall for words as a function of semantic, graphic, and syntactic orienting tasks. *Journal of Verbal Learning and Verbal Behavior, 12*, 471–480.

13 Ormrod, J. E. (2008). *Human learning* (p. 373). Upper Saddle River, NJ: Prentice-Hall.

14 Palincsar, A. S., & Brown, A. L. (1984). Reciprocal teaching of comprehension-fostering and comprehension-monitoring activities. *Cognition and Instruction, 1*, 117–175; Palincsar, A. S., Brown, A. L., & Campione, J. C. (1993). First-grade dialogues for knowledge acquisition and use. In E. A. Forman, N. Minick, & C. A. Stone (Eds.), *Contexts for learning: Sociocultural dynamics in children's development* (pp. 43–57). New York: Oxford University Press.

15 Although the type of extrinsic motivation used in this example is much superior to extrinsic motivation related to giving presents or money for good grades.

16 Barrow, R., & Woods, R. (2006). *An introduction to philosophy of education* (4th edition) (p. 129). New York: Routledge.

17 Stipek, D. (2002) *Motivation to learn: Integrating theory and practice* (p. 108). Boston, MA: Allyn and Bacon.

18 Otterman, S. (2011). Ed Schools' pedagogical puzzle. *The New York Times*, July 21 Retrieved from http://www.nytimes.com/2011/07/24/education/edlife/edl-24teacher-t.html?_r=1&ref=sharonotterman.

19 Incidentally, I wonder what medical doctors would say if it were suggested that students in medical schools should learn only how to prescribe medicine without studying anatomy and physiology?

9 What Do Students Learn in "Traditional" Schools?

1 The international standing of the U.S. fourth and eighth graders in the fields of math and science is less troubling; in particular, it does not fall as much below the performance of their Finnish peers as is the case for American fifteen-year-olds (see *Highlights From TIMSS 2011: Mathematics and Science Achievement of U.S. Fourth- and Eighth-Grade Students in an International Context,* retrieved from http://nces.ed.gov/pubsearch/pubsinfo.asp?pubid=2013009). An explanation of this phenomenon will be suggested in the concluding section of this chapter.

2 The statement of Education Secretary Arne Duncan on the results of the Program for International Student Assessment (December 7, 2010). Retrieved from http://www.ed.gov/news/press-releases/education-secretary-arne-duncan-issues-statement-results-program-international-s.

3 Burson, G. (1989). A lack of vision: The Bradley Commission report. *The History Teacher,* **23**(1), 59.

4 *Ibid,* p. 61.

5 Brophy, J. E., & VanSledright, B. (1997). *Teaching and learning history in elementary schools* (p. 23). New York: Teachers College Press.

6 Burson, G. (1989). A lack of vision: The Bradley Commission report. *The History Teacher,* **23**(1), 65.

7 Hammack, D. C., Educational Testing Service., National Center for Education Statistics., United States., & National Assessment of Educational Progress (Project). (1990). *The U.S. history report card: The achievement of fourth-, eighth-, and twelfth-grade students in 1988 and trends from 1986 to 1988 in the factual knowledge of high-school juniors.* Princeton, NJ: Educational Testing Service.

8 Ravitch, D. (2005) American History 101 (May 17). *Slate.* Retrieved from http://www.slate.com/articles/arts_and_life/history_book_blitz/features/2005/american_history_101/dontknow_much_about_history.html.

9 University of Illinois at Urbana-Champaign (2009). Rote Memorization Of Historical Facts Adds To Collective Cluelessness. *ScienceDaily* (February 12). Retrieved from http://www.sciencedaily.com/releases/2009/02/090212125135.htm?utm_source=feedburner&utm_medium=feed&utm_campaign=Feed%3A+sciencedaily+%28ScienceDaily%3A+Latest+Science+News%29.

10 Davydov, V. V. (1990). *Types of generalization in instruction* (p. 152). Reston, VA: National Council of Teachers of Mathematics. (Original work published 1972).

11 NSTA Issues Statement Regarding the Science Results of the 2011 National Assessment of Education Progress (2012). National Science Teachers Association (May 10). Retrieved from http://www.nsta.org/about/pressroom.aspx?id=59379.

12 Labudde, P., Reif, F., & Quinn, L. (1988). Facilitation of scientific concept learning by interpretation procedures and diagnosis. *International Journal of Science Education*, **10**(1), 81.

13 Bruer, J. T. (1993). *Schools for thought: A science of learning in the classroom* (p. 131). Cambridge, MA: MIT Press.

14 *Ibid*, p. 130.

15 *Ibid*, p. 130.

16 Berger, E. (2009). In science class, students are learning to hate science. *Houston Chronicle* (April 10). Retrieved from http://www.chron.com/neighborhood/baytown-news/article/In-science-class-students-are-learning-to-hate-1744302.php.

17 Inspiring the Next Generation of Innovators: National Findings on Science Education from Speak Up 2007 (July 2008). Project Tomorrow and PASCO scientific. Retrieved from http://www.tomorrow.org/speakup/scienceReport.html.

18 Davydov, V. V. (1990). *Types of generalization in instruction*. Reston, VA: National Council of Teachers of Mathematics. (Original work published 1972); Talyzina, N. F. (1981). *The psychology of learning*. Moscow: Progress. (Original work published 1975).

19 Bruer, J. T. (1993). *Schools for thought: A science of learning in the classroom* (p. 90). Cambridge, MA: MIT Press.

20 *Ibid*, p. 92.

21 Zakaria, E., & Zaini, N. (2009). Conceptual and procedural knowledge of rational numbers in trainee teachers. *European Journal of Social Sciences*, **9**(2), 202.

22 Bruer, J. T. (1993). *Schools for thought: A science of learning in the classroom* (p. 81). Cambridge, MA: MIT Press.

23 *Ibid*, p. 100.

24 *Ibid*.

25 Raytheon U.S. Middle School Students Math Habits Study (August 2009). Retrieved from http://www.raytheon.com/responsibility/rtnwcm/groups/public/documents/content/rtn_stem_math_study.pdf.

26 Davydov, V. V. (1990). *Types of generalization in instruction* (p. 126). Reston, VA: National Council of Teachers of Mathematics. (Original work published 1972).

27 *Ibid*.

28 Fuson, K. C., Stigler, J. W., & Bartsch, K. (1988). Grade placement of addition and subtraction topics in Japan, Mainland China, the Soviet Union, Taiwan, and the United States. *Journal for Research in Mathematics Education*, **19**, 449–456.

29 Ingersoll, R. M. (1999). The problem of underqualified teachers in American secondary school. *Educational Researcher*, **28**(2), 26–37.

30 Boris Slutsky: *"Scientists and Poets"* (translated by Inna Kouper). Retrieved from http://inkouper.blogspot.com/2009/08/poem.html.

31 Sahlberg, P. (2010). *Finnish lessons: What can the world learn from educational change in Finland*. New York: Teachers College, Columbia University.

32 *Ibid*, p. 5.

33 *Ibid*, p. 70.

34 *Ibid*, p. 71.

35 Ravitch, D. (2002) *Commentary on the results of the 2001 National Assessment of Educational Progress in U.S. History* (Press Release). U.S. Department of Education, OERI, NAEP, Washington, DC.

36 Carrol, T. (2009). The next generation of learning teams. *Phi Delta Kappan*, **91** (2), 8–13. Retrieved from http://nctaf.org/wp-content/uploads/2012/01/Tom-Carroll-PDK-Article-Oct.-09-v91n2.pdf.

37 Sahlberg, P. (2010). *Finnish lessons: What can the world learn from educational change in Finland* (p. 26). New York: Teachers College, Columbia University.

38 *Ibid*, p. 5.

39 *Ibid*, p. 32.

40 *Ibid*, p. 35.

41 *Ibid*.

42 Sorensen, C. W. (1994). Success and education in South Korea. *Comparative Education Review*, **38**, 12.

43 Heitin, L. (2012). U.S. found to recruit fewer teachers from top ranks. *Education Week* (August 5). Retrieved from http://www.edweek.org/ew/articles/2010/10/15/08teachers.h30.html.

44 Ingersoll, R. M. (1999). The problem of underqualified teachers in American secondary school. *Educational Researcher*, **28**(2), 26–37.

45 Lee, Y. (2010). Views on education and achievement: Finland's story of success and South Korea's story of decline. *KEDI Journal of Educational Policy*, **7**(2), 384.

46 Sorensen, C. W. (1994). Success and education in South Korea. *Comparative Education Review*, **38**, 28.

47 *Ibid*, p. 24.

48 Goslin, D. A. (2003). *Engaging minds: Motivation and learning in America's schools*. Lanham, MD: Scarecrow Press.

49 Sorensen, C. W. (1994). Success and education in South Korea. *Comparative Education Review*, **38**, 21.

50 Kim, S., & Lee, J-H. (2010). Private tutoring and demand for education in South Korea. *Economic Development and Cultural Change*, **58**(2), 259–296.

51 Ripley, A. (2011). Teacher, leave those kids alone. *Time* (September 25). Retrieved from http://www.time.com/time/magazine/article/0,9171,2094427,00.html.

52 *Ibid*.

53 Sorensen, C. W. (1994). Success and education in South Korea. *Comparative Education Review*, **38**, 33.

54 *Ibid*.

55 Kim, S., & Lee, J. -H. (2010). Private tutoring and demand for education in South Korea. *Economic Development and Cultural Change*, **58**(2), 289.

56 Sorensen, C. W. (1994). Success and education in South Korea. *Comparative Education Review*, **38**, 29.

57 *Ibid*, p. 27.

10 Does Constructivist Instruction Present a Good Alternative to "Traditional" Teaching?

1 Brown, A. L., & Campione, J. C. (1994). Guided discovery in a community of learners. In K. McGilly (Ed.), *Classroom lessons: Integrating cognitive theory and classroom practice* (p. 230). Cambridge, MA: MIT Press.

2 Quoted in Clark, R. E. (2009). How much and what type of guidance is optimal for learning from instruction? In S. Tobias & T. M. Duffy (Eds.), *Constructivist instruction: Success or failure?* (p. 161). New York: Routledge.

3 Sweller, J. (2009). What human cognitive architecture tells us about constructivism. In S. Tobias & T. M. Duffy (Eds.), *Constructivist instruction: Success or failure?* (p. 127). New York: Routledge.

4 It is worthy of note that some advocates of constructivist instruction clearly contrast Vygotsky's emphasis on "the importance of formal definitions and of the teacher's explicit explanations" with their own emphasis on "inquiry mathematics," which is "interactively constituted in the classroom" (see Cobb, P., Wood, T., & Yackel, E. [1993]. Discourse, mathematical thinking, and classroom practice. In E. A. Forman, N. Minick, & C. A. Stone [Eds.], *Contexts for learning: Sociocultural dynamics in children's development* [p. 100]. New York: Oxford University Press).

5 Vygotsky, L. S. (1986). *Thought and language* (p. 152). Cambridge, MA: MIT Press. (Original work published 1934).

6 Luria, A. R. (1961). *The role of speech in the regulation of normal and abnormal behavior*. Oxford: Pergamon Press.

7 Vygotsky, L. S. (1998). R. W. Rieber (Ed.), *The collected works of L. S. Vygotsky, Vol. 5: Child psychology* (p. 182). New York: Plenum. (Original work published 1984).

8 Sweller, J. (2009). What human cognitive architecture tells us about constructivism. In S. Tobias & T. M. Duffy (Eds.), *Constructivist instruction: Success or failure?* (p. 136). New York: Routledge.

9 Arocha and Patel, 1995 as cited in Kirschner, P. A., Sweller, J., & Clark, R. E. (2006). Why minimal guidance during instruction does not work: An analysis of the failure of constructivist, discovery, problem-based, experiential, and inquiry-based teaching. *Educational Psychologist*, **41**, 83.

10 Ibid.

11 Kirschner, P. A., Sweller, J., & Clark, R. E. (2006). Why minimal guidance during instruction does not work: An analysis of the failure of constructivist, discovery, problem-based, experiential, and inquiry-based teaching. *Educational Psychologist*, **41**, 77.

12 Brown, A. L., & Campione, J. C. (1994). Guided discovery in a community of learners. In K. McGilly (Ed.), *Classroom lessons: Integrating cognitive theory and classroom practice* (pp. 229–270). Cambridge, MA: MIT Press.

13 Chang-Wells, G. L. M., & Wells, G. (1993). Dynamics of discourse: Literacy and the construction of knowledge. In E. A. Forman, N. Minick, & C. A. Stone (Eds.), *Contexts for learning: Sociocultural dynamics in children's development* (p. 84). New York: Oxford University Press.

14 Wise, A. F., & O'Neill, D. K. (2009). Beyond "more" versus "less": A reframing of the debate on instructional guidance. In S. Tobias & T. M. Duffy (Eds.), *Constructivist instruction: Success or failure?* (p. 101). New York: Routledge.

15 Gagné, R. M. (1966). Varieties of learning and the concept of discovery. In L. S. Shulman & E. R. Keislar (Eds.), *Learning by discovery: A critical appraisal* (p. 143). Chicago: Rand McNally.

16 Zakaria, E., & Zaini, N. (2009). Conceptual and procedural knowledge of rational numbers in trainee teachers. *European Journal of Social sciences*, **9**(2), 204.

17 Ormrod, J. E. (1995). *Human learning* (p. 267). Englewood Cliffs, NJ: Prentice Hall.

18 Tudge, J. (1992). Vygotsky, the zone of proximal development, and peer collaboration: Implications for classroom practice. In L. C. Moll (Ed.), *Vygotsky and education: Instructional implications and applications of sociohistorical psychology* (pp. 155–172). Cambridge: Cambridge University Press.

19 Cobb, P., Wood, T., & Yackel, E. (1993). Discourse, mathematical think-
    ing, and classroom practice. In E. A. Forman, N. Minick, & C. A. Stone
    (Eds.), *Contexts for learning: Sociocultural dynamics in children's devel-*
    opment (p. 98). New York: Oxford University Press.
20 Heller, J. I., & Gordon, A. (1992). Lifelong learning. *Educator*, **6** (1), 10.
21 Confrey, J. (1991). Learning to listen: A student's understanding of
    powers of ten. In E. von Glaserfeld (Ed.), *Radical constructivism in*
    mathematics education (p. 122). Dordrecht, The Netherlands: Kluwer
    Academic Publishers.
22 Cobb, P., Wood, T., & Yackel, E. (1991). A constructivist approach to
    second grade mathematics. In E. von Glaserfeld (Ed.), *Radical construc-*
    tivism in mathematics education (p. 158). Dordrecht, The Netherlands:
    Kluwer Academic Publishers.
23 Heller, J. I., & Gordon, A. (1992). Lifelong learning. *Educator*, **6**
    (1), 16.
24 Brown, A. L., & Campione, J. C. (1994). Guided discovery in a com-
    munity of learners. In K. McGilly (Ed.), *Classroom lessons: Integrating*
    cognitive theory and classroom practice (pp. 229–270). Cambridge, MA:
    MIT Press.
25 Mayer, R. E. (2004). Should there be a three-strikes rule against pure
    discovery learning? *American Psychologist*, **59**(1), 17.
26 Sweller, J., Kirschner, P. A., & Clark, R. E. (2007). Why minimally guided
    teaching techniques do not work: a reply to commentaries. *Educational*
    Psychologist, **42**(2), 117.
27 Anderson, J. R., Reder, L. M., & Simon, H. A. (1995). *Applications and*
    misapplications of cognitive psychology to mathematics education (p. 18).
    Retrieved from http://www.psy.cmu.edu/~mm4b/misapplied.html.
28 *Ibid.*
29 Bruer, J. T. (1993). *Schools for thought: A science of learning in the class-*
    room (p. 254). Cambridge, MA: MIT Press.
30 *Ibid.*
31 *Ibid,* pp. 253–254.
32 Ball (1997) as cited in Windschhitl, M. (2002). Framing constructiv-
    ism in practice as the negotiation of dilemmas: An analysis of the con-
    ceptual, pedagogical, cultural, and political challenges facing teachers.
    Review of Educational Research, **72**(2), 149–150.
33 Heller, J. I., & Gordon, A. (1992). Lifelong learning. *Educator*, **6** (1),
    pp. 4–6.

34 Schwartz, D. L., Lindgren, R., & Lewis, S. (2009). Constructivism in an age of non-constructivist assessments. In S. Tobias & T. M. Duffy (Eds.), *Constructivist instruction: Success or failure?* (p. **42**). New York: Routledge.

35 Ausubel (1968) as cited in Anderson, J. R., Reder, L. M., & Simon, H. A. (1995). *Applications and misapplications of cognitive psychology to mathematics education* (p. 13). Retrieved from http://www.psy.cmu.edu/~mm4b/misapplied.html.

36 Anderson, J. R., Reder, L. M., & Simon, H. A. (1995). *Applications and misapplications of cognitive psychology to mathematics education* (p. 13). Retrieved from http://www.psy.cmu.edu/~mm4b/misapplied.html.

37 Chall, J. (2000). *The academic achievement challenge: What really works in the classroom.* New York: Guilford.

38 Gresalfi, M. S., & Lester, F. (2009). What's worth knowing in mathematics? In S. Tobias & T. M. Duffy (Eds.), *Constructivist instruction: Success or failure?* (p. 282). New York: Routledge.

39 Spiro, R. J., & DeSchryver, M. (2009). When it's the wrong idea and when it's the only idea. In S. Tobias & T. M. Duffy (Eds.), *Constructivist instruction: Success or failure?* (p. 106). New York: Routledge.

40 *Ibid.*

41 *Ibid*, p. 109.

42 *Ibid*, p. 113.

43 Clark, R. E. (2009). How much and what type of guidance is optimal? In S. Tobias & T. M. Duffy (Eds.), *Constructivist Instruction: Success or Failure?* (p. 165). New York: Routledge.

44 Palincsar, A. S. (1998) Social constructivist perspectives on teaching and learning. *Annual Review of Psychology*, **49**, 345–375.

45 Kirschner, P. A. (2009). Epistemology or pedagogy, that is the question. In S. Tobias & T. M. Duffy (Eds.), *Constructivist instruction: Success or failure?* (p. 149). New York: Routledge.

46 Gagné, R. M. (1966). Varieties of learning and the concept of discovery. In L. S. Shulman & E. R. Keislar (Eds.), *Learning by discovery: A critical appraisal* (p. 148). Chicago: Rand McNally.

47 Klahrl, D. & Nigam, M. (2004). The equivalence of learning paths in early science instruction. *Psychological Science*, **15**(10), 661.

48 Kirschner, P. A., Sweller, J., & Clark, R. E. (2006). Why minimal guidance during instruction does not work: An analysis of the failure of

constructivist, discovery, problem-based, experiential, and inquiry-based teaching. *Educational Psychologist,* **41**(2), 82.

49 Clark, R. E. (2009). How much and what type of guidance is optimal? In S. Tobias & T. M. Duffy (Eds.), *Constructivist instruction: Success or failure?* (p. 176). New York: Routledge.

50 Kirschner, P. A., Sweller, J., & Clark, R. E. (2006). Why minimal guidance during instruction does not work: An analysis of the failure of constructivist, discovery, problem-based, experiential, and inquiry-based teaching. *Educational Psychologist,* **41**(2), 83–84.

51 Anderson, J. R., Reder, L. M., & Simon, H. A. (1995). *Applications and misapplications of cognitive psychology to mathematics education* (p. 1). Retrieved from http://www.psy.cmu.edu/~mm4b/misapplied.html.

52 Sweller, J. (2009). What human cognitive architecture tells us about constructivism. In S. Tobias & T. M. Duffy (Eds.), *Constructivist instruction: Success or failure?* (p. 128). New York: Routledge.

53 Clark, R. E., Kirschner, P. A., & Sweller, J. (2012). Putting students on the path to learning: The case for fully guided instruction. *American Educator,* **36**(1), 8.

54 Schmidt, H. G., & Loyens, S. M. (2007). Problem-based learning *is* compatible with human cognitive architecture: Commentary on Kirschner, Sweller, & Clark (2006). *Educational Psychologist,* **42**(2), 92.

11 The Vygotskian Theoretical Learning Approach as an Alternative to "Traditional" Explicit Instruction and to Constructivist Instruction

1 Davydov, V. V. (1986). *Problemy razvivayuschego obucheniya* [Problems of developmental-generating learning]. Moscow: Pedagogika; Davydov, V. V. (1990). *Types of generalization in instruction.* Reston, VA: National Council of Teachers of Mathematics. (Original work published 1972); Elkonin, D. B. (1976). *Kak uchit detei chitat* [How to teach children to read]. Moscow: Znanie; Galperin, P. Y. (1985). *Metody obucheniya i umstvennoe razvitie rebenka* [Methods of instruction and the child's mental development]. Moscow: Izdatelstvo MGU; Talyzina, N. F. (1981). *The psychology of learning.* Moscow: Progress. (Original work published 1975).

2 Bruer, J. T. (1993). *Schools for thought: A science of learning in the classroom* (p. 95). Cambridge, MA: MIT Press.

3 Vygotsky, L. S. (1984). *Sobranie sochineniy, Tom 4: Detskaya psikhologiya* [The collected works, Vol. 4: Child psychology] (p. 35). Moscow: Pedagogika.

4 The students had been informed that their grades for the projects would not depend on whether or not the lesson was a success as long as the lesson was properly described and analyzed.

5 For the survey data, see Aguilar Fernandez, P., & Humlebaek, C. (2002). Collective memory and national identity in the Spanish democracy: The legacies of Francoism and the civil war. *History & Memory, 14*(1&2), 121–164.

6 Talysina, N. F. (1973). Psychological bases of programmed instruction. *Instructional Science, 2*, 243–280; Talyzina, N. F. (1981). *The psychology of learning.* Moscow: Progress. (Original work published 1975).

7 *Ibid.*

8 Schmittau, J. (1993). Vygotskian scientific concepts: Implications for mathematics education. *Focus on Learning Problems in Mathematics, 15*(2&3), 35.

9 Davydov, V. V. (1986). *Problemy razvivayuschego obucheniya* [Problems of developmental-generating learning]. Moscow: Pedagogika; Galperin, P. Y. (1985). *Metody obucheniya i umstvennoe razvitie rebenka* [Methods of instruction and the child's mental development]. Moscow: Izdatelstvo MGU; Talyzina, N. F. (1981). *The psychology of learning.* Moscow: Progress. (Original work published 1975).

10 Davydov, V. V. (1986). *Problemy razvivayuschego obucheniya* [Problems of development-generating learning]. Moscow: Pedagogika; Galperin, P. Y., & Talyzina, N. F. (1961). Formation of elementary geometrical concepts and their dependence on directed participation by the pupils. In N. O'Connor (Ed.), *Recent Soviet psychology* (pp. 247–272). New York: Liveright. (Original work published 1957).

11 Davydov, V. V. (1986). *Problemy razvivayuschego obucheniya* [Problems of development-generating learning]. Moscow: Pedagogika.

12 Davydov, V. V., Pushkin, V. N., & Pushkina, A. G. (1972). Zavisimost razvitiya myshleniya mladshikh shkolnikov ot kharaktera obucheniya [Dependence of the development of elementary school students' thinking on the type of instruction]. *Voprosy Psikhologii* [Questions in Psychology], *6*, 124–132; Maksimov, L. K. (1979). Zavisimost razvitiya matematicheskogo myshleniya shkolnikov ot kharaktera obucheniya [Dependence of the development of students' mathematical

reasoning on the type of instruction]. *Voprosy Psikhologii* [Questions in Psychology], **2**, 57–65; Zak, A. Z. (1984). *Razvitie teoreticheskogo myshleniya u mladshikh shkolnikov* [Development of theoretical thought in elementary school children]. Moscow: Pedagogika.

13 It is worth noting that, as a rule, under traditional instruction, even adults demonstrate such an approach only when dealing with problems in their area of expertise (Chi, M. T. H., Feltovich, P. J., & Glaser, R. [1981]. Categorization and representation of physics problems by experts and novices. *Cognitive Science*, **5**, 121–152; Novick, L. R. [1988]. Analogical transfer, problem similarity, and expertise. *Journal of Experimental Psychology: Learning, Memory, and Cognition*, **14**, 510–520).

14 Kozulin, A. (1998). *Psychological tools: A sociocultrural approach to education* (p. 55–56). Cambridge, MA: Harvard University Press.

15 Vygotsky, L. S. (1986). *Thought and language* (p. 188). Cambridge, MA: MIT Press. (Original work published 1934).

16 Otterman, S. (2011). Ed Schools' pedagogical puzzle. *The New York Times*, July 21 Retrieved from http://www.nytimes.com/2011/07/24/education/edlife/edl-24teacher-t.html?_r=1&ref=sharonotterman.

Conclusion

1 A similar idea is expressed by some American researchers: "Genes do not shout commands to us about our behavior. At the very most, they whisper suggestions." (Ehrlich, P. R. [2000]. *Human natures: Genes, cultures, and the human prospect* [p. 7]. Washington DC: Island Press).

2 Luria, A. R. (1936). The development of mental functions in twins. *Character and Personality*, **5**, 35–47.

3 Scarr, S. (1992). Developmental theories for the 1990s: Development and individual differences. *Child Development*, **63**, 11.

4 Plomin, R. (1989). Environment and genes: Determinants of behavior. *American Psychologist*, **44**(2), 106.

5 For a review, see Nisbett, R. E. (2009). *Intelligence and how to get it: Why schools and cultures count*. New York: Norton.

6 *Ibid*, p. 35.

7 Sternberg, R. J., & Detterman, D. K. (Eds.), (1986). *What is intelligence? Contemporary viewpoints on its nature and definition*. Norwood, NJ: Ablex.

8 Eysenck, H. J. (1985). Revolution in the theory and measurement of intelligence. *Psychological Assessment*, **1**(1–2), 99–158; Jensen, A. R. (1982). Reaction time and psychometric g. In H. J. Eysenck (Ed.), *A model for intelligence* (pp. 93–132). New York: Springer-Verlag; Jensen, A. R. (1998). *The g factor: The science of mental ability*. New York: Praeger; Luciano, M., Wright, M. J., Smith, G. A., Geffen, G. M., Geffen, L. B., & Martin, N. G. (2003). Genetic covariance between processing speed and IQ. In R. Plomin, J. C. Defries, I. W. Craig, & P. McGuffin (Eds.), *Behavioral genetics in the postgenomic era* (pp. 163–181). Washington, DC: American Psychological Association; Posthuma, D., de Geus, E. J. C., & Boomsma, D. I. (2003). Genetic contributions to anatomical, behavioral, and neurophysiological indices of cognition. In R. Plomin, J. C. Defries, I. W. Craig, & P. McGuffin (Eds), *Behavioral genetics in the postgenomic era* (pp. 141–161). Washington, DC: American Psychological Association; Rindermann, H., & Neubauer, A. C. (2004). Processing speed, intelligence, creativity, and school performance: Testing of causal hypotheses using structural equation models. *Intelligence*, **32**, 573–589.
9 Jensen, A. R. (1982). Reaction time and psychometric g. In H. J. Eysenck (Ed.), *A model for intelligence* (p. 99). New York: Springer-Verlag.
10 Haywood, H. C. (1989). Multidimensional treatment of mental retardation. *Psychology in Mental Retardation and Developmental Disabilities*, **15**(1), 1–10; Haywood, H. C., Tzuriel, D., & Vaught, S. (1992). Psychoeducational assessment from a transactional perspective. In H. C. Haywood & D. Tzuriel (Eds.), *Interactive assessment* (pp. 38–63). New York: Springer-Verlag.
11 Danthiir, V., Wilhelm, O., & Schacht, A. (2005). Decision speed in intelligence tasks: Correctly an ability? *Psychology Science*, **47**, 216.
12 Joseph, J. (2001). Is crime in the genes? A critical review of twin and adoption studies of criminality and antisocial behavior. *The Journal of Mind and Behavior*, **22**, 179–218.

Index

concepts (*cont.*)
    spontaneous, 155. (*see also*
        knowledge, everyday life)
constructivism
    as a developmental theory, 6–8, 17,
        48
    in education, 2, 7–8, 11, 168–184,
        202

Daly, Martin, 2
Darwin, Charles, 1–2
Dewey, John, 168
Duncan, Arne, 148
dynamic assessment. *See* zone of
    proximal development, and
    assessment

egocentric speech. *See* self-regulation,
    and egocentric (private) speech
egocentrism
    as a characteristic of preschooler
        thinking, 7, 68
    its overcoming as a component of
        school readiness, 68
    its overcoming within sociodramatic
        play, 72
    and Vygotskian early childhood edu-
        cation. (*see* Vygotskian early child-
        hood education, and overcoming
        of egocentrism)
Elkonin, Daniel, 103
emotional interactions between infants
    and caregivers
    and gestural communication, 39–41
    as leading to attachment.
        (*see* attachment, Vygotskian
        explanation of)
    mediation of, 31–34, 42–43
    as a preparation for object-centered
        explorations, 35–39
Erikson, Erik, 109, 116

factual knowledge, 129–131, 151–153,
    169, 174
    its processing, 141, 148
Ferguson, Christopher, 2
formal-logical thought, 7–8, 98–99,
    109–110, 113–114, 120
    as a prerequisite for transition to
        adolescence. (*see* adolescence, and
        formal-logical thought)
    school instruction and development
        of, 8, 98–99, 114
Freud, Anna, 119
Freud, Sigmund, 109

Galton, Francis, 2, 3

Hirsch, Eric, 130–131

knowledge
    conceptual. (*see* concepts)
    everyday life, 94–95, 132–133.
        (*see also* concepts, spontaneous)
    factual. (*see* factual knowledge)
    metacognitive. (*see* metacognitive
        knowledge)
    procedural. (*see* procedures)
    scientific, 94–95, 125, 144, 154,
        168–169, 173, 185. (*see also* con-
        cepts, scientific)
    See also knowledge (information)
        processing
knowledge (information) processing,
    135–143, 148
    and attention, 137–138
    and long-term memory,
        140
    model of, 136
    and sensory register, 135–136
    and short-term (working) memory,
        138–142
Köhler, Wolfgang, 4